This brilliant book reminds me of *History*. *Đức* is a compelling and elegantly-written memoir. But it is much more than that. Uwe Siemon-Netto challenges facets of our flawed historical memory of the Vietnam War. He exposes the false virtue of Vietnamese Communist forces that brutalized innocents in their quest to impose their totalitarian system on the South Vietnamese people. And he sheds fresh light and understanding on the experiences of those who endured that brutality, wartime reporters, and South Vietnamese and American troops as well as the interactions between them.

– Maj. Gen. H.R. McMaster, U.S. Army, Ph.D., author of *Dereliction of Duty: Lyndon Johnson, Robert McNamara, the Joint Chiefs of Staff and the Lies that Led to Vietnam*

Siemon-Netto, a young German reporter not naïve about communism, fell in love with the Vietnamese. He found Saigon filled with armchair reporters praising each other's dissent on the war. In the countryside he saw the truth: the horror of the North Vietnamese massacre of mothers dressed for the festival of Têt, the self-sacrifice of GIs and South Vietnamese troops, the heroic comedy of two WWII veterans—a German and an English journalist—bringing order to the chaotic defense against the Viet Cong. Every page has an eccentric or brave or charming or cowardly or villainous individual—Vietnamese or Western—brought to life on it. *Đức* is an angry account of the betrayal of a nation. But there is hope about people on every page too.

– John O'Sullivan, Executive Editor
Radio Free Europe/Radio Liberty, 2008–2011
Editor-in-Chief, UPI, 2001–2004
Editor, National Review, 1988–2007

In this captivating memoir of his time in South Vietnam, Uwe Siemon-Netto describes what that country was really like. Having served there as a U.S. diplomat at about the same time, I can thoroughly vouch for the accuracy of his observations. The book abounds in incidents and episodes amusing, heartwarming, heartbreaking, depressing, frightening and thought provoking. Uwe did not shun danger and witnessed some fierce combat, notably at the bloody 1965 Ia Drang battle.

He demonstrated both physical courage and the courage of his convictions, not hesitating to expose and condemn the Communist enemy regime as cruel and intrinsically evil. This was most dramatically illustrated by the notorious 1968 Huế massacre, which he depicts in detail. When Communist forces captured the old imperial capital of Huế during the Tết Offensive they came with prepared lists of leading citizens and foreigners whom they systematically executed. It is believed that there were as many as 6,000 victims. After the enemy was driven out, a mass grave with nearly 3,000 bodies was found, some buried alive.

Uwe has rendered a useful service in bringing attention to this greatest atrocity of the war, which so many in our media minimized. Throughout, Uwe demonstrates an abiding affection for the Vietnamese people. He fittingly begins the book by noting it "has been written in memory of the countless victims of the Communist conquest in South Vietnam," and then lists them. A word of note: when one begins to read this book, it is hard to put down.

– William Lloyd Stearman, Ph.D., Director
White House National Security Council
Indochina Staff, 1973–1976

Forty years ago, at the time of this writing, Henry Kissinger—then America's Secretary of State—shook hands with his North Vietnamese counterpart in Paris and signed the agreement that seemed to guarantee the long-awaited peace in Indochina, ending the bitter war between North and South Vietnam. Prior to signing, Washington told Saigon not to worry. Should the Communists strike again, the United States would respond, immediately and rigorously.

But, of course, this promise was not kept. Two years later, Hanoi attacked with massive conventional armed force, just as it had in the spring of 1972. Then the South's valiant soldiers threw back the Communist assault. But in April 1975, South Vietnam fell to Communism, spawning hundreds of thousands of "boat-people," a large number of who found refuge in the United States, while many others drowned.

Throughout much of the Vietnam War, Germany's *Axel Springer Verlag* in Berlin, Europe's largest publishing house with dozens of magazines and papers, had relied on Uwe Siemon-Netto's splendid reporting for general and specialized coverage of the armed and political conflict in Vietnam.

The Vietnamese called him Đức, meaning the German. Now he has chosen this nickname as the title of his memoir. This fine book is the proclamation of "A reporter's love for the abandoned people of Vietnam," as its subtitle states. It wraps up a rare, distinguished career in the trenches.

– **H. Joachim Maître, former editor of**
Die Welt / Welt am Sonntag
Brookline, Mass., March 2013

It seems appropriate that this meaningful and poetic book, written from well ingrained memories going back forty-plus years, comes to our attention just as we prepare to celebrate and honor the hundreds of thousands surviving Vietnam veterans who were sent away to defeat communism only to come home abandoned and mistreated by the country that sent them into this hellish war. I had the great pleasure of supervising Uwe during his tenure at the St. Cloud, Minnesota Veterans Affairs Medical Center early in my career as a Clinical Psychologist treating combat veterans with PTSD. His earlier book, *The Acquittal of God*, helped many of our veterans overcome longstanding, painful spirituality issues and this current release will certainly help my generation to better fully understand the horrifying mindset and trauma enforced upon a culture and people by their fellow countrymen.

– James R. Tuorila, Ph.D., L.P.
VFW Surgeon General 2012–2013

Every reader will gain much from this book's empathetic portrait of the countless tragedies the freedom-loving South Vietnamese suffered during and after the Vietnam War, a war that still haunts many Americans who do not know or remember that their leaders, with the compliance of the American public, opted to enter this war with the commitment of protecting and saving the South Vietnamese from the Communist Viet Cong. Uwe Siemon-Netto, a German war correspondent for five years in Vietnam, shows how Americans at home, unwilling to support their soldiers in a protracted war, together with their throw-away disposition, jettisoned their commitment. They withdrew their forces, enabling Communists to slaughter millions in pursuit of "liberation," a duplicitous term the new journalists, as social-advocates, a byproduct of the Vietnam War, did not question.

– Rev. Alvin J. Schmidt, Ph.D.
Professor of Sociology, Emeritus, Illinois College

I was a so-called "'68er," part of the rebellious youth movement of the 1960s. In those days my knowledge derived largely from the media of the time. By reading Đức, I now realize this was insufficient to give me a real picture of the conflict. What has not changed, and was underpinned by Uwe Siemon-Netto's book, are my feelings about the cruelties and absurdities of war in general.

– Wolfgang Drautz,
former Consul-General of Germany in Los Angeles

Uwe Siemon-Netto's memoir about his years as a war correspondent in Vietnam is one of the most touching and moving books I have read in a long time. It is also hilarious. This renowned journalist, a longtime war correspondent for various German newspapers, made me both sad and happy. I did cry at times, but I also laughed. He took me on a splendid journey from Saigon to Huế and back again, always captivating me with his memorable talent and his unique way with engaging words and phrases. I couldn't get enough of his anecdotes about his little friends, a group of street urchins. They slept in his ramshackle car at night, protesting they were doing him a favor by guarding it. His vivid writing brings alive all kinds of unusual cosmopolitan "characters" he met, as well as the innocent victims and brave survivors of this war, in particular the everyday people of Vietnam. His genuine sympathy for the Vietnamese and his understanding of the war that engulfed them help to make this a powerful read.

– Barbara Taylor Bradford, author of
A Woman of Substance and
Secrets from the Past

Uwe Siemon-Netto's account of the Vietnam War provides many new details and important insights. It is impossible to read the book without being reminded of Graham Greene's *The Quiet American* and Bernard B. Fall's *Street Without Joy*. It is beautifully written and relates very captivating stories.

– Col. (ret.) Duong Nguyen, MC,
former Division Surgeon, 1st Armored Division U.S. Army
former Captain, ARVN Medical Corps

ĐỨC THIRD EDITION

Triumph
of the
Absurd

A reporter's love for the
abandoned people
of Vietnam

UWE SIEMON-NETTO
Foreword by Peter R. Kann

BOOKS

An imprint of
1517.The Legacy Project

Đức Third Edition: Triumph of the Absurd — A reporter's love for the abandoned people of Vietnam

Published by:

NRP Books, an imprint of 1517.The Legacy Project
2151 Applegate Drive
Corona, California 92882
www.1517Legacy.com

Library of Congress Control Number: 2015937843

ISBN 978-1-945500-00-8

All illustrations published by permission.
Cover photo: Uwe Siemon-Netto during a lull in the 1968 Têt Offensive in Huế. Photo: Hilmar Pabel.

1517.The Legacy Project is committed to packaging and promoting the finest content for fueling a new Lutheran Reformation. We promote the defense of the Christian faith, confessional Lutheran theology, vocation and civil courage.

To Gillian

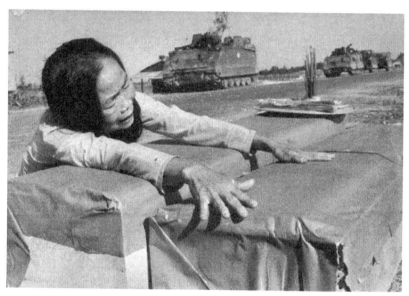

A mother weeps over the coffins of her children killed in a North Vietnamese artillery attack on her village near Huế in 1972.

IN MEMORIAM

This book has been written in memory of the countless innocent victims of the Communist conquest in South Vietnam, notably:

- The hundreds of thousands of men, women, and children massacred in villages and cities, especially Huê;
- The hundreds of thousands of South Vietnamese soldiers and officials who were executed, tortured or imprisoned after the end of the war;
- The millions who were driven from their country and the hundreds of thousands who drowned in the process;
- The brave ARVN soldiers who fought on when all was lost, and their valiant generals who took their own lives in the end;
- The young South and North Vietnamese conscripts who died in this so-called war of liberation, which brought no liberty;
- The 58,272 American, 4,407 South Korean, 487 Australian, 351 Thai and 37 New Zealand soldiers who made the ultimate sacrifice in Vietnam;
- My German compatriots who were murdered by the Vietnamese Communists, notably Dr. Horst-Günther and Elisabetha Krainick, Dr. Alois Alteköster, Dr. Raimund Discher, Baron Hasso Rüdt von Collenberg and many others, who came as friends and paid for it with their lives.

UWE SIEMON-NETTO

i

CONTENTS

ABOUT THE AUTHOR

U we Siemon-Netto, an international journalist from Germany, has reported about major world events for 57 years and covered the Vietnam War over a period of five years, from 1965 until 1969 and then again in 1972. At age 50 he interrupted his career to earn an M.A. at a Lutheran seminary in Chicago and a doctorate in theology and sociology of religion at Boston University. As part of his theological studies he served as a chaplain to Vietnam veterans in Minnesota and wrote a highly acclaimed book on pastoral care titled, *The Acquittal of God—A Theology for Vietnam Veterans*. Dr. Siemon-Netto now lives in southern California as a writer, educator and founding director emeritus of the *Center for Lutheran Theology and Public Life* in Capistrano Beach. Part of the year he and his British-born wife, Gillian, spend their time at their home in southwestern France.

FOREWORD

by Peter R. Kann

Uwe Siemon-Netto, the distinguished German journalist, has written a masterful memoir of his many years covering the Vietnam War. He captures, as very few others have, the pathos and absurdities, the combat, cruelties and human cost of a conflict which—as he unflinchingly and correctly argues—the wrong side won. From the street cafés of Saigon to Special Forces outposts in the central highlands, from villages where terror comes at night to the carnage and war crimes visited on the city of Huế at Tết, 1968, Uwe brings a brilliant reportorial talent and touch.

Above all, Uwe writes about the Vietnamese people: street urchins and buffalo boys, courageous warriors and hapless war victims, and the full human panoply of a society at war. As a German, Uwe had, as he puts it, "no dog in this fight," but he understood the rights and wrongs of this war better than almost anyone and his heart, throughout this powerful and moving volume, is always and ardently with the Vietnamese people.

Peter R. Kann, former correspondent with the Wall Street Journal in Vietnam and 1972 Pulitzer laureate, was named the Journal's publisher in 1988. From 1992 to 2006 he was CEO and chairman of the board of Dow Jones & Company.

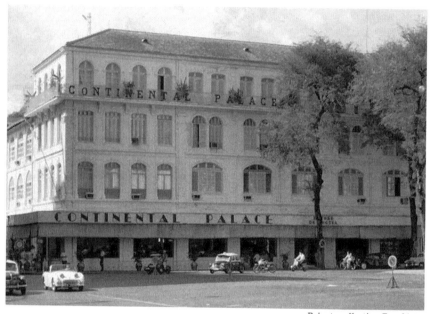

The author's home in Saigon: the *Continental Palace*

Preface to the Third Edition

Đức, or, Triumph of the Absurd

Forty years ago, absurdity triumphed in South Vietnam. On April 30, 1975, the wrong side conquered this tortured country. The Communists did not achieve their victory because they owned the moral high ground, as their adulators in the Western world would have us believe. They crushed South Vietnam with torture, mass murder and other horrendous acts of terror committed with cold strategic intent in violation of international law. I lived in Paris when their tanks crashed through the gates of the Presidential Palace in Saigon. As I watched this on television, I wondered: How did they manage to gain the upper hand after their clear military defeat I had witnessed as a combat correspondent during the Tết Offensive in Huế in 1968?

The answer can be found in the sinister prediction by General Vo Nguyen Giap, the North Vietnamese defense minister: "The enemy [i.e., the West] ... does not possess the psychological and political means to fight a long, drawn-out war." In his commentary on the fall of Saigon, Adelbert Weinstein, the brilliant military specialist of Germany's renowned *Frankfurter Allgemeine Zeitung*, summed up the reason for the victory of this totalitarian power in one short, elegiac sentence: "America could not wait."

Giap's prophetic words and the adjective "absurd" will reappear time and again in several chapters of this book. They are meant to be a recurrent theme intended to remind my readers why, four decades later, I wrote this memoir of my five years in Vietnam.

I would like this leitmotif to shine through the potpourri of mirthful or sad, erotic as well as lethal episodes in my narrative. Equally important is a second theme underlying these reminiscences: my declaration of love for the wounded, betrayed and abandoned people of South Vietnam whom the authors of many other books about this war have arrogantly and absurdly assigned a subordinate place.

This is why, beginning with the second edition, I have renamed this memoir *Triumph of the Absurd*, replacing the initial title, *Đức*. But I would like to make it clear that this original title is still very much on my mind, for three reasons: 1. *Đức* is the Vietnamese term for German, and these are, after all, the reminiscences of a German war correspondent. 2. *Đức* was the nickname my Vietnamese friends gave me when I lived among them. 3. *Đức* was the name of two of my protagonists, one a buffalo boy in central Vietnam, and the other a feisty and amusing urchin I befriended in Saigon.

That latter *Đức*, whom I will now introduce in this preface, was the spindly leader of a gang of homeless kids roaming the sidewalks of "my" block of Tu Do Street. We met in 1965 when Tu Do, the former *Rue Catinat*, still displayed traces of its former French colonial charm; it was still shaded by bushy and bright green tamarind trees, which would later fall victim to the exhaust fumes of tens of thousands of mopeds with two-stroke engines and prehistoric cars such as my grey 1938 *Citroën 15 CV Traction Avant*, the "gangster car" of French film classics. This car was nearly my age, a metric ton of elegance on wheels—and very thirsty; eight miles were all she gave me for a gallon of gasoline, provided her fuel tank had not sprung a leak, which my mechanic managed to seal swiftly every time with moist Wrigley gum harvested from inside his cheeks.

As you will presently see, my friendship with *Đức* and my love for this car were entwined. In truth, it wasn't really my automobile. I had leased it from Ariane, the comely concessionaire of an international car rental company, who, as I later found out, was also the agent of assorted Western European intelligence agencies, including the BND, Germany's equivalent of the CIA. I had often wondered why Ariane rummaged furtively through the manuscripts on my desk when she joined my friends and me for "sundowners" in Suite 214 of the *Continental Palace*. I fantasized that she was attracted by my youthful and slender Teutonic looks and my stiff dry martinis. She never let on that she read German; why would she want to stare at my texts if they were incomprehensible to her? Well, now I know: She was a spook, according to the Dutch station chief, who was possibly one of her lovers. But that was alright! I loved her car and she loved my martinis, which she handed around with amazing grace, and she was welcome to my stories anytime; after all, they were written for the public at large.

But my mind is wandering. Let us return to Đức. He was a droll twelve-year old with a mischievous grin reminding me of myself when I was his age, a rascal in a large wartime city. True, I wasn't homeless like Đức, although the British Lancaster bombers and the American Flying Fortresses pummeling Leipzig night and day during the final years of World War II tried their best to render me that way.

Like Đức, I was an impish, big-town boy successfully bossing other kids on my block around. But Đức was also different. He was an urchin with a high sense of responsibility. He protectively watched over a gang of much younger orphans living on Tu Do Street between Le Loi Boulevard and Le Than Ton Street, reporting to a middle-aged *Mamasan* headquartered on the sidewalk outside *La Pagode*, a café famed for its French pastries, and the renowned rendezvous point of pre-Communist Saigon's *jeunesse dorée*. *Mamasan* was the motherly press tycoon of that part of the capital. She squatted there outside *La Pagode* surrounded by stacks of newspapers: papers in Vietnamese and English, French and Chinese—the Vietnamese were avid readers. She handed them out to Đức and his wards and several other bands of children assigned to neighboring blocks.

From what I could observe, Đức was *Mamasan*'s most important lieutenant, the head paperboy at the busiest end of his block. His turf was the sidewalk between *Givral*, a restaurant renowned for its Chinese noodle soup as well as the most authentic French onion soup in all of Southeast Asia, and the entrance to the shopping passage in the Eden Building, which housed the consular section of the West German embassy at that time and the offices of the Associated Press. I fancy that I was one of Đức's favorite clients because I bought the *Saigon Daily News* and the *Vietnam Guardian* from him every day, and the *Saigon Post* and the *Journal d'Extrême Orient*. Sometimes I allowed him to cajole me into paying for a couple of Vietnamese-language papers; not that I could read them, but I was intrigued by their frequent empty spaces, the handiwork of government censors.

One late afternoon, at the onset of the monsoon season, Đức and I became business partners. The massive clouds in the tropical sky were about to burst. Sheets of water threatened to descend on me with the force of a guillotine blade transforming Saigon's principal thoroughfare into a gushing stream. I hastily squeezed my *Traction* into a tight parking space outside *Givral's*, a muscle-building exercise given that this front-wheel-driven machine lacked power steering and was propelled by a heavy six-cylinder motor made of cast iron. Exhausted, I switched off the engine by which time I was lusting for a bottle of *Bière Larue* on the *Continental Palace*'s open-air terrace when Đức stopped me.

The old *Traction's* front doors opened forward, thus in the opposite direction of the doors of all modern cars. As I tried to dash out, Đức stood in my way pointing at the windscreen sticker I had been issued that morning by my embassy. It bore the German national colors, black, red and gold, and identified me as *"Báo Chí Đức,"* a German journalist. This was meant to protect me in case I ran into a Viet Cong roadblock on my occasional weekend jaunts to Cap Saint-Jacques, now called *Vũng Tàu*, a seaside resort once known as the St. Tropez of the Orient. It actually did shield me in those days. Whenever I ran into a patrol of black-clad Communist militiamen, they would charge me a toll and let me go, but not before issuing me a stamped receipt.

"You Đức!" he shouted delightedly. "My name Đức. We both Đức. We like brothers!" We shook hands. Now I had a younger brother in Saigon; later I learned that his remark meant even more: it was wordplay. Đức is also the Vietnamese word for virtuous.

Having established our bond, he wouldn't let me go, though. "Okay, okay," he said. "Rain coming, Đức, rain numbah ten." I knew Saigon street jargon well enough to realize that my new brother wasn't talking of the tenth rainfall. No, "numbah ten" meant the worst, the pits, something definitely to avoid.

"Okay, okay," Đức continued. "You Đức, you numbah one (the best). You and I do business, okay?"

Then he outlined our deal: I was to allow him and his wards to seek shelter in my *Traction*. It would become their bedroom, which they promised to keep immaculately clean. If I wanted to leave any valuables in the car, they would be safe. Its lock no longer worked; this much Đức had already ascertained.

"Okay, okay, Đức?" he pleaded impatiently.

I nodded. He whistled, and at once nine toddlers rushed out of several doorways and piled into my *Traction*. Three curled up on the back seats, two on the jump seats, one each in the legroom separating them, one girl took the right front seat, another squatted on the generous floor space under her feet, and Đức naturally took his place behind the steering wheel.

"*Bonne nuit*, Đức, you numbah one!" he said, slamming the door and winding up the window. At this moment a torrent of rain poured down on the *Traction* and on me. The kids were safe. I was drenched to the bones within seconds. I ran into the *Continental Palace*, needing more than a *Larue*.

First I had a shower in my room, then a whisky on the covered terrace. As night fell I kept staring across Tu Do Street at my large *Citroën* with steamed up windows outside *Givral's*. This sight pleased me. These children were warm and dry. In all my years in Vietnam I rarely felt as happy as on that evening, an uncommon sensation in a reporter's life.

I am honoring Đức in this book too because in my mind he personified many qualities that formed my affection and admiration for the people of South Vietnam, and my compassion for them after their abandonment by their protectors and their betrayal by some, though not all, members of my profession. Like Đức, they are feisty and resilient; they don't whine, but pull themselves up by their bootstraps, and they care for each other. When they are down, they rise again and accomplish astonishing things.

I am in awe of the achievements of the hundreds of thousands of South Vietnamese living and working close to my home in southern California. I am full of admiration for those former boat people and survivors of Communist reeducation camps, those former warriors suffering in silence from Post-Traumatic Stress Disorder and other severe ailments caused by torture and head injuries received in combat.

I hope that Đức's adolescence and adulthood turned out to be a success story as well, but I don't know. We lost contact 18 months after our first encounter. Was he drafted into the South Vietnamese army and eventually killed in combat? Did he join the Viet Cong and perhaps die in their service? Was he among the thousands of civilians butchered by the Viet Cong during the Tết Offensive of 1968? Or did this crafty kid manage to flee his homeland after the Communist victory of 1975? Perhaps he is alive at the time of this writing and is a successful 58-year old businessman or professional in Westminster, California, just up the road from me; perhaps he is reading this book.

I thought of Đức when two wonderful Vietnamese friends, Quy Van Ly and his wife QuynhChau, better known as Jo, invited me to address a convention of former military medical officers of the South Vietnamese Army. They had been urging me for some time to write my wartime reminiscences. "Do it for us," they said, "do it for our children's generation. They want to know what it was like. You have special credibility because as a German you had no dog in this fight." Then, after listening to my anecdotes (such as the one about my encounter with Đức) several of those retired physicians, dentists and pharmacists in my audience said the same thing, and some bounced my speech around the Internet.

I do not presume to rewrite the history of the Vietnam War or even give a comprehensive account of the nearly five years I spent in Indochina as a correspondent, first of the *Axel Springer* group of German newspapers and subsequently as a visiting reporter of *Stern*, an influential Hamburg-based magazine. I beg my readers not to expect me to take sides in the domestic squabbles between South Vietnamese factions, quarrels that are being perpetuated in the huge communities of Vietnamese exiles today. When I mention former Vice President Nguyen Cao Ky, for example, this does not mean that I favor him over former President Nguyen van Thieu, or vice versa; I am just here to tell stories, including some about Ky and some about Thieu, without wishing to pass judgment on either. Theirs was an unenviable lot, and they deserve my respect for having taken up an appalling burden.

As I stated in the first paragraph of this preface, I did not welcome the victory of the Communists in 1975. They deserved this triumph as little as the Taliban in Afghanistan will deserve the triumph, which I fear will be theirs once NATO forces have left their country. It is also with this latter sinister prospect in mind that I have written this book.

In Vietnam, I have been a witness to heinous atrocities the Communists committed as a matter of policy, a witness to mass murder and carnage beside which transgressions against the rules of war perpetrated on the American and South Vietnamese side— clearly not as a matter of policy or strategy—appear pale in comparison. I know that many in the American and international mass media and academe have unjustly, gratuitously and arrogantly maligned the South Vietnamese and are still doing so. I was disgusted by the way returning GIs were treated by their fellow countrymen and am shocked by the fact that the continued suffering of South Vietnamese veterans is not deemed worthy of consideration by U.S. journalists.

This book is a collection of personal sketches recounting what I saw, observed, lived through and reported in my Vietnam years, and about the people I met. It is a series of alternating narratives about experiences ranging from the horrific to the absurd, about pursuits ranging from the glamorous to the frivolous, and about life ranging from despair to hope. All the persons mentioned here are authentic, though in some cases I changed their names to protect them or their next of kin.

Vietnam has had a significant impact on my spiritual life as well. But this process, which took decades, will not be a major feature in the present volume because I intend to elaborate on it in a different kind of memoir later. But I will mention it briefly in this preface: Gradually, my war experiences in Vietnam have led me back to the Christian faith to which my maternal grandmother, Clara Netto, introduced me in our air raid shelter in Leipzig as blockbuster bombs detonated all around us. It was in those fearful moments that she taught me to place my trust in God: She held me tightly and sang to me softly Lutheran hymns, especially one that was to remain in my ears for the rest of my life:

> Abide, O dearest Jesus,
> Among us with Thy grace,
> That Satan may not harm us,
> Nor we to sin give place.

To say that I was filled with Christian fervor in the 1960s would be mendacious. Like my contemporaries, I indulged in a lifestyle filled with worldly pleasures of which chain-smoking was the least iniquitous, particularly as nicotine has a seemingly numbing effect in combat situations, as almost all frontline soldiers and war reporters will affirm. The photograph on the cover of this book shows me sucking grimly on a cigarette during a lull in the battle of Huế in 1968. We chose this picture because it is authentic and realistic. This is how people look after they have seen others die all around them for many days and nights; this is how I looked as a young man in an unforgettably terrifying situation, which determined the course of the rest of my life.

Though a hedonist then, I was never an atheist. I spoke the Lord's Prayer frequently, subsequently humming in my head the Lutheran offertory versicle based on the 51st Psalm: "Create in me a clean heart, O God, and renew a right spirit within me. Cast me not away from Thy presence, and take not Thy Holy Spirit from me." When I was in heavy combat, holding the hand of a dying soldier, I chanted to myself the *Kyrie eleison*: Lord, have mercy!

Today I am grateful for having been brought up with the rich liturgy of the Lutheran Church in Saxony. Its words, all taken from Scripture, have become deeply ingrained in my memory. But following Saint Augustine's example, I had relegated God to the waiting room of my biography. Too enticing were those dark-haired beauties in whose arms we reporters found solace from the war, too wonderful were the food and wine in Saigon's French restaurants, too jolly was the fellowship of my witty British colleagues.

Then in 1973, the year the Americans turned their backs on South Vietnam, I was shocked to hear myself profess my faith in Christ in the absurdly godless environment of a German newsroom where I was the managing editor. The circumstances of this sudden commitment during a fierce slugfest with extreme leftwing members of my staff will make a hilarious chapter of a future book. Suffice it to say that this was a turning point in my life, which, after many temptations and inner strife, led me to enroll in the Lutheran School of Theology at Chicago thirteen years later.

Slowly, almost homeopathically, Vietnam had changed me. At first I thought I was called to the ordained ministry, until my astute wife, Gillian, set me straight, convincing me that my acerbic manner, nurtured as a battle-scarred reporter, would split any congregation within 24 hours. "Your place in church is neither at the altar nor in the pulpit but in one of the back pews from which you can seek refuge at the nearest pub when you hear a bad sermon," she said. And she was right.

Before opting for the strictly academic route to theology, though, I enrolled in a Clinical Pastoral Education program that is a prerequisite for ordination in the United States. I took this course at the Veterans Hospital in St. Cloud, Minnesota, where I asked my superiors to assign me to Vietnam veterans. I immediately encountered hosts of broken men describing to me the bone-headed cruelty with which their fellow Americans, especially young women, disowned them. I discovered that almost all of them were convinced that God had long condemned them to hell for all eternity. God, they said, had deserted them in Vietnam.

This gave me an excellent starting point for providing them with pastoral care, especially as I had concentrated heavily on Dietrich Bonhoeffer's take on the Lutheran Theology of the Cross in my studies. Together with VA psychologist James Tuorila I formed therapy groups of 30 men each, ranging from former private to lieutenant colonel. I made them read Bonhoeffer's *Letters and Papers from Prison*. What fascinated them most about this stirring book was Bonhoeffer's emphasis on Jesus' words to his disciples in Gethsemane, "Could you not stay awake with me one hour?" (Matthew 26:40). "This is the reversal of everything a religious person expected from God", Bonhoeffer wrote. "The human being is called upon to share in God's suffering in a godless world."

This was the first time these former warriors were told a basic Christian verity: The Christian is called to suffer with God in this world as an act of discipleship. Their suffering in Vietnam and after their return home was the cross God had placed on their backs. But this means that God himself also suffers in the world from the godlessness these men of war experience daily. That being so, God is clearly not the deserter they thought he was. Quite to the contrary, he is a fellow sufferer, a comrade.

I taped these discussions, edited and commented them, and thus turned them into my M.A. thesis, which I presented to the Lutheran School of Theology. In 1990, this thesis was published as a book, which is still in print and used as a textbook for providing pastoral care to veterans.

Then I found an entirely different occasion for dealing with the topic of Vietnam. After earning my M.A. in Chicago, I transferred to Boston University to study for my interdisciplinary doctorate in theology and sociology of religion. This triggered my interest in the sociological phenomenon of thinking in clichés.

Used as a metaphor for a particular way of thinking, clichés distinguish themselves by "their capacity to bypass reflection and thus unconsciously to work on the mind, while excluding potential relativizations," according to the Dutch sociologist Anton Zijderveld (Zijderveld, Anton: *On Clichés*, London 1979). "Having been fully socialized in a particular society," Zijderveld writes, "the clichés of this society will lie in store in man's consciousness, ever ready to be triggered and used."

Clichés, or stereotypes, thus become "containers of old experiences" that have "grown stale and common through repetitive overuse," Zijderveld continues. They are exchanged "like the many coins of our inflated economic system." A cliché should be seen "as a specimen of human expression which has lost much of its original ingenuity and semantic power, but gained in social functionality."

Zijderveld saw a strong affinity between clichés and modernity. In my doctoral dissertation I took this thought a step further: If Zijderveld is right, then stereotypical thinking is a twin of the *Zeitgeist*, which also does not allow for any relativizations. The *Zeitgeist* shares a property Zijderveld attributes to clichés: "They become tyrannical in that stereotypes are hard to avoid in a fully modernized society; they are prone to become the molds of consciousness, while their functionality penetrates deeply into the fabric of socio-cultural and political life."

To be sure, Vietnam was not the topic of my dissertation, with which I refuted the widely held stereotype that Martin Luther had paved the way for Adolf Hitler. I did this by pointing to a large number of relativizing factors disproving this contemptible slander. In the present book, however, I am attempting something similar concerning Vietnam, though just by relating my personal experiences and observations rather than in a scholarly manner.

Forty years after the communist conquest of Saigon, a stereotypical lump lairs heavily on peoples' collective consciousness: the absurd cliché that this victory, which was accomplished by means of torture and mass murder, was actually an act of liberation and thus a good thing. In its tyrannical way, as Zijderveld would say, this cliché allowed for no relativizing factors of the kind I describe graphically in order to counter a historical lie.

To remind my readers and myself that this is ultimately a book about a tragic war that ended in defeat for the victims of aggression, I will insert a brief reflection underscoring this fact every few chapters, beginning with a description of a mass murder the Communists committed during the 1968 Têt Offensive.

I owe gratitude to many people, but especially to my faithful friends Quy and Jo who steadfastly stood behind me as I wrote this book giving me every conceivable support while I labored over the manuscript. Every time I had finished a chapter, Quy translated it immediately into elegant Vietnamese with the help of his friend Nguyen Hien. He did the layout, designed the cover and gave me sound advice on cultural and historical questions. I am proud to have become part of Quy's and Jo's very traditional Vietnamese family in Orange County. I thank Quy's brother-in-law, Di Ton That, and his wife, Tran, who were the first to contact me when I moved to southern California, and who introduced me to the huge and thriving Vietnamese community in Orange County.

I am grateful to the absent Đức, and to the countless other Vietnamese, American, French, British and German friends I made in Vietnam. I also wish to thank the Vietnam veterans for whom I served as a chaplain intern at the VA Medical Center in St. Cloud, Minnesota, and the psychologists and ministers with whom I worked in order to provide those former soldiers with pastoral care. I am very thankful to my friend Perry Kretz for allowing me to publish some of his magnificent photographs from our reporting trip to Vietnam in 1972 in this volume.

I thank my friend and editor Peggy Strong and, most importantly, my wife Gillian who, in our 50 years of marriage, has stood by me and endured our long periods of separation caused by my assignment to an enchanting war-torn country I have come to love.

Uwe Siemon-Netto
Laguna Woods, California
January 2015

A *Citroën 15 CV Traction* just like the car the author drove in Saigon, allowing street urchins to use it as their bedroom.

Reflection One

When warriors wept

"One becomes so accustomed to all the dead being men that the sight of a dead woman is quite shocking."

– Ernest Hemingway

Fighting men don't weep easily, especially not in combat. But in early February 1968 I saw warriors in tears. I was traveling with a battalion of the 5th Marines as it advanced slowly from Phú Bài airfield toward Huế, which was then occupied by Communist forces. As we entered the southern outskirts of this beautiful city that was once Vietnam's imperial capital, there were so many corpses on the road that the leathernecks had to move them aside under sniper fire to create a free passage for their convoy.

Some of the dead were old men with wispy white beards, but most were women and children, all festively clad for Tết, the Vietnamese New Year. We could tell from their wounds and the way they lay that they had not been killed by shrapnel; they had not died accidentally in crossfire. No, these noncombatants were shot at point-blank range, massacred by the Viet Cong, like the thousands of other Huế residents, whose cadavers were found later.

Hemingway was understating his case when he wrote, reminiscing about his service as a Red Cross volunteer in World War I, "[The] sight of a dead woman is quite shocking." For normal men—especially fighting men—this spectacle is unbearable. So it was a natural reaction by these young Americans to cry, for they were simple, decent men who deeply believed that God had created women to be loved, not slaughtered.

There was something particularly eerie about this scene—eerily elegant. Even in death these women looked sublime as their bodies were draped protectively around those of their children. We could see that they had just donned their freshly cleaned national dress, the *Áo dài*, to welcome the Vietnamese New Year. We saw that their fingernails had just been carefully manicured and their faces made up in preparation for the highest feast of the year.

Disgracefully, some very prominent American apologists for the Hanoi regime, such as philosopher Noam Chomsky and historian Marilyn P. Young, claimed that the Huế Massacre never happened. To me they seemed intellectually dishonest, not unlike the holocaust deniers or those shameful Western intellectuals of the 1920s who visited the Soviet Union when Stalin's goons killed hundreds of thousands of kulaks, or land-owning farmers, but chose to ignore this crime.

I am stating it here and will repeat it later in this book: I saw what the Communists have done in Huế, and I stood at the rim of shallow mass graves where they had buried their victims while many of them were evidently still alive: Some of these sites were discovered because the manicured fingers of dying women had protruded through the surface in a vain effort to escape their fate; they never made it out.

Chapter One

Comme la mer, comme le ciel

My home during most of my stints in Vietnam between early 1965 and late 1969, and then again in 1972, was Suite 214 in the *Continental Palace*. It was an abode with agreeable features, including the way two servants on the second floor attended to my whims. They knew that I preferred the ceiling fan to the dilapidated air conditioner, which might have kept the mosquitoes out, but kept me awake all night, rattling, and would not allow me to regulate the temperature. With this in mind, the two kindly men caught geckos in the corridor and released them in my room to eat the malaria-causing bugs.

I cannot think of a more convenient address for a reporter in the center of Saigon than Suite 214. My side windows faced southwest. Below was Tu Do Street, the former *Rue Catinat*, running from *Notre Dame* Cathedral down to the Saigon River docks. I could hear a cacophony of chirping mopeds, gurgling, blue-and-white *Renault 4CV* taxis, bicycle bells, limousines and military trucks. Between these two windows stood my desk. Late in the afternoon it doubled as a bar where I mixed dry martinis for guests like my friend Peter Heller, a U.S. government spokesman, after he had survived the usually exasperating *Five O'Clock Follies*. He merited a stiff drink as a reward for regaling me with witty summaries of these press conferences which he directed every day in an office building nearby, next to a statue we newsmen dubbed *Buggery Statue* because it symbolized two charging soldiers in a position validating this odious description.

I seldom wasted time on the *Follies*, which were dominated by braggadocios like Joe, the highly-strung and prosecutorial correspondent of a large American tabloid. He rarely ventured into the hinterland where the inconveniences of combat would have curtailed his risk-free way of life. According to Richard Pyle and Horst Faas of the Associated Press, seventy percent of the accredited correspondents covered the war by staying close to Saigon and thus disregarding the wise counsel of Barry Zorthian, the legendary chief press officer of the U.S. government in Saigon: "Get out of town and look for yourself." (Pyle and Faas in *Lost over Laos*, Cambridge, MA, 2003). It figures that these were the most persistent carpers against the conduct of this conflict; real war correspondents, hazarding injury and death, were too busy staying alive and getting their stories out to engage in media posturing.

My big front windows opened to the southeast, overlooking the intersection of Tu Do and Le Loi streets, the busiest in the city. Lam Son Square, formerly *Place du Grand Théâtre*, was below. A French colonial building patterned after *Le Petit Palais* in Paris flanked this square on the left. In the pre-Communist era it housed the National Assembly but has since become the Municipal Opera House. Across Lam Son I saw the *Caravelle* Hotel, which was allegedly owned by the Catholic diocese of Saigon. I found its atmosphere sterile, though others treasured it as a secure refuge, for it admitted no strangers: notably no ladies of the night. The *Caravelle* was the preferred haunt of the species Pyle termed, "celebrity columnists and political prognosticators," although some less lofty friends and colleagues of mine stayed there as well. As the Romans said, *de gustibus non est disputandum:* in matters of taste there can be no disputes.

When media stars popped into Saigon for short sojourns, they found comfort in the rarified atmosphere of the *Caravelle's* restaurant and bar, where they pontificated about the war with highly placed sources, and with each other. The *Caravelle's* roof terrace afforded a generous view of enemy territory: the mangrove swamps on the far shore of the Saigon River. As the war progressed, this terrace became the front-row position to observe what we named *son et lumière*, after the nightly summertime open-air shows in France. Saigon's *son et lumière* was a lethal spectacle performed by "Puff, the Magic Dragon." This was our nickname for U.S. Air Force gunships of the *C-47 Spooky* type. With fierce bursts of fire drowning out, like colossal eruptions of flatulence, every other noise, these planes "sprayed" Viet Cong positions at the rate of 100 bullet rounds per second.

For all its security, I never cared for the *Caravelle's* roof terrace, which impressed me as a soulless venue in a colorful land. Like most European correspondents, along with the hard-working, hard-drinking, brave, but uncelebrated troopers among our American colleagues, I preferred the raucous ambiance of the *Continental's* covered terrace, which in a more elegant era had been equal to the terraces of the *Carlton* in Cannes, *Shepheard's* in Cairo and *Raffles* in Singapore. Here *le tout Saigon* could be found: colonels and generals, senior civil servants and diplomats; members of the local *haute volée*; remnants of the old French community, Corsican opium lords, and lustful but suicidal female freelance photographers with stomachs full of shrapnel, a result of their habit of charging ahead of advancing forces determined to shoot the most sensational pictures; obese American contractors in the company of transvestites, and other nasty practitioners of the horizontal enterprise; pundits, spies, adventurers, nefarious deadbeats; teetotaling doctors and nurses of the local Seventh Day Adventists Hospital nipping at large glasses of *citron pressé*; and doubtless many undercover Viet Cong agents whose very presence protected us from being blown up by their infiltrators.

This was once Graham Greene's terrace. It couldn't have looked much different from when he was here in the 1950s covering the French Indochina War, except that then it was surely more stylish. The *Continental's* terrace featured in *The Quiet American*, Greene's novel about that conflict. This novel used to lie on every respectable Saigon correspondent's bedside table alongside two other significant books: *People's War, People's Army*, the manual of guerilla warfare by North Vietnamese Gen. Vo Nguyen Giap, and *The Two Viet-Nams*, by Bernard Fall (London: Pall Mall Press, 1967). This is a "political and military analysis" of the nature and roots of this hot proxy of the global Cold War. Later I shall discuss the mysterious failure of many analysts of the Vietnam tragedy to draw the proper conclusions from Giap's and Fall's works. As for Graham Greene, I am still chortling about his passage concerning Vietnamese women in *The Quiet American* (London: Heinemann, 1955):

"To take an Annamite to bed with you is like taking a bird: they twitter and sing on your pillow."

Perhaps Suite 214 was Greene's room; perhaps here, in this bed that was now mine, he made his enthralling observation. However, my own impressions of these superb creatures were shaped by visual rather than acoustic sensations. Every morning, I took my breakfast of croissants, mango, papaya, mangosteen fruit and *café noir* in a colonial-era leather armchair by one of my front windows, and then delighted in the most glorious sight. Beginning soon after six, when the nightly curfew was lifted, streams of beauty flowed down the thoroughfares of central Saigon: tens of thousands of women and men on foot, riding bicycles and mopeds, and reclining in the passenger seats of bicycle rickshaws called *cyclo-pousses*. My male Vietnamese friends will forgive me for focusing chiefly on females who moved provocatively in their national dress called *Áo dài*, a garment so erotic that it has no match in any other culture; for as the saying goes, the *Áo dài* "covers everything but hides nothing."

The *Áo dài* is probably the most captivating example of a perfect Eastern-Western blend in aesthetics and sensuality. It has its origins in Vietnamese culture, but under the inspiration of Paris fashions was redesigned in the 1920s by artists associated with Hanoi University. Subsequently the Saigon couturiers of the 1950s refined it even more alluringly. The *Áo dài* consists of a silk tunic hugging the upper torso more tightly even than the Chinese *Cheongsam*, and then splitting above the waist into two long flaps, one in front and one in the back.

Underneath these flaps, Vietnamese women wear pantaloons, leaving an inch or two of skin exposed on both sides at the upper end of the split. If these pantaloons are white and light, as is often the case, the attentive admirer will spot just a hint of briefs shimmering through. This arrangement of female legs covered by pantaloons and feet shod with high-heeled sandals pushing the silk tunic's silk flaps forward results in an inimitably elegant stride. No twenty-first century pornographer possesses the imagination or concupiscence needed to conjure up such sensuality. Top this with a shock of thick black hair over a pair of almond-shaped eyes, and you are in love with an entire nation. Or at least I was.

I beg my readers of postmodern persuasion to indulge me for discussing the attractions of Vietnamese womanhood with such passion early in this volume. This has to do with age. I proudly belong to a generation of Western men who thought it normal to love, court, adore and wish to protect the opposite sex. Like Ernest Hemingway, I found "the sight of a dead woman quite shocking," which has caused me to dedicate these memoirs to "the wounded people of Vietnam" or, as the subtitle of my second and subsequent editions reads, to "the abandoned people of Vietnam." To be precise, when I think of Vietnam, the first thing that comes to my mind is the beauty of its women. And this goes logically in tandem with my memory of the horrific images of these butchered creatures, some of whom the Communists buried alive, as my readers will discover in Chapter Fifteen.

This is what came to mind when my ophthalmologist Anna Phuong Nguyen in Costa Mesa, California, tried to draw out of me, with a bemused glint in her eyes, a disclosure of the romantic aspects of my life in Saigon.

"So, have you left, hee hee, the great love of your life behind in Saigon, haven't you?" she asked.

"Hundreds of thousands," I answered evasively, "I adored every woman I watched from my windows in the *Continental*."

Did she think I would turn her shop into a confessional? But I loved Anna's barefaced curiosity, just as I delighted in the unabashed inquisitiveness of a dozen Vietnamese women in the first nail salon I ever visited. It was in Irvine.

"You want drink?" asked the receptionist after she had guided me to my chair.

Remembering one word from my small Vietnamese vocabulary, I said: *nước*, meaning water.

"You speak Vietnamese!" shouted the girl soaking my left hand.

"He speak Vietnamese!" echoed the gorgeous creature sitting on a stool by my left foot, ready to soak it in a bowl of lukewarm *nước*.

"You speak Vietnamese! You been in Vietnam War? You made babies in Saigon, right?" said her colleague while ministering to the toes of a morose blonde in the chair to my right.

"Everybody listen! *Ông* (this man) made baby in Vietnam. You have daughter, right? For sure: you have daughter. Your daughter blond like American, eyes like Vietnamese, right?"

"I am not an American, I am German—I am a Đức," I corrected her. By now the sullen blonde to my right cracked a smile. The Indian lady in the chair to my left laughed out loud. Soon half a dozen Vietnamese giggling manicurists, pedicurists and shop assistants had assembled around me.

"Okay, okay," continued my inquisitor, "you German, you tall, you blond. You have blond daughter with Vietnamese eyes, okay?"

Pause.

"There she is," she cried, pointing to a strapping colleague of mixed ancestry. "Kelly. That's her. Everybody listen! We have found Kelly's father. He Đức."

By this time we had reached a point where cheerful pandemonium quashed any reasonable argument involving age and timeframe in this Irvine nail salon. Never mind that Kelly was born in Saigon in late 1973, one year after I had left this city for the last time. In half an hour I had acquired a daughter, plus an extended family of amusing females. The one who claimed jokingly that I was Kelly's father embraced me firmly on my way out.

This interlude in Irvine reminded me of the paradoxical qualities I enjoyed in Vietnamese women half a century ago. On the one hand they look deliciously frangible, fitting the sweet songs and tweets they emit on a gentleman's pillow, if we follow Graham Greene. Yet they can be as earthy and unabashed, even maliciously blunt, including in carnal matters, as any self-assured German lady I have ever met. Being German, I found this combination hugely attractive, especially when compared with the strident narcissistic feminism of the baby boomer generation, which the 1960s spawned, and which I always considered a sign of weakness. Vietnamese women are not posing as strong—they *are* strong. That's the difference.

I won't deny that this display of genuine female can be over the top sometimes. I suspect that the hostility of certain American scribes to the Saigon government stemmed in part from their misapprehension of what they dubbed the "dragon ladies" in the presidential Palace. The fiercest of these was the late Trần Lệ Xuân, better known as Madame Nhu, whose loud mouth and voluptuous beauty seemed an incongruous match, especially if judged by the standards of a prissy culture that spawned that hideous malignancy called political correctness.

She was the sister-in-law of President Ngô Đình Diem, a bachelor, and served as his *de facto* first lady; her husband was Diem's powerful younger brother and chief political adviser, Ngô Đình Nhu. These two men, both Catholics, were assassinated in a *coup d'état* in November of 1963, following mass protests by Buddhists against alleged religious discrimination. This crisis had culminated in the fiery self-immolation of Thich Quang Đức, a Buddhist venerable, in downtown Saigon. Madame Nhu commented on this event with a distinct dearth of kindliness. It takes a sardonic sense of irony to stomach her televised remarks delivered in French-accented English, while waving a delicate fan under her aristocratic chin:

"What (rhetorical pause) have the Buddhist leaders done...? They have barbecued one of their own monks whom they have intoxicated—whom they have abused the confidence. Isn't that barbecuing?"

She topped these words by adding:

"It was done not even by self-sufficient means because they used imported gasoline."

Well, this was callous; it was macabre; it wasn't "nice." But when her arrestingly lush lips spoke these arrestingly cruel words she looked arrestingly lovely. And let's face it: You knew where she stood.

That said, I must add one personal note to my ode to Vietnamese womanhood. Honesty demands that I not fob off Anna the optician with a generic copout. Not that I am confessing anything, but there was Josephine.

One Saturday morning I boarded my *Citroën 15 CV Traction* for a day trip to the beach with a friend I will call Fabian Fuchs for the purposes of this narrative. Fabian represented a West German non-governmental organization aiding the Saigon government in social matters. He had just acquired a delectable new girlfriend called Monique whose father was a Frenchman married to a Catholic refugee from Hanoi. On this occasion, she brought along another *métisse*, or half-breed, who was the most glamorous woman I ever saw in Saigon: tall with lips like Madame Nhu's, very dark, large moist eyes and thick black hair falling down beyond her hips. Her name was Josephine.

Đức, my car's minder and leader of a gang of homeless children on Tu Do Street, was invited along. I offered to reimburse *Mamasan*, his boss, for the loss of income resulting from Đức's brief vacation, but she waved me off: "No, no, he needs a rest! Go, go, Đức, go have good time!" He turned us down, though: "Other kids no go, I no go. Come back safely; we need your car tonight."

My *Traction* was, after all, their bedroom. That was my Đức, the imp filled with a sense of responsibility.

So off we drove in a southeasterly direction along National Route 5 to the South China Sea. My car must have done this eighty-mile journey scores of times—before World War II, during the Japanese occupation, before the French defeat in Dien Bien Phu and after Vietnam's division in 1954. We weaved in and out of gaps between trucks and jeeps, armored vehicles and self-propelled howitzers; we passed passenger coaches billowing out black clouds, mopeds carrying families of five; three-wheeler Lambretta buses—known as Lams—with two dozen peasants on board, air-conditioned limousines belonging to members of Saigon's *haute bourgeoisie* and the colonies of Europeans and Asians. All displayed *laissez-passers* from their embassies on their windshields: French, German, Italian, British, Canadian, Australian, Japanese, Thai, Indian, Pakistani and Israeli. At that stage of the war nobody expected guerilla attacks on a Saturday when foreigners fled the muggy capital for some relief at the "Indochinese Riviera."

We had to be back in Saigon by nightfall because after dark National Route 5 belonged to the Communists. Just as it became hot late in the morning, our *Traction* stopped dead, fortunately only 500 yards from a gasoline station. Monique, Fabian and I got out; Josephine, whose former husband had taught her to drive, took the steering wheel, barely capable of moving it as we pushed this ton of steel meter by meter into the garage, which had a French-speaking mechanic on duty.

"*Pas d'essence,*" he stated, "*pauvre vieille bagnole*"—no gas, poor old jalopy.

He crawled underneath, found a crack in the gasoline pipe connecting the tank with the engine and instructed me how to fix it: just stick a moist piece of chewing gum on it; it will hold. It did. I later taught my Saigon mechanic this trick. It always worked. The hole in the gasoline pipe was never properly mended.

We continued our journey in the midday sun and were drenched in sweat when we arrived in Cap St. Jacques, so we headed directly to the white sandy beach at the *Baie des Cocotiers*, or Coconut Bay (Bài Truoc in Vietnamese), and threw ourselves into the waves of the South China Sea. When we were a fair distance from shore and alone, Josephine began swimming in circles around me. Closer and closer she came. She grabbed me by my arms, saying: "Let us dance." So we danced in the water to the music in our heads, as her long hair floated on the waves, forming a circular black carpet around both of us.

"Je t'aime comme la mer, comme le ciel," she said; I love you like the sea and the sky.

We danced on for a while and returned to the beach. We were back in Saigon before the tropical night set in.

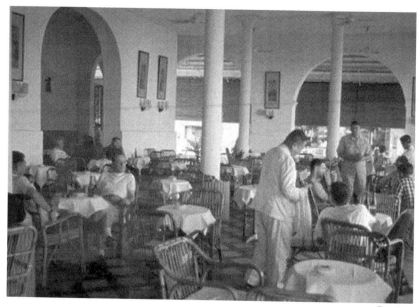

Ron Yates

Graham Greene's old watering hole:
The legendary terrace of the *Continental Palace*

Chapter Two

The Gillian factor

Je t'aime comme la mer, comme le ciel, Josephine had said.

These words have since defined my relationship with Vietnam but in the end not with Josephine, though by no fault of hers. After our Terpsichorean swim we saw each other often when I was not "up country" accompanying Vietnamese troops or American Special Forces on combat missions. Her loveliness added to my dining pleasure at my favorite restaurant, *Le Royal*, on Nguyen Huê´ Boulevard. The *Royal* was an old-fashioned French establishment with starched white tablecloths. Its Corsican owner, Jean Ottavi, was a droll, emaciated septuagenarian with the phenomenal capacity to humor his Vietnamese wife. Her years on earth equaled the number of opium pipes he smoked every day—35 on each count at the time we met, or so I was told.

I took Josephine with me to concerts and parties. On some Saturdays we drove to the *Club Nautique* to water-ski on the Saigon River; this was still possible in 1965 but became too dangerous as the fighting closed in on the city.

Once I rendered Josephine an almost sacrificial service, when she asked me to bring back from a reporting trip a rare fish sauce that had become unavailable in Saigon stores because of the war. This assignment degenerated into an excursion to Dante's first circle of hell; but this metaphor requires elucidation: Since my childhood I have suffered from a seafood allergy. Eating fish or shellfish can kill me. This disposition, called ichthyophobia, doesn't make life easy if one is living in a culture with a cuisine the most important ingredient of which is *nuoc mam*, a protein-rich condiment made from fermented fish. Not that this is an exclusively Oriental oddity because jars containing a sauce like *nuoc mam*, called *garum*, used to be on every dinner table of the

13

Roman Empire. I am grateful that when the Roman Empire collapsed 1,500 years ago, it left us Westerners with merely one benign vestige of *garum* in the shape of rotten anchovies contained in Worcestershire sauce.

When invited to dinner at a private home in Southeast Asia I usually warned my hostess beforehand that I was a vegetarian. This was a little white lie she would appreciate more easily than any claim to an allergy, for my predicament put me in a class with the brown-robed monks of Mahayana Buddhism, Vietnam's principal religion, who are also vegetarians. But Josephine's request entailed a spirit of self-sacrifice on my part when I traveled to Phú Quốc island to research a story about a camp for Communist prisoners of war.

To *nuoc mam* aficionados, Phú Quốc is what the Médoc is to lovers of Bordeaux wines. On this largest island in the Gulf of Siam the fish sauce equivalent of *Château Margaux* or *Château Latour* is created in wooden vats with the help of gadgets resembling sauerkraut presses. The day had an entertaining start: as I toured a POW camp, an inmate in black pajamas read the nametag on my fatigues identifying me as a German journalist.

"Where in Germany are you from?" he asked me in a Saxon accent, the most ridiculous of all German dialects.

"The place where you learned German," I replied in the same accent.

"Leipzig?"

"Yes, Leipzig, I fled from Leipzig to West Germany when I was a child."

"I studied German in the Herder Institute," said the inmate, a North Vietnamese medical officer who had trained in East Germany.

"What a coincidence! This was once the *Gaudig-Schule*, the best girls' school in Germany, before World War II. My mother graduated from there. You might have sat in her classroom," I told him.

We jested for a while in Saxon, making my American and South Vietnamese guides very nervous because they suspected us of exchanging information in an alien tongue; so they rushed me along.

What followed was less jolly. I subjected myself to a tour of twenty small *nuoc mam* factories, bravely enduring the sights and smells of layers of decomposing fish separated by layers of sea salt. It was a miracle that I did not faint from the stench and even managed to avoid tasting samples of the liquid, which is the end product of this process, without offending my smiling hosts.

On my way back to Saigon calamity struck: I boarded an *Air Vietnam* DC-3 carrying a gift box containing six bottles of "grand cru" *nuoc mam*, as did all other passengers, soldiers and Vietnamese civilians alike. Most stowed their bottles away on the hand baggage racks, while I kept mine firmly wedged between my legs on the floor. No sooner did we take off than the old plane hit turbulence. It shook furiously from side to side, roared downward steeply and upward again like the German *Stukas* of World War II; Vietnamese pilots really are good! I ducked when other passengers' *nuoc mam* containers came crashing down on all of us, bouncing off seats, windows and cabin walls, and bursting on the floor, splashing their contents on stewardesses and travelers, including me. *Nuoc mam* was everywhere, dripping on us from the walls, luggage compartments, raining down from the ceiling, and gushing through the aisle.

The journey back was long and odiferous. After intermediate stops at Rach Gia, a coastal town, and My Tho, a large city in the Mekong Delta, I arrived at Saigon's Tan Son Nhut airport in a wretched state. My hair, my brand-new tropical fatigues, and my jungle boots were soaked, but all of my *nuoc mam* bottles had miraculously remained intact. "Stinky, stinky," noted the driver of the *Renault* taxi taking me back to the *Continental Palace*, where Monsieur Loi, the Chinese manager, turned sideways holding his nose discreetly as I passed him in the lobby. I sent out my fatigues, underwear and jungle boots to be dumped. The loss of the very expensive boots pained me the most because I had just bought them on the black market; they were the newest model of military footwear, with steel-lined soles to protect me against anti-personnel mines; no single GI in the field had yet been issued with a pair of these, and here I had to throw mine out.

Six times I showered and shampooed, and then drove to Josephine's house taking Đức with me. "Hee hee, you stink of fish," he said, winding down the window on his side of the *Traction*. "*Tu ne sens pas du tout bon, mon cher ami*" (you don't smell at all good, my dear friend), protested Josephine, keeping her distance from me as I deposited the *nuoc mam* in her doorway. I drove back to the *Continental Palace*, showered and shampooed one more time, ponged myself from top to toe with Hermès aftershave and then indulged defiantly in very European dining pleasures at the *Royal*, wondering grimly whether Kipling didn't have a point after all, when he wrote, "East is East and West is West and ne'er the twain shall meet," but this mood passed soon enough. Differences in culinary tastes not withstanding, Josephine and I were well suited and would have made a fine pair had it not been for one paramount consideration: the Gillian factor.

Gillian is my wife. By the grace of God—and this I state in the most profound theological sense—our marriage has survived 50 perilous and exciting years at the time of this writing. By the grace of God, too, I have come out of my dangerous assignments in Vietnam and other war zones alive and without lasting damage to my body like my father who had lost his eyesight in World War I; hence I am now here to write what I remember.

I had met Gillian three years earlier in London, my first foreign posting as a journalist, and we were married in New York after a brief courtship. She was, and still is, a bubbly, bright and intensely loyal woman; she was a very pretty young woman with a laughing round face and the peachy complexion admired by continental Europeans. Perhaps most importantly, she was, and is, the "good sport" a peripatetic reporter needs as a partner, lest his marriage fail as happens so often in our business.

As a case in point, I don't believe many brides would uncomplainingly accept the cancellation of their wedding to accommodate their suitor's career schedule. Gillian did. We were set to marry in London's Chelsea Old Church and on the following day, in lieu of a honeymoon, board the *Queen Mary* to New York, my next position. The upcoming nuptials were announced in the *Daily Telegraph* and *The Times*. My future father-in-law had ordered hundreds of bottles of champagne. My mother, a professional oratorio vocalist, had already bought her plane ticket to London and rehearsed the arias she was to sing at the service.

Late one evening, less than a month before the nuptials, Julius Hollos, my editor-in-chief in Hamburg, called me in my office in the *Daily Telegraph Building* on Fleet Street.

"Do you have your American visa, Uwe?" he asked in his Hungarian-accented German.

"Yes, Julius."

"And your plane ticket?"

"No, Julius, I am taking the Queen Mary next month. You know that."

"There is not enough time to take a ship. You must go now. Don't you read the papers? There's a serious world crisis brewing; it's b-i-g! And Henk wants to return to Germany. He is scared."

Of course I knew this. The world was in the middle of the Cuban Missile Crisis of 1962, and the cable traffic from New York to our head office in Hamburg passed through our London bureau and thus landed on my desk. The "Henk" Hollos mentioned was Henk Ohnesorge, our political correspondent who also covered the United Nations; I was scheduled to replace him. His family name meant "without worry."

"Why is he in such a rush?" I asked.

"He is afraid of nukes. He doesn't want to get bombed again. He says he has had enough of that in the last war."

"So have we all, Julius. I'll go next month, but first I am getting married as planned."

"What are you, Uwe?" Hollos barked, "Are you a journalist or a bridegroom-to-be?"

"A journalist, Julius."

"Then my apologies to Gillian. Take her along if you want, but you pay for her flight. I'll reimburse you only when you have married her in New York. We don't encourage living in sin."

The wicked sod!

On the next evening, October 25, 1962, my 26th birthday, Gillian and I took a *British Overseas Airways* VC-10 jet to Idlewild Airport in New York. The plane was almost empty because everybody was traveling in the opposite direction, away from Khrushchev's Cuba-based nukes. Gillian's father, Sidney, was content. He did not have to pay for all that champagne. Her mother, Ethel, took us to the Knightsbridge Air Terminal, crying; she was sure that this foreigner was abducting her only child. We soon became friends, though, but until she died she never quite trusted the authenticity of our wedding certificate issued by *Immanuel Lutheran Church* on 88th Street and Lexington Avenue six weeks later. Its design was too kitschy for her taste. "No official document looks like that!" she huffed. Julius kept his promise, though. He sent me a check for our tickets.

But this was only the beginning of Gillian's ordeals. A little more than two years later we were separated for long periods of time because of my assignment in Vietnam. In 1966, we were forced to spend a total of eight months apart. Many weeks went by without any communication between us. Emails did not exist in those days. The postal service was unreliable. It took hours, sometimes days, to get a telephone connection and when we did, it was outrageously expensive and the lines were so bad that we couldn't hear each other's voice. We therefore corresponded via colleagues carrying letters and gifts in and out of the country. At first Gillian remained in our apartment in New York; later she moved back to England to be close to her parents, hoping that I would show up in her life again eventually.

As I said: Only by the grace of God did our union not suffer the fate of the marriages of so many war reporters and 90 percent of all U.S. soldiers fighting in Vietnam. It wasn't just that couples drifted apart because of long periods of separation; the husbands' combat experiences often caused grave psychological damage their wives could not possibly grasp. When I reunited with Gillian during home leaves I hurt her deeply by my inability to get close to her during the first days after each return, not because my love for her had lessened, but because I felt abject and contaminated, having seen hundreds of maimed or dead Vietnamese women only days before. As I held her hands I feared defiling her because in my confused imagination her hands became the hands of mortally wounded soldiers gripping me as they cried out first to their mothers and then to God—always in that order.

A BBC correspondent, a Welshman whose name I will not expose here, tipped off Gillian about my friendship with Josephine. Before he returned to Britain I entrusted him with a package containing a letter and a pearl necklace I had bought for her during a stopover in Hong Kong before arriving in Saigon. He promised to deliver it to Gillian who was staying with her parents in their pub, *The Ham and Blackbird*, in Farnborough, Hampshire.

What happened next, I must reconstitute from secondary sources because Gillian never told me: The Welshman came, stayed beyond the midday pub hour, sat down with Gillian for a drink in the lounge, handed her my parcel and proceeded to say, "I am telling you this in confidence, as one Brit to another: do not expect Uwe to come back to you because we see him all the time around Saigon in the company of Josephine, a very beautiful Vietnamese woman." He then had the impertinence to proposition her, "Come up to London to see me someday." Gillian stopped him abruptly, rose, opened the door and said coldly:

"Get out of here, now! Out! You are very cruel. You have no right to hurt me with this gossip. What's more, you are a bad and disloyal colleague to my husband. You are a disgrace! Get out!"

She gave the Welshman a hard push making him stumble into the street. This shocked him so much that, strangely, he confided this episode that same evening to a colleague at Bush House, the BBC's headquarters in London. This other reporter was on his way to Vietnam as the Welshman's replacement. Three days later we met at *Aterbéa's*, Saigon's best French restaurant, where a small group of European journalists assembled once a week for a very expensive stag meal that served one single goal: *not* to discuss the war, politics, Vietnam or America; our purpose was to purge our minds just for this one night of our Vietnamese preoccupations.

"So you are *that* German," he said when we were introduced, "Be careful! Your wife knows about Josephine." The rest of the story I learned later from Gillian's mother who had eavesdropped on her conversation with the Welshman.

A few weeks on, Gillian and I were reunited at a hotel at Orly Airport in Paris. The next morning she said softly, "You mentioned the name, Josephine, several times in your sleep. I never want to hear it again!"

I saw Josephine one more time briefly under the extreme circumstances of the 1968 Têt Offensive. But this is a story for another day and a later chapter.

Cyberart by Manfred Märschenz

Gillian and Uwe Siemon-Netto as newlyweds.

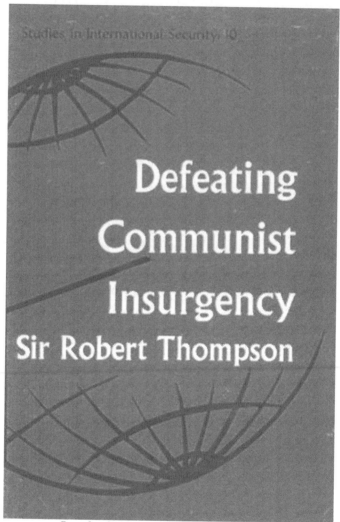

Sir Robert Thompson, a brilliant counterinsurgency theorist, headed the British Advisory Mission in Saigon. The U.S. defense establishment ignored his counsel. His masterpiece, *Defeating Communist Insurgency,* was published by Palgrave Macmillan in England in 1978.

Reflection Two

The curse of impatience

The enemy [i.e., the West]...*does not possess...the psychological and political means to fight a long, drawn-out war.*

Gen. Vo Nguyen Giap,
Defense Minister of North Vietnam
from Bernard Fall, *The Two Viet-Nams.*
London: Pall Mall Press, 1967; p. 119

Peoples' Revolutionary Wars are by their nature destined to be long, arduous, protracted struggles; but I have no doubt at all that if the means are correctly deployed and applied they can be won... If we plan for a long haul, we may get quick results. But if we go for quick results, we may at best get a long haul.

Sir Robert G. K. Thompson,
"Squaring the Error,"
Foreign Affairs, April 1968

It is all very well having B-52 bombers, masses of helicopters and tremendous firepower, but none of these will eliminate a communist cell in a high school which is producing 50 recruits a year for the insurgent movement.

Sir Robert G. K. Thompson, *ibid.*

The Americans... did not have the patience for this sort of war.

Sir Robert G. K. Thompson, *ibid.*

There is no concern here for the fate of the South Vietnamese who, encouraged by the American commitment, have stuck their necks out against the Viet Cong.

Sir Robert G. K. Thompson, *ibid.*

Chapter Three

Homage to Captain Ngu

Only once did I meet Sir Robert G. K. Thompson briefly in my years in Vietnam. This happened mere weeks before the British Advisory Mission, which he headed, went out of business in 1965 and Sir Robert, the world's most influential expert on counterinsurgency warfare, left Saigon. An English reporter had introduced us. I was intrigued by Sir Robert's conviction that weight of firepower, preponderance of manpower, and sophistication of equipment counted for nothing compared to the willingness to meet and defeat the enemy on his own terms.

This strategy had worked well for the British in Malaya. It was one of the many tragic aspects of what seemed to me a Theatre of the Absurd in Vietnam that Sir Robert could not persuade the intellectual "eggheads" in the cabinets of Presidents John F. Kennedy and Lyndon B. Johnson in Washington. According to *The Times* of London, "[Sir Robert] contended that the underground cadres in the villages were more important than the Viet Cong guerillas in the jungle, and that these [underground cadres] must have priority for attack; that an effective police force and intelligence organization were decisive (and lacking); that soldiers, policemen and government officials must act within the law; and that aid for development was effective only if it produced a growing rural economy with local people trained to run it, instead of being dissipated on eye-catching projects, which would collapse as soon as the money to maintain them no longer came from outside."

When the Vietnam War was over in 1975, Sir Robert Thompson said, "The Americans never could see Vietnam in the time frame of Malaya; they did not have the patience for this sort of war."

Much has been written about the difference in emphasis between Thompson's proposals and the boisterous military policies of the United States seeking quick results. It is not the purpose of this book, nor does it lie within my competence, to adjudicate strategic matters, but this is a reporter's tale; I have always been an insatiably inquisitive reporter, and here I was offered an opportunity to satisfy my curiosity: I wanted to see how Sir Robert's strategy worked after he had been advising successive Saigon governments for four years, so I grabbed this opportunity.

I asked Sir Robert to direct me to one place where his "clear and hold" concept had succeeded—in other words, where an area had been cleared of insurgents in a military operation, where their return was prevented, and where the government had therefore won the support of the populace.

A member of his staff suggested that I visit Long Khôt near the Cambodian border. Long Khôt is a dusty village that is part of Tuyen Binh, the capital of a district by the same name, and Capt. Ngu was its chief. I instantly liked this impressive officer, a seasoned, brave and wiry man with an earthy sense of humor, military wisdom and a predilection for subjecting me to practical jokes involving exotic animals.

It wasn't easy to get to him, even though Long Khôt lies a mere 150 miles to the west of Saigon. To travel to Long Khôt by car would have been too dangerous; too many guerilla attacks occurred on the circuitous road every day. As an accredited correspondent, I was allowed to fly almost anywhere in South Vietnam by military aircraft, provided there was space available. But reporters, carrying assimilated military ranks of majors or lieutenant colonels, had a high priority status, and a seat on a plane was not yet the rare commodity it became a few months later as the war heated up. In early 1965, when I went to see Capt. Ngu, only 27,000 American servicemen were stationed in South Vietnam and, of those, no more than 4,000 operated as advisors, pilots, helicopter crews and support staff in the field; the rest led comfortable lives in Saigon, the "Pearl of the East" and "Paris of the Orient."

Similarly, the Saigon press corps was still quite small. So the U.S. military treated us generously, chauffeuring us in staff cars from our hotels to Tan Son Nhut airbase, but there the bliss ended and the lunacy of military routine took over, notably the rule of the thumb, "hurry up and wait."

At 3 a.m. an air-conditioned U.S. Air Force (USAF) sedan pulled up in front of the elegant hotel *Majestic*, where I lived in my first weeks in Vietnam, to take me on a twenty-minute ride to the military terminal at the airport. For the next eleven hours, I sat on the floor waiting for my 7:30 a.m. flight, which was delayed— again and again and again. I was sweltering and starving. Somebody handed out combat rations, commonly referred to as "C Rats," and I emptied a tin of "franks and beans," the bloating properties of which did not make a good diet for the tropics.

When my plane finally showed up, the flight to My Tho in the Mekong Delta only took 20 minutes, but that was long enough for me to develop a dislike of the vintage *C-123 Provider* transport aircraft that in those early days of the war was the USAF workhorse: a shivering, drafty, but extremely reliable torture chamber on wings propelled by two deafening piston engines. It was a relief to transfer in My Tho to a marginally quieter and smaller U.S. Army *Caribou*, a Canadian-built machine with turboprop motors. It took me as far as Moc Hoa but no further. The evening approached. It would have been foolhardy now for a small military convoy to begin a three-hour trip to Tuyen Binh. Capt. Ngu had to wait.

It turned out to be my good fortune that I got stuck for the night in Moc Hoa, where the U.S. Special Forces Detachment B-41 was based. The Special Forces, or Green Berets, played a pivotal role in the counterinsurgency effort I was researching, prompted by my brief encounter with Sir Robert Thompson. French intelligence agents mingling with their American, Australian, and Vietnamese counterparts in "the spooks' hangout," as we journalists called the *Chéval Blanc* bar and restaurant in a narrow side alley in Saigon, used to be full of praise for the Green Berets, "Three of these are worth more than an entire regular company," they used to say.

Because of the Green Berets' professionalism, headgear and international flair, these Frenchmen considered them akin to the paratroopers in the French Foreign Legion, who also wore green berets. More than 35,000 Legionnaires, 70 percent of them Germans, had fought in the previous Indochina War; Vietnam's soil was drenched with the blood of 10,483 of these mercenaries, and half of them were Germans, often young *Wehrmacht* veterans of World War II.

In many ways, the Special Forces in Moc Hoa resembled this French élite force. They too were paratroopers; they also represented the cream of foreign-born soldiers in the service of the United States. There was Captain Sully H. de Fontaine, a nobleman from Belgium. He became one of the most celebrated counterinsurgency officers of this theater. There were two native Germans as well: staff sergeants Hans Koch and Walter Rübel. Later in the war I ran into many more of my fellow countrymen in American, Australian and New Zealand uniforms; some were grunts, some noncommissioned officers, some company commanders, helicopter and fighter pilots. When I wrote about Detachment B-41 in the German daily *Die Welt,* I compared it with a miniature United Nations: in addition to these Europeans, I met Filipinos and Latin Americans, native Cambodians and especially Nung tribesmen; the Nung are an ethnic minority living in Vietnam but originating from China and were renowned for their ferocious ability to hunt down the Viet Cong wherever they happened to be, especially in the jungle.

That evening in the Special Forces compound produced a rich harvest of information. Over many good drinks, I heard for the first time details about one of their most effective and dangerous missions, which later evolved into the CIA's controversial *Phoenix Program.* It featured in particular techniques to assassinate

Communist cadres as they slept in their nightly hideaways. Tipped off by local informers, who were crucial to the counterinsurgency effort, small units of no more than a dozen Special Forces officers and NCOs would disappear into the jungle for several weeks at a time. Carrying a gadget consisting of a wire attached to two wooden handles, they'd sneak into the Viet Cong commissars' or commanders' tents, place the wire around their sleeping victims' throats, and quickly pull it tight, decapitating them.

When these clandestine operations, then carried out by the CIA, became public knowledge in the late 1960s, the American and worldwide peace movements went apoplectic. Congressional hearings were held and reams of editorials written against this practice. As one who spent some of his childhood years in air raid shelters trying to avoid British and American bombs, I found this agitation annoyingly disingenuous. If only the allies had found similar ways to rid the world of Nazi bigwigs, *gauleiters*, Gestapo and SS officers, some civilian lives could perhaps have been spared!

Journalists of the old school, whom professional soldiers could trust, followed the iron rule that a news source's confidence must never be breached. Keeping a secret was a reporter's virtue, just as much as his ability to dig up information reflected his professional skill. This is why I have never written about this until now, even though I heard many titillating details that night. For example, I was told that if I wanted to come along on such a mission, I would have to start preparing myself at least three weeks beforehand: no smoking, no dairy products, no scented aftershave or deodorants. Why no butter and cheese, I wondered? Because, the Green Berets explained, to the finely tuned nose of Asian partisans, the consumption of milk derivatives causes a uric body odor. It will linger on for days in the stale air of quadruple-canopy jungles after a Westerner has camped out for hours or even days. This would betray their presence to seasoned Viet Cong fighters, who would literally sniff you out.

I did not have to give up my cheese, nor did I stop smoking until a decade later, for it would have made no journalistic sense to come along on such a perilous mission about which I wasn't even allowed to write.

Early in the morning, a small convoy left the Moc Hoa camp for Long Khốt. I traveled in a jeep driven by First Lieutenant Kenneth Crabtree of the Special Forces. A boyish 24-year old from Colorado, Crabtree introduced himself as Capt. Ngu's advisor but quickly added with a laugh, "It's quite ridiculous. Capt. Ngu is twice my age and one hundred times more experienced. He has already fought the Viet Minh as a career soldier in the French Army. In reality, he is my teacher and I am his pupil. But we have become very good friends."

He handed me a 0.45 Colt pistol, showed me how to release its safety catch and said, "I know journalists are not supposed to carry guns in war zones, but in case of an ambush, you might have to defend yourself because we might be quickly outgunned."

"An ambush here? This area is as flat as a flounder, where could anybody hide?" I asked, scanning the dusty and arid landscape.

"You'd be surprised," Crabtree replied. "Those peasants up the road, those kids riding on the backs of water buffaloes over there—they could all be Viet Cong, or at least enemy scouts. I won't feel secure until I am in Capt. Ngu's territory. He has everything under control, but here you can never be sure."

Capt. Ngu's territory covered 80,000 hectares, or 309 square miles. Only 500 yards separated his headquarters and residence, a white villa built in the French colonial style, from Cambodia. As we approached the house, we observed a stream of Cambodians carrying fruit, vegetables, fish, textiles, bottles of Chinese pineapple liqueur and strong French *Gauloises* cigarettes—my brand in those days—to the Long Khốt market.

"Much of this is contraband, but that doesn't worry us," said Lt. Crabtree. "We are only interested in the folks crossing the border at night. They are the enemy—the Viet Cong. Cambodia is their sanctuary, never mind what Sihanouk says."

Back in 1965, ten years before the genocidal Khmers Rouges regime murdered two million people—one-third of Cambodia's population—this kingdom was an enchanted fairyland. It was the last peaceful part of former French Indochina, a neutral nation whose ruler, Prince Norodom Sihanouk, proved his brilliance in many fields: as a statesman, choreographer, film star and director, poet, literary polemicist, gourmet chef, saxophonist, pianist, accordion player and composer of instrumental music reminiscent of Charlie Chaplin's romantic tunes, but there was one thing he lacked: military power; his 34,000-man army could not control Cambodia's easternmost region, which the Viet Cong used as a safe haven and logistical base, even back in 1965; I saw their men cross the frontier with impunity. On the other hand, Capt. Ngu, a lowly South Vietnamese district chief, had agents on the other side of the border; they told him when the Communists were on the move and what they were carrying with them. This was the case on the day I met him.

He was dressed in an undershirt and shorts as Lt. Crabtree and I entered his office.

"*Voilà*, there they are," said Ngu standing over a large map and pointing excitedly at a spot less than a mile from his house, on the Cambodian side. "My men have discovered a whole Viet Cong company carrying 2,000 bags of rice. This means that they are planning a long march. Let's welcome them with a firework. I have already alerted BTT."

BTT was the military acronym for *Binh Thanh Thon*, a nearby base where two South Vietnamese Army (ARVN) companies and the Special Forces' A-413 team consisting of 12 officers and NCOs were stationed. They had enough firepower to stop the Communist intruders in their tracks.

Most Vietnamese men I know speak with quite a high pitch. Not Ngu. He had a dark, raspy voice like Jean Gabin, perhaps a legacy of his many years of service in the French military, most of them spent in combat.

He put on his uniform in order to show me around his district but first beckoned me to take a closer look at the map.

"We have 10,295 residents, and of these 6,834 live in areas I control. The others are under Communist rule. Still, that's quite a change from five years ago when I arrived here. Then the Communists owned more than two-thirds of my district."

"What changed all that?" I wanted to know.

He pointed at 13 settlements. "Take these fortified villages as an example, this is where we moved many of our people the way the British did in Malaya when Sir Robert Thompson was there."

Before he took me around in a small U.S. Army landing craft moored a few yards from his house on a branch of the Mekong River, he pulled the first of his practical jokes on me, probably to test my nerves. We went to the village grocery store, ostensibly to buy some supplies. When we entered, a huge pet python came from behind the counter and wrapped itself around me resting its head on my right shoulder, causing much merriment to Ngu, Crabtree, the shopkeeper, his family and assorted onlookers.

I eyed the 0.45 Colt in Lt. Crabtree's holster, wondering if I could grab it with my left hand and blast the beast's head off should it suddenly decide to constrict me, but I couldn't move my arm. My arm was pinned by this very heavy animal, which, thankfully, did not constrict, but returned to its place behind the counter on a signal from its master.

"Voilà, Monsieur, this goes to show that we know how to handle security around here," Ngu said, roaring with laughter. "No robber would break into this shop at night. If he did he would soon be strangled and gobbled up by a snake, and, take a look, there is another python behind the counter. It is still small. But it will be ready for action soon enough."

With that in mind we started our boat trip to some of Capt. Ngu's fortified villages.

"You are not wearing a pistol. How come?" I asked him.

"The French taught me that a gentleman takes off his gun when entering somebody's private home."

"But...?"

"No 'buts.' These villages *are* the private homes of people. Therefore I enter them unarmed. People appreciate this."

As the boat sputtered along, pointing at his map Ngu described three villages, "In this village here, one-third of the residents are Viet Cong sympathizers. In that one there we have three, and in the one next to it only two VC followers."

"Sir Robert Thompson says that underground cadres in the villages are more important than Viet Cong guerillas in the jungle," I said.

"Thompson is right on target. But I know who these underground cadres are. I know every one of them, and this neutralizes them. I could arrest them, of course," said Ngu. "But what good would that do? Leaving them where they are helps us to keep an eye on our enemies, on their contacts and their moves. I even know the names of the two Viet Cong infiltrators in one of the two ARVN companies over in BTT; we leave them where they are. They might not know it, but are actually doing us a favor by being there. A close-meshed network of intelligence agents is one the most important criteria of successful counterinsurgency, and I do have a substantial web of agents."

We entered one of his fortified villages and went straight to the brand-new dispensary in a mud hut, where Sgt. William Nichols, a Special Forces medic who had come along for the ride with us, immediately went to work assisted by a male ARVN nurse. They handed out pills, gave injections, advised pregnant women, bandaged wounds, checked peoples' lungs using a stethoscope, and tried to comfort on old man dying of tuberculosis.

"He is brilliant," said Lt. Crabtree. "I have seen him perform sophisticated surgical operations."

We went outside and received a shock. Armed men carrying M-1 rifles and wearing black pajamas, the usual peasants' clothing in Vietnam, seemed to be all over the place.

"Good God, Captain," I said. "There are VC everywhere."

"*Calmez vous*," Ngu answered, relax! "These are my men. They just look like Viet Cong but are part-time soldiers of the Popular Forces. They live here with their families. Their job is to protect their village, especially at night, to make sure that it doesn't fall under Viet Cong control when it gets dark. If they need reinforcement they can get it quickly from the units stationed in BTT."

"So they are an important part of your counterinsurgency program?"

"Precisely. They don't look like much, but they are very effective. You have to fight this war the way the Viet Cong do. It would be crazy to fight it with conventional means, as more and more people suggest these days. Conventional warfare does not give rural people the sense of security they need. But our methods do. You see it here."

On the way back to Long Khôt, Ngu said with a poker face, "You are German. You like goose, right? I have known many Germans serving in the Foreign Legion. They all loved goose."

I quickly replied, "Yes, we all do, at Christmas: roast goose with red cabbage and potato dumplings—a marvelous meal in the winter, but it wouldn't be very good in this tropical climate."

"This evening you will get goose: cold goose salad," he announced with an evil grin.

I was ready for another practical joke. When evening came, we sat down at a white-cloth-covered dining table by open French doors leading out to Capt. Ngu's garden. There was a restless monkey on a chain swinging between the house and a tree. Capt. Ngu's wife served Beaujolais wine in pop-top cans, which she had probably bought from the Cambodian traders.

A maid brought in a glass bowl filled with a red liquid containing bits of flesh.

"Voilà, goose," said Ngu, laughing uproariously. "Raw goose salad. Quite delicious." Perhaps it was, perhaps he was having me on. I never found out what kind of meat it really was. I placed a little on my plate and piled a lot of rice on it intending to just eat a little of that. But the blood-colored liquid seeped up to the top of the pile at which point the monkey swung inside the dining room landing squarely on my head.

I looked at the blood-colored rice while the monkey pulled my hair. I heard the other diners' laughter and suddenly felt sick. Ngu pointed me to the lavatory. I couldn't find a light switch but, suspecting this to be one of those squat-job toilets I had come to appreciate in France, I stepped up on what I presumed to be a lavatorial socle, and urinated and vomited in the direction of where I expected the hole to be.

Suddenly, the ground began to move, pulling my feet further and further apart. I found my Zippo, lighted it and saw that I was standing on two giant turtles as I aimed full-blast at two other giant turtles. It was time to go. After all, that night I intended to accompany Lt. Crabtree and his mixed detachment of Vietnamese and American soldiers on an operation intercepting Viet Cong infiltrators. I bade farewell to Captain and Madame Ngu.

"See you tomorrow at your parachute jump."

My parachute jump? Another practical joke?

That night, Lt. Crabtree and I lay on our bellies under a mosquito net 200 yards from the border, staring into the darkness. Nobody came our way. But then, perhaps half a mile to our right, all hell broke loose: there was small arms and machine gun fire, mortar rounds detonating. I saw the night sky light up.

"Our men must have surprised the Viet Cong company with their 2,000 sacks of rice Capt. Ngu was talking about," said Crabtree.

The next morning we drove to *Binh Thanh Thon* where a U.S. Army *Caribou* had just arrived on a dirt strip ready for the obligatory parachute jumps required of the Green Beret officers and soldiers in order to maintain their Airborne badges. Capt.

Ngu was already there, grinning broadly. The crew automatically put a parachute on my back. I didn't protest. I had never jumped before in my life, but I didn't want to lose face before Capt. Ngu. As Kenneth Crabtree had said, he was such a good guy. I was crazy, young and supple in those days, weighing only 140 pounds, and there was no wind. I figured the risk was small and there was little to fear.

The next thing I knew, we were in the air. I got up with all the others and, like them, was hooked up on the overhead cable. I heard the jumpmaster's yell. In rapid successions the others jumped out of the rear of the *Caribou*. I had no time to reflect that my turn was next. I was out, falling. The chute opened as planned. Somebody had told me that when you hit the ground you must roll forward, which I did. It was over. I was alive and intact. We had come down in a dry field. I rolled up my chute with the help of a soldier, and then followed the others. We came to a halt.

Suddenly, the ground gave way under my feet. I stepped aside. Then the ground came up again on the same spot where I had just been standing. I jumped on it with full force and heard a groan. Stepping aside again, I realized that somebody must have been hiding there. Carefully, I scraped the soil cover off what turned out to be a primitively camouflaged plastic helmet of the kind Viet Cong fighters usually wore. Next to it I spotted a gun muzzle. I grabbed it and pulled it out of the ground; it was an M-1 rifle of World War II vintage in my hand. A Green Beret helped me yank a skinny middle-aged man in black pajamas out of the hole. He was shivering.

"*Courage, camarade, pour toi la guerre est fini,*" I said: take courage, buddy, for you the war is over. He gave me a thin smile.

The Americans took charge of the gun and handed the prisoner of war over to the ARVN officers. I kept his helmet as a souvenir. It lived for decades on a bookshelf behind my desk in the library of my house in France. I looked at it often and wondered: Where are you now, Capt. Ngu, you good, tough guy with your wicked sense of humor, your bloody python, monkey, raw goose salad and giant turtles? Have you survived the violent battles that in later years engulfed Long Khốt and your district? Have you survived the Viet Cong victory in 1975? Would the Communists have won had Sir Robert Thompson's and your theories prevailed?

Yes, you were a good guy. You were the best. This chapter is written in your honor, Capt. Ngu, and those who wish to pay homage to you are invited to go to the Vietnam War Museum in Westminster, California. That's where my trophy, the helmet of the Viet Cong I captured after my visit with you, has found its final home.

Capt. Ngu and Lt. Crabtree on the Mekong in 1965.

Chapter Four

Death in town

My return trip to Saigon involved many hours of travel by jeep and then three flights and it was even more draining than the journey to Long Khốt had been. Once back in my cool room in the *Majestic*, I was in no mood to venture afar, not even in pursuit of the familiar food I had dreamed of since my traumatic confrontation with Capt. Ngu's raw goose salad, or whatever that exotic dish might have been. I had fantasized about a sturdy Alsatian dinner, such as Madame Eudel's *choucroute garnie* in the *Guillaume Tell*, or of lentils and sausages at a small and unpretentious Corsican restaurant called *Chez Henri*, where French expatriates drank strong Algerian red wine while reminiscing about past colonial glories, and bragging about chance encounters with Viet Cong guerilla leaders during their visits to French-run plantations in the hinterland. To my reporter's ears, and doubtless to the ears of several intelligence officers who were regular guests at *Henri's*, these tales sounded like an excellent yarn, though it was not always trustworthy information. That evening I could not face a heavy meal; I could not even bring myself to visit my black market moneychanger around the corner on Tu Do Street. He was a French-speaking Indian from Madras, who gave me ten times the amount of South Vietnamese piasters for my dollar than I would have received at a bank.

I showered, poured myself a Scotch, stretched out on my bed, however my bliss was brief. There was a knock at my door. I wrapped a bath towel around my waist and opened it. Lanh entered, looking grave. Lanh was not his real name, but it means "peaceful" and therefore seems fitting.

"Big story," he said. "Big, big story."

Lanh always looked earnest, unlike most of the bubbly people of Saigon who were quick to smile, even in hard times. He was cerebral, highly-strung, and tetchy. As soon as he sat down, his legs began twitching nervously; they always did. I was told that these were the marks of many natives of Huế, the gracious former imperial capital city in central Vietnam. Lanh was born in Huế.

I liked Lanh. In fact, I liked him a lot, not least because of his admirable command of my mother tongue, which he had acquired when working with a German-speaking battalion of the French Foreign Legion for whom he played the trombone in their military band.

Thanks to his language skills, he had a secure job as an interpreter and assistant for German television teams when they came to Vietnam, and as their network's local point man in their absence. Lanh was a decent, loyal and competent partner who knew how to trounce government bureaucracy; he knew how to get airplane tickets even when all flights out of Saigon were booked; how to obtain seemingly unobtainable travel and filming permits; how to expedite films by airfreight to Germany the quickest way; how to handle South Vietnamese customs and tax authorities trying to profit from the presence of foreign journalists, and how to arrange for interviews with officials who would not normally speak to anybody in the media. He was fearless in combat, and very proud. When one crude and stout middle-aged correspondent—the only boor among a succession of gentlemanly colleagues—commanded Lanh to procure a girl for him, Lanh replied, "German television has not employed me as a pimp." The inebriated reporter slapped him in the face, and Lanh quietly walked out of his room. He came to me to let off steam in a rare show of personal emotion.

"I could *cat dau* this fat slob," he said, using a common and very disagreeable Vietnamese term for cutting someone's head off.

"Cool it, Lanh," I warned him, "this klutz will bury himself in the end; you won't have to do it for him, and then spend the rest of your life in prison. He has already been drummed out of India for his repulsive manners."

"You might be right," Lanh replied, "Perhaps I should just bite the bullet and get him a girl—but a girl he won't forget for a long, long time. You know what I mean: medically speaking..."

I laughed: "Well, of course one shouldn't be vengeful, but if you must, the latter course would be much less dangerous for you."

Lanh departed, grinning maliciously; this was the first and only time I ever saw him smile.

When no German TV team was in town, Lanh worked for me, or at least came to see me every day, as he did on that late afternoon after my return from Long Khôt.

"You look more intense than usual, my Lanh," I teased him. "What's the big story?" I asked.

"This morning a rich woman was murdered at the Central Market, a very handsome woman."

"How was she killed?"

"Somebody cut her throat from behind, garotte-style. The killer sneaked up on her, placed a wire with two handles around her neck, and then quickly pulled it tight. Very swift, very messy, lots of blood, no arrest."

"Phew," I said, remembering that the same method was being applied to kill Viet Cong cadre while they slept in jungle camps.

"Did the Viet Cong do this?" I inquired.

"I'm not sure, but I don't think so," Lanh answered. "The circumstances suggest otherwise. This woman was a Chinese grain merchant living in Cholon (Saigon's Chinatown). There is a strong suspicion that she was the leader of a group of speculators responsible for driving up rice prices to dramatic levels."

"How?"

"By hoarding rice to dry up the market," Lanh explained.

"Couldn't it be that the Viet Cong killed her to look good in the eyes in the Vietnamese public?"

"If so, why didn't the VC make this public? This way, they are getting no publicity mileage out of it. That's not the way the VC operate," said Lanh. "After all, propaganda has a huge role in their strategy."

"So?"

"Look, there was a storm of unrest brewing over the grain prices, and our government couldn't get a handle on this situation."

"Are you suggesting that a government agency might have been behind this killing?" I asked.

"That's what many think—either that or some people with a strong business interest in bringing the prices down. The bet around town is that this must have been the work of a 'dirty tricks' department in government. Chances are we'll never find out. But we have some pretty hardnosed and efficient people on our side."

"I bet you do," I answered without telling him of my discussions with Special Forces officers in Moc Hoa.

Lanh walked to the door. "I am not shedding a tear over the death of this woman. As of tomorrow it will be cheaper to feed my family. See you in the morning."

I dressed and went to the *Majestic's* fifth-floor restaurant, which afforded its guests a splendid view of the Saigon River, the busy harbor filled with warships and freighters as well as sampans and fishing vessels. The elegantly laid tables in the restaurant were empty except for one, where a tall trim American and a striking Asian woman in her mid-thirties dressed in a tight-fitting, purple *cheongsam*—purple suggesting noble birth—were beginning the evening with a bottle of *Dom Pérignon*, the finest champagne available in Saigon. I knew them vaguely. He was a full colonel staying in the room next to mine. She belonged to a prominent local Chinese family and was working as an interpreter in one of the U.S. government offices in town. We journalists who met her at diplomatic parties admired her not only for her beauty but also for her talents as a linguist; she spoke English with a refined British accent, flawless French, Vietnamese, Cantonese, Mandarin Chinese, some German, and probably other languages as well. As the colonel's neighbor, I also knew that they were lovers, and I admired him for his taste in women. I walked over to their table to greet them.

"Celebrating?" I asked.

"Having a farewell dinner," he said. "My tour is up. Tomorrow I am returning to the States."

I said goodbye to him and told her: "I am sure we'll meet again at your office or a reception." She nodded and smiled sadly. Someone had told me that the colonel was rejoining his wife and children in America. He and his Chinese friend had made an extraordinarily stylish couple.

The *Majestic* featured a buffet with fresh *crudités*. A plate of hors d'oeuvres followed by cheese with French bread and a bottle of chilled red *Brouilly*, my favorite Beaujolais, was all I needed on that hot evening. I chose a table near a window overlooking the river. Below me, to the right, I see the lights and hear the chatter and laughter coming from the *My Canh Café*, a floating restaurant renowned for its Chinese and Vietnamese cuisines and expensive French wines. Four months later, on June 25, 1965, while I was out of the country, this happy place would make the headlines of every major newspaper around the globe: two time bombs planted by Viet Cong terrorists blew the *My Canh* out of the water, killing 42 diners and waiters and injuring 80 more. Of the victims, 14 were Americans but all the others were Vietnamese, including many women and children. In its propaganda, the Viet Cong proudly took credit for this odious act that was the starkest reminder thus far that the conflict in Vietnam had reached a crescendo of phase two of the "war of national liberation," according to the textbook by North Vietnamese Defense Minister Vo Nguyen Giap. Said book lay on every self-respecting correspondent's bedside table; phase two included guerilla activity, terror and intimidation, and was the prelude to phase three, conventional warfare, the first major battles of which I would cover later in the year.

I went to bed early and immediately fell asleep. A scream woke me, a shriek so loud, fearsome and unusual that I did not associate it with a human being at first. My overhead light went on, and the "boy" assigned to my room stood at the foot of my bed, shivering; in French-colonial jargon, *boy* was the term for a manservant, the female equivalent being *boyesse*. Political correctness had not yet polluted Western speech.

"*Venez vite*, Monsieur," shouted the *boy*, who in truth was a dignified gentleman in his fifties. I followed him out. From the corner of my eyes I saw a slender woman in purple running down the dimly lighted corridor, her long, black hair streaming behind her.

The door to the colonel's room next to mine was open. I heard a groan and a nervous high-pitched giggle. On the bed I saw the colonel in a pool of blood. There was blood on the walls, blood on the floor, blood shooting into the air from his groin, blood all over the Vietnamese *boy* assigned to his room who was desperately trying to stem the flow by pressing his right fist against the American's dorsal artery. The boy was laughing nervously. The falsetto snigger some Asian men emit in extreme situations has always perturbed Westerners; later I learned that many American soldiers sadly misunderstood it as an expression of amusement, and this sometimes had tragic consequences during combat. Nobody had told them that it was an attempt to camouflage their reaction to horror, a sign of embarrassment.

The colonel was by now unconscious. Next to his body lay his penis and a razorblade with which it had been cut off at the stem. This made it almost impossible to stop the bleeding.

"Have you called a doctor and an ambulance?" I asked my *boy* who for a few minutes had left the room and returned.

"Yes, but it will take some time for them to get here. You understand: the curfew…"

"And what about the woman?"

"She couldn't get away because of the curfew. She was stopped at the door and is now under arrest by our security people."

By the time the doctor arrived in the company of stretcher-bearers, Vietnamese cops and American military police, the colonel had bled to death. A French-speaking Vietnamese officer asked me to return to my room and stay there until he visited me the next morning, which he did in the company of one of his colleagues. Our discussion was extremely brief, very professional and marked by what I found a moving display of humanity. It went roughly like this:

"Tragic event," said the officer.

"Indeed," I said, "they seemed a happy couple."

"You knew them, correct?"

"Only superficially. I spoke with them briefly at the restaurant yesterday evening."

"How did she seem to you?"

"Very, very sad; this was their farewell dinner."

"*Pauvre fille*," he went on, poor girl. "Any idea of what might have made her do this? Anything she said? Any facial expression? Any gesture? You are a journalist; you might have noticed."

I shook my head: "It beats me. Jealousy? I am not Vietnamese. Is this something that happens often in your culture?"

"Not really," he answered, "certainly not in her milieu. She seems to have snapped, but why? This seems so out of character. We had always admired her for her beauty, self-discipline, and her gentility."

When he and his colleague left my room, I wanted to hug them both for their humanity. These weren't two hard-nosed cops; they were two men deeply saddened by what they saw as an unfathomable personal tragedy.

Later an acquaintance in the prosecutors' office offered a possible explanation for her seemingly inexplicable act. They had gone to bed and made love for the last time, but then the colonel brusquely turned on his side and fell asleep, leaving her alone and disconsolate in her sorrow. The court seemed to accept her assertion that she emasculated her lover without aforethought, but rather acted on the spur of the moment out of hurt, using the blade from the colonel's razor, which he had used to shave himself before their last embrace.

If I am correctly informed, the Saigon court termed her act as a crime of passion and sentenced her to 15 years. Three or four years later she was out. A haggard, slender woman in a very modest dress and without makeup or jewelry stopped me briefly in Tu Do Street: "Do you know who I am?" she asked.

"My God, what happened to you? Have they mistreated you in prison?" I asked.

"Absolutely not," she answered, "Everybody was kind to me, including the police, the prosecutors, the court and the prison wardens. Even the room *boy* at the Majestic and some Americans came to see me in jail. What you see is a perplexed and sad woman full of remorse, a woman who killed the person she loved most in her life and still does not comprehend why." She melted into the rush hour crowd on Saigon's busiest boulevard. I never saw her again.

Chapter Five

Death in the village

The *Majestic* was a hotel built in the architectural style of the French Riviera. I loved its fading glamour and the stories I heard about its colorful past, especially the yarn surrounding its concessionaire, an epic character in the Corsican milieu of Indochina. His name was Mathieu Franchini. He arrived in Saigon from Marseilles soon after World War I as a ship's steward and wasted no time making a career for himself, albeit one with seedy elements.

Franchini married into one of the richest Vietnamese families, became a celebrated hotelier and allegedly the godfather of Saigon's Corsican syndicates. For decades Franchini was the chief financial advisor to the *Binh Xuyen*, an independent politico-military force within the Vietnamese army, which ultimately destroyed it. Some revered the *Binh Xuyen* as oriental Robin Hoods; others feared them as ruthless gangsters. They had started out as river pirates but eventually ran the opium trade, prostitution and, for a while, the police of southern Vietnam. I was told that at one time Franchini owned most of the brothels in town. Being the ever-curious journalist, I was sorry I never met Mathieu Franchini. By the time I arrived in Saigon, he had returned to France where he died in the autumn of 1965.

But the impressions of that fatal evening were too deeply imprinted on my mind to stay in the *Majestic*: meeting this graceful couple in the restaurant; hearing the tortured scream from next door a few hours later; seeing the woman in purple run down the corridor with her long black hair flapping wildly behind her, and then watching powerlessly as her American lover bled to death from his groin with his penis and a razor blade lying by his side. For two or three days, the room next to mine remained sealed off while the police and forensic specialists completed their work. Then painters arrived to conceal the damage, but I checked out.

As I was paying my bill, Bernard B. Fall moved in. He was the French political scientist whose book, *The Two Viet-Nams*, I considered indispensable reading for any reporter covering this intriguing country.

"You are writing for *Die Welt*, aren't you?" he asked me in German. "Are you leaving? What a pity."

I was amazed. Bernard Fall was born in Vienna of Jewish parents and fled to France with them when Germany occupied Austria. In France, the Gestapo tortured Fall's father to death, while his mother was deported to Auschwitz and murdered in a gas chamber. And yet this man was sorry to see a German go!

"I read your stories," he explained, "You seem to love Vietnam und are trying to understand it. That's what we have in common: I dedicated *The Two Viet-Nams* to the valiant and long-suffering Vietnamese."

"I am just moving up the road to the *Continental Palace*," I said. "How about lunch at *Ramuntcho's* on Le Loi? They have artichokes fresh in from Da Lat. They are the best in the world and in season now."

"*Ramuntcho's* at one, then," replied Fall.

I drove my suitcases up Tu Do Street to the *Continental Palace*, an even older French-style hotel that was to become my Saigon home for the next four years. Built in 1880, it was run by Mathieu Franchini's son, Philippe, a Corsican-Vietnamese artist, author and historian married to an enchanting Chinese woman. Philippe became a friend of mine, and an invaluable source of information about his country's history and the byzantine nature of Saigon society.

At *Ramuntcho's*, Bernard Fall seemed glum. He had written extensively about the Communist terror in North Vietnam and clearly did not wish that fate on the South Vietnamese. He supported the U.S. war effort but despaired over American naïveté and lack of stamina.

"Vo Nguyen Giap must be rubbing his hands: He predicted that democracies will not have the patience to see this thing through."

"I know, I read it in your book," I said.

"In the next months, Washington is going to Americanize this war to get it over with quickly instead of patiently creating secure areas for the Vietnamese people and giving them a sense of safety. This city, this whole country, will soon be crawling with GIs. American soldiers will be returning home in body bags; the antiwar movement in America will grow rapidly, putting pressure on the administration to seek a quick way out. I bet Gen. Giap is ecstatic. It seems such a tragic contradiction, but I know that America does not possess the staying power to defeat a vicious tyranny in a guerilla war. This scares me as one who has experienced tyranny in his youth and done battle against it."

Bernard Fall had fought in the French Resistance against the Nazis and served in the regular French Army before moving to the United States as a graduate student; by the time we met he was a full professor at Howard University in Washington, D.C.

I told him about Long Khôt and Capt. Ngu.

"You see?" Fall said, "That's Sir Robert Thompson's strategy at work. Washington wouldn't listen to him. [Secretary of Defense] Robert McNamara simply does not understand this war. So Sir Robert is leaving."

"The Green Berets sound like you," I told him.

"I know. They are good men and have done a fine job. Go to the Central Highlands and you'll see. Do this before the American divisions arrive. Go see for yourself where the Special Forces have succeeded and where they were left stranded." Fall said this with great sadness in his voice.

"The Communists are gaining ground," he continued. "They are infiltrating from the North via Laos and Cambodia in large numbers. And the South Vietnamese villagers are left defenseless at night. Large American forces will conduct 'search and destroy' operations killing lots of Communists with air power. The point is that the Communists don't care how many of their men die. They have plenty. American ground troops will return to their bases at night; they won't be in the business of clearing a terrain and holding it, and thus protecting the people, because this would require a commitment for decades."

In these few sentences, Bernard Fall outlined America's Vietnamese dilemma long before it became apparent to political leaders and military strategists in the United States. A year earlier, Fall had gone public with his belief that the U.S. could not win the Vietnam War for precisely the reasons he gave me at *Ramuntcho's*. Not that Fall *wanted* America to lose; not that this former soldier was a mindless "peacenik" or, worse, pro-Communist; not that he was not staunchly pro-American, on the contrary, he made his pessimistic prognosis about America's inability to win a protracted war with sorrow and great personal regret.

J. Edgar Hoover's FBI placed Bernard Fall under observation for his views. Washington simply did not get his point, just as it had not got Sir Robert Thompson's point until years later when President Richard M. Nixon sought this former British colonel's advice—too late. Going through clippings of my articles of that period, I found a news analysis published on September 7, 1967, in *Die Welt*. It was titled, *"Verfolgen die USA eine falsche Strategie?"* (Is the U.S. Pursuing the Wrong Strategy?), and was based in part on my discussions with Fall and on a commentary by Sir Robert Thompson in the British magazine, *The Spectator*.

Written one year after his departure from Vietnam, and after the Americans had lost their first 4,000 men in battle, this *Spectator* article was yet another appeal by Sir Robert to the United States to pursue a "strategy leading to victory": by all means use maximum military might against North Vietnam's core forces, but minimize civilian casualties; deploy American and South Vietnamese troops primarily to conquer and hold and secure population centers, denying the Viet Cong valuable pools for recruitment and supplies. This was also Bernard Fall's message.

After our first encounter, I met Fall several more times in Saigon and once or twice at Howard University in Washington. On February 21, 1967 he stepped on a *Bouncing Betty* land mine and was killed, along with Gunnery Sergeant Byron G. Highland, a U.S. Marine Corps photographer. Fall died on the *Street Without Joy*; this was the name the French Expeditionary Corps had given to the perilous 70-mile stretch of National Route 1 between Huế and Quang Tri. It was also the title of Fall's most celebrated book about the first Indochina War. In his autobiography, *My American Journey*, former U.S. Secretary of State and General Colin Powell wrote about this work:

"I recently reread Bernard Fall's book on Vietnam, *Street Without Joy*. Fall makes painfully clear that we had almost no understanding of what we had gotten ourselves into."

In the morning after my lunch with Fall I went to Tan Son Nhut Airbase to hitch a ride on a C-123 to Plei Ku in the Central Highlands. My final destination was the triangle-shaped Special Forces camp at Plei Me, 25 miles south of Plei Ku, which eight months later became the arena of the first major clash between conventional North Vietnamese and United States forces. I was anxious to visit Plei Me because of what the Green Berets in Moc Hoa, as well as Fall and Sir Robert Thompson's people had told me: In this war the side that controlled the Central Highlands would have the upper hand. How important the Highlands were became clear when, in the week before my trip, the Viet Cong had attacked Camp Holloway, a nearby helicopter base, killing eight defenders, wounding 108 and destroying 18 aircraft. This prompted President Lyndon B. Johnson to start a bombing campaign against North Vietnam.

Waiting for my C-123 flight to Plei Ku, my hypochondriac disposition played a trick on me. I sat on the floor of the Tan Son Nhut military departure lounge next to a U.S. Air Force lieutenant colonel whose fatigues bore a patch showing the snake-entwined staff of Aesculapius.

"Are you a doctor?" I asked.

"Dentist," he answered. "I am the chief Air Force dentist in Vietnam, inspecting our facilities in the boonies."

Suddenly I had a toothache and told him so.

"You are in luck. When we get to Plei Ku, follow me. Our clinic is right at the airport."

We landed. I went with him to a tent, saw a pedal-powered drill, heard its hideous pitch and the groan of a patient. I was instantly cured. Outside this makeshift clinic somebody called my name: "Siemon-Netto for Plei Me!" Thank God! My face was saved. I bade the dentist farewell, rejoiced in my miraculous cure, and rejoiced in a jeep-ride to a military camp I enjoyed very much.

Plei Me was the home of Special Forces Team A-313, which consisted of 12 men under the command of Captain Ronnie A. Mendoza, a feisty Filipino-born officer who, five years later as a lieutenant-colonel, lost his life when the *Air America* plane he was traveling in crashed in the Central Highlands; *Air America*, nicknamed *Spooky Airlines*, was owned and operated by the CIA.

The other residents of Plei Me were some 250 Jarai tribesmen speaking *Mon-Khmer*, a Malayo-Polynesian language. They were fierce fighters and just as fiercely loyal to the Americans, whom they preferred over the Vietnamese majority, Communist or otherwise. The Green Berets visibly loved these tiny men who would slip into Laos on reconnaissance missions and return with reliable intelligence. Mendoza and several of his men spoke their tongue and also managed to keep up with their habit of sucking through bamboo canes huge amounts of their rice wine, a foul-tasting beverage fermenting quietly in large crocks. In the years to come, mountain tribesmen like these tested my manliness often by promising me the loveliest girl in their village if I succeeded in drinking a given quantity of that vile stuff. Inevitably I failed the test, keeling over backwards before even laying eyes on the promised beauties.

I carried a bottle of Scotch, which made the rounds of the Green Berets as we spoke of their successes and frustrations. Their best story concerned a black Special Forces captain who became inducted into a Rhadé family. Related to the Jarai, the Rhadé are a matriarchal society. If the daughter of a Rhadé village chief falls in love with a man there will be serious consequences. This happened to the captain. The girl's family insisted that he marry her.

Had he rejected her advances this Rhadé community might well have taken revenge against the Special Forces by switching their loyalty to the Viet Cong. So the officer, though already married with three children in America, went through the tribal nuptials and then moved in with her in her family's bamboo longhouse, even learning the Rhadé way of communicating with God through music played with suspended gongs, flutes and string instruments. Every morning, like a good Rhadé family man, he went off to work, meaning to war.

Then his 12-month tour in Vietnam ended. He had to return to his family in the United States. But how?

"We faked his death," said one of the Green Berets. "We brought her his dog tags, bloodstained pieces of his fatigues, some of his hair, his canteen and his Zippo lighter, and told her that he had been blown to bits by a Viet Cong mortar round. In the truth we had rushed him out of the country. We couldn't have solved this problem in any other way. This way we even reinforced their opposition against the Communists!"

We had a good laugh, but suddenly the Green Berets turned solemn. "What's happening in these villages, whether they are inhabited by Vietnamese or *Montagnards* (mountain tribesmen), is no laughing matter," one of them said. "The horrendous acts of terrorism against village chiefs loyal to Saigon are multiplying at an alarming rate. It's suicidal for local leaders to be on our side. They get slaughtered, usually at night because there's nobody there to defend them. The North Vietnamese are pouring over the border. Our scouts bring us reliable intelligence about plans to attack on South Vietnamese bases soon. As we speak, Victor Charlie (the Viet Cong) seems to be planning an attack on the headquarters of the 45th ARVN regiment near Nha Trang, which has Special Forces advisors. It doesn't look good."

I got a seat on the military "milk run" connecting Central Highland cities. The plane, once again a C-123, took me to Nha Trang, a coastal resort town with spectacular white sandy beaches by the South China Sea. In February of 1965 it seemed a beleaguered place. The evening curfew was imminent. There were no taxis at the airport. A young Vietnamese lieutenant offered me a ride on his 125-cc Honda motorbike and I asked him to drive me to the 45th ARVN regiment's headquarters near Nha Trang, just off National Route 1. The sentry stopped me at the gate and telephoned his superiors.

Minutes later, a wild-eyed Special Forces captain materialized: "Who are you?" he snarled.

"I am an accredited correspondent of the largest West German publishing house," I answered showing him my press cards issued by the U.S. Military Assistance Command Vietnam (MACV) and the Vietnamese government.

"I don't believe you," he said. "You don't sound like a German. I was stationed in Bavaria. I know what Germans sound like. I trained with West German Rangers in the Alps. You don't speak like them. You are a phony. I think you are a Communist spy. Go to hell."

"Well, I am sorry I don't talk like Hogan's Heroes. Take a look at my press cards and my West German passport. I'm for real. There'll be a curfew on in a few minutes. Where am I to go?"

"I don't give a damn. Go to hell." He turned on his heel and walked back into the base.

In hindsight, this must surely have been one of the funniest experiences in my five years in Vietnam. It became even funnier when 22 years later I met this officer at a VA hospital where he was treated for Post-Traumatic Stress Disorder. We have been laughing about our first meeting ever since. At the time of this writing, a quarter of a century later, we have become good friends, which is why I won't embarrass him by revealing his real name. Let's just call him Lt. Col. Bradford Jones, U.S. Army (ret.).

In 1965, he was an adviser to Lt. Col. Ba Tong Ly, the commander of the 45th Regiment and one of the most competent officers in the South Vietnamese army. Col. Ba later rose to the rank of brigadier-general and commanded the celebrated 23rd division. "We were expecting to be hit that night," Jones explained, "That's why Col. Ba was very nervous when you showed up at the camp and sent me to find out if you were for real. And I thought you weren't because I had never met a German before who didn't sound like Sergeant Schultz."

Fortunately the Vietnamese lieutenant who had given me a lift on his motorbike was still there and offered to take me to the only "hotel" he knew in the neighborhood. It turned out to be a bordello, another "first" that evening; never before had I spent a night in a bagnio. The owner was a nice old man with two silver teeth, the only ones left in his mouth. Unlike Capt. Jones, he accepted me for who I was.

"Báo Chí Đức," he said cheerfully, reading the nametag on my fatigues, "You German journalist. Long time no see a Đức. *Beaucoup* German legionnaires came through here. They were good customers. Fine, fine soldiers, they were. Come in, Monsieur Đức, I will give you my best room."

I explained that a clean room was really all I wanted—and perhaps a ham sandwich and a beer or two, but nothing else; I hadn't eaten all day. The room was impeccable but sparse, furnished only with a bed under a spotlessly white mosquito net. There was one wooden chair, one bedside table, a ceiling fan, an overhead neon light, and a bathroom with a cold-water shower, which I used with grateful abandon. When I stepped out of the shower I found a one-liter bottle of *Bière Larue* and a French *sandwich jambon* on the bedside table: a *baguette* with ham, butter and *cornichons*. I was ecstatic.

In the distance, I heard the rumblings of mortar fire and the rat-tat-tat of machine guns. The fighting seemed to be coming closer and closer. Was this the Viet Cong attack the Green Berets had predicted? Never mind! I was tired. I dropped off, but not for long. The neon light woke me. A childlike creature with a short boyish haircut and no discernible curvature came crawling under my mosquito net.

"Go," I said. "I don't need company tonight. I need sleep, and I don't sleep with boys."

"No, no, no! I no boy," whispered the creature, taking off her blouse without proving her point.

"Toi la mot co gai" — I am a girl, she said.

I made gestures explaining how tired I was. She pointed to the window, held her hands over her ears began to cry. I understood what she was trying to say: "There is a war going on out there, please don't send me away."

She gently took my right hand, sat up and moved her tiny body next to my head. There she sat, just as Graham Green had written, singing and twittering on my pillow until I fell asleep again. When I woke in the morning she was gone.

"You didn't like girl I sent you?" asked the patron as I paid my bill. He seemed hurt.

"I am not a child molester," I replied.

"She is no child. She is a war widow. Her husband, a lieutenant, was killed in combat last month. Poor woman; she is very sweet."

"That she is," I agreed.

The brothel owner drove me back to the base. This time I had no difficulty getting in. An American press officer was on duty. He picked me up at the gate and drove me straight to the helicopter field where a swarm of American UH-1 choppers, called Hueys, were waiting with whining engines and flap-flap-flapping rotor blades for the command to take off.

"There's a big operation on," said the press officer, "One ARVN battalion was mauled by the VC last night. It has lost all of its officers and senior NCOs and run almost out of ammunition. We are flying in new officers and supplies, and will try to give them some air support. So if you want to see some action, hop on the colonel's ship here. He is in charge. Good luck."

I took my place behind a lieutenant colonel who was "riding right-seat," meaning that he was in command of this helicopter. That was a rarity; normally lieutenants, captains or warrant officers pilot these flying workhorses of the American army. Wedged in between the door gunners sat three Vietnamese: a major, a first lieutenant and a staff sergeant. We flew in a westerly direction over a beautiful mountainous terrain, which looked deceptively peaceful.

Below us we spotted scenes of hopeless confusion in a large clearing: men running around like headless chickens and mortars firing off their rounds in chaotic abandonment. We came down briskly.

"Shiiiiiiiit!" screamed the colonel as a mortar round whooshed past our chopper, followed by a second one and a third one. "That's friendly fire. They'll kill us all."

"Stop firing," he shouted into his microphone, but he had no radio contact with the ground.

"This unit is leaderless," he explained (nearly half a century later, Bradford Jones told me: "It must have been part of the 44th regiment, which was in a horrible mess at that time").

"Let's go down quickly or they'll shoot us out of the sky," the colonel went on, "I won't even land. You jump out as soon as you can, and run."

As the helicopter hovered for a minute or two about three meters above the ground, the three Vietnamese and I jumped and hit the ground for cover while the aircraft regained height as quickly as possible.

There was pandemonium all around us. Giggling nervously, young soldiers tried to get 81-mm mortars going. Some of these guns sent their grenades heavenward, with no discernible target in sight. Others failed to function altogether because the humidity had rendered the ammunition unusable.

A few yards from where we lay, three young men fumbled perilously with a mortar that hadn't shot off its round. One guy tried to loosen the grenade by poking a tree branch into its nozzle!

"Noooooooo!" shouted the staff sergeant who had flown in with me. He jumped up to show the soldiers how to handle the faulty weapon in such a situation: one guy should lower it very gently and another catch the dud grenade as it slid out. But these three teenagers in uniform were no longer in a condition to follow orders; they were by now hysterical, whirling the mortar irrationally in a circular direction thus endangering everybody.

We ran as fast as we could. It took the officers and NCOs from Nha Trang two hours to restore some order within this leaderless unit. The helicopters came back. I jumped on the colonel's aircraft.

"Welcome back," he grinned. "After Tohuwabohu, now let me show you hell."

As we headed further west he explained, "What you just saw was a company of one of the worst regiments in the South Vietnamese Army. It's bad because it has lost most of its leadership. It should really be thoroughly retrained and re-equipped before being sent back into combat. This is sheer butchery. Now we have been sent to a unit of one of the best regiments. It is on a dangerous mission pursuing a team of murderous Viet Cong thugs who have left a long trail of blood in this area."

He dropped me off in a jungle clearing with the headquarters company of an ARVN battalion of about 450 men. It was the exact opposite of the anarchic bunch of young men I had experienced earlier that day. This battalion belonging to the 45th regiment, if I remember correctly, totally defied the asinine bias of many members of the Saigon press corps that the South Vietnamese made lousy soldiers. Though it had been in the field for several weeks trying to establish a modicum of a government presence in outlying villages, its officers and men were in astonishing shape:

58

motivated, smart, physically fit, disciplined and well informed. Their American advisors, three Green Berets, told me that this particular unit had reliable scouts and informers in communities normally dominated by the Viet Cong after dark, villages and hamlets where the pro-government elders had been decimated by communist killer squads.

The American advisors shared their C-rations with me. I remember eating franks and baked beans cold out of a can, followed by fruit salad, then wrapping myself in my poncho to catch some sleep. At about 3 a.m. we received the urgent order to proceed to a remote village that had just been "visited" by a Viet Cong unit. Our battalion approached the target from three directions unhindered by the enemy who clearly must have been observing us. For psychological reasons inherent in Vo Nguyen Giap's "People's War" strategy, they wanted us to see what they had just done: an unspeakable act of inhumanity, which showed the true and horrific face of the Vietnam War, but a face the peace activists, who paraded through the streets of the United States and Europe a few years later, chose to ignore.

In his book, *The Real War* (New York: Warner Books / Random House, 1980), President Richard Milhous Nixon quoted my report about this incident. He wrote: "…German journalist Uwe Siemon-Netto provided a vivid illustration of how communist guerilla groups use terrorism to effect their purpose. Siemon-Netto, who accompanied a South Vietnamese battalion to a large village the Viet Cong had raided in 1965, reported: 'Dangling from the trees and poles in the village square were the village chief, his wife, and their twelve children … including a baby…'"

The Viet Cong had ordered everyone in the village to witness this family first being tortured, and then hanged. "They started with the baby and then slowly worked their way up to the elder children, to the wife, and finally to the chief himself. … It was all done very coolly, as much an act of war as firing an anti-aircraft gun…"

The image of the dead mayor and his sons was gruesome enough. The Communists had ripped out their tongues. Then they cut off their genitals and stuffed them into their bleeding mouths. But I was even more shaken by sight of his wife and daughters who had their breasts lopped off before they were hanged, reminding me of Hemingway's words, "One becomes so accustomed to all the dead being men that the sight of a dead woman is quite shocking."

Nixon explained that this is how the Communists "won the hearts and minds of the rural population." They did not win hearts and minds by acts of compassion but by the most merciless forms of intimidation. I interviewed several villagers, including a highly articulate French-speaking elder who told me that the Viet Cong cadre had entered the village several times before and warned the chief that if he did not stop cooperating with the South Vietnamese government, there would be severe consequences.

But the chief remained loyal, so they returned in the middle of the night and woke everybody in the village to witness the massacre during which a propaganda officer announced: "This is what will happen to you if you side with the Saigon puppet regime; remember that!" I am ashamed to admit that I can no longer recall the name of that village. But that doesn't really matter because this sort of thing went on all over South Vietnam every night back then.

The combat unit to which I had attached myself left the village less than two hours later, after a team of military intelligence officers had arrived to investigate this atrocity and interview eyewitnesses. They also took down the bodies from the trees.

"Why haven't the villagers done this?" I asked one of the American advisers.

"Fear," he answered. "They were afraid of Communist informers in their midst. The Viet Cong would have interpreted this as an act of sabotage against their handiwork and killed them the same way they had punished the village chief. Such is the nature of terrorism."

While preparing this chapter I spoke about this incident with Bradford Jones, the Green Beret officer who in 1965 had turned me away from the Nha Trang base believing that I was a Communist spy. "We arrived at that village on the same day almost the same time as you," he said. "I remember the dead bodies of that man, his wife and their children. This was not the only massacre I saw in Vietnam, but it was the worst."

Bradford Jones also gave me a different motive for this mass killing: "From what our intelligence people told me, the village chief had been so loyal to the central government in Saigon that he had hidden weapons and ammunition left behind by the French, burying them in the jungle. He didn't want them to fall into Communist hands. But a neighbor betrayed him to the Viet Cong. They found the cache and then tortured him and his family to death."

I told Jones about my discussions with Sir Robert Thompson and Bernard Fall.

"They were right," he replied, "This is why we tried so hard to provide the rural Vietnamese with security. We did not do enough to protect the population. The Viet Cong assassinated many civilian leaders while I was there. We tried appointing some of the most able South Vietnamese officers to these village positions, men who would train local defense forces."

"That's what Thompson did in Malaya and wanted to do in Vietnam," I said.

"He was right."

"What went wrong?" I wanted to know.

"The American media shot down this idea, claiming that we intended to militarize the countryside."

The American public was largely unaware of these atrocities because they were seldom described in U.S. media reports. In the daily press briefings in Saigon—nicknamed *Five O'Clock Follies*—these episodes were reduced to a mere statistic. The briefers would routinely inform correspondents of the huge number of "incidents" that occurred in the previous 24 hours.

But these briefings sounded like a sales report: "I Corps, 184 enemy incidents; II Corps, 360 incidents; III Corps, 225; IV Corps, 480." That was that. No details. What was related were numbers, not the fate of men, women and children. In fairness, it would have been impossible for reporters to follow up every one of these statistics, and it would have also been very hard to get such stories published. As a smug senior editor of the left-of-center magazine *Der Stern* told me when I tried to discuss this topic with him in Hamburg: "The problem with you, Uwe, is that you are too close to the scene. It's much wiser to evaluate such stories from a distance."

Courtesy of USIA

Protecting civilians was a key to the success in counterinsurgency, according to Sir Robert Thompson. Local militias, including women, fulfilled that function.

Reflection Three

Journalism—a calling

Somehow, over the years, those engaged in journalism... have acquired a certain aura of irreverence. Perhaps it's because they have seen too much of the unsavory side of human nature and have also seen some of the skeletons in organized religion's closets. It becomes hard to hang on to religion of any kind. More often than not this irreverence is a prickly covering hiding a deep-seated commitment to a deity and to religious values.

Alfred P. Klausler and John DeMott eds.,
The Journalist's Prayer Book
(Minneapolis: Augsburg Publishing House, 1972); p. 7

I can't pretend that in my Vietnam years I lived the life of a fervent Christian, quite to the contrary. Not that I was an atheist. I had the "deep-seated commitment to a deity" described in the *Journalist's Prayer Book*. But I was also an ambitious and hedonistic fool relegating God to the waiting room of my biography. Yet I was thoroughly instructed in the Christian faith, chiefly by my grandmother in the air raid shelters of World War II. I spoke the Lord's Prayer often and occasionally chanted out loud, especially in combat situations, the *Kyrie eleison* from the Lutheran liturgy I had learned in my childhood: "Lord have mercy." There were also dangerous moments when I sang in my head the offertory canticle based on Psalm 51:10–12: *"Create in me a clean heart, O God, and renew a right spirit within me. Cast me not away from Thy presence and take not thy Holy Spirit from me."* On a more practical level, I never doubted one central point of Lutheran doctrine: that all human beings have divine assignments in their secular lives, and that my vocation to serve my fellow man was that of a journalist. In Vietnam, it became clear to me that a newer breed of "colleagues" lacked this sense of calling and therefore used journalism as means to further only their own interests. These were the ones who caused today's widespread loathing of the media. But to be fair to most of my contemporaries, they would certainly have agreed with this moving old prayer for the members of my craft:

God, you called some to be teachers, and some to be preachers, and some to be deacons, and drawers of water, and hewers of wood; and some who were fit for none of these worthy occupations you called to be writers of words. Help them, God, to get their stories factual and straight. Guide their fumbling fingers on the typewriter keys, and for whatever good it may do, strengthen the connection between their fingers and their minds. And such hearts as they have, bid them use them freely that their printer's ink might evoke the flowing not of blood but of fellowship. Give them a good story now and then, to keep their editors civil, their readers happy, and their minds off their own degradation. And when that day comes for their final thirty-dashes, mercifully grant them just a glimpse of their glory before they travel to that eternity to which they have been consigned so frequently by so many.

Almighty God, we recognize that of ourselves we are impotent to achieve the radiant goals, which thou hast inspired us to set for ourselves. Let us not say of our best deeds that we accomplished these with our own puny powers. Thy hand, unseen and often unrecognized, has been upon our shoulders in good works, and we bow before thee. We do not ask to go unfettered. We willingly wear the bonds of thy making. Make us prisoners of a lively conscience. Make us captives also of an acute justice toward our fellow man. Bind us to the post of journalistic duty.

The Journalist's Prayer Book, p. 100

Chapter Six

Media Theatre of the Absurd

An unpleasant surprise awaited me when I returned to the *Continental Palace* after my introduction to the unvarnished character of the Vietnam War in the Central Highlands. It was a telegram from Julius Hollos, my editor-in-chief in Hamburg, and contained what in American wire service jargon is called a "rocket," meaning a reprimand. The cable read:

WE HEAR YOU DRUNK EVERY PRESS BRIEFING STOP
DEMAND EXPLANATION EXCLAMATION HOLLOS

I was stunned. This imputation was patently false and could have ended my career as an international reporter. While I do enjoy my Scotch or dry martini, and always have wine with dinner, I never touched alcohol before the day's end, and for good reason: evidence of the dangers of liquor and drugs in a tropical warzone abounded in Saigon and, though immature, I was not suicidal. Moreover, I rarely attended the *Five O'Clock Follies*, as we called the daily briefings by the South Vietnamese government, the American embassy and the U.S. military. So I shot back angrily:

NAME SOURCE ADVISE SLANDEROUS SWINE OF
LOOMING PERDITION STOP UWE

Julius was the consummate pro. He could handle my furious outburst, and a few weeks later sent me a conciliatory letter explaining that he had seen the preview of a play in London about the Vietnam War, titled, "US." It was sprinkled with hilarious scenes from official press conferences always featuring an inebriated German reporter's wacky questions preceded by a guttural "AAARRRRRGH."

"The audience was informed that these scenes were authentic," Julius wrote. "As I did not know of any other regular German correspondent in Saigon, I just assumed that this drunkard must have been you. If I was mistaken, please accept my apologies."

Many German reporters flew into Saigon for short-term assignments. They included some of the most capable journalists in the business, and we will meet some of them later in this book. But until this incident, I had thought of myself as the only semi-permanent German correspondent in town. Eventually my street urchin friend, Đức, taught me that I was wrong.

"Hey, Đức," said the imp, using the Vietnamese word for German, which is also his name, "You not only Đức here. That man there also Đức and a journalist like you."

The boy pointed to a red-faced man nursing an orange juice on the *Continental's* covered terrace. I had noticed him before. He always sat by himself at the same table from early in the morning until evening.

"Đức, this guy can't be a German. Germans don't drink juice all day," I objected.

"Hee hee, this man, he no drink juice. He drink screwdriver. *Beaucoup* screwdriver. He always drunk. Hee hee hee."

Screwdrivers are shots of vodka camouflaged by orange juice.

My friend Ronald Ross, the British-born correspondent of the *Minneapolis Tribune*, happened to overhear this dialogue and laughed. Ronald's assignment in Vietnam included filing a daily report, which obliged him to attend the daily press briefings, a grim fate I was spared because my job was writing feature stories, backgrounders and news analyses while leaving "spot news" to the wire services.

"Don't you know him? This guy is hilarious," said Ronald. "His AAARRRRRGH is the highlight of the *Follies*."

I won't mention the real name of this colleague, a lovable eccentric who has since died of alcoholism. Let's just call him Eberhard Budelwitz. He worked as a staff correspondent for a German wire service, writing chiefly straight news items without byline, which is why my boss was not aware of his existence. Much later I came across erudite feature stories about Vietnam, which Budelwitz had crafted in his sober moments (which followed his repeated detoxification stints in German clinics), but sadly, these moments of sobriety never lasted long.

One day I accompanied Ronald to the *Follies* for the sole purpose of hearing Eberhard. He staggered into the briefing hall next to the *Buggery Statue* on Le Loi Boulevard and picked up the daily handouts distributed by the Saigon Government, the U.S. Embassy and the military. As usual, we were immediately rendered drowsy by dry statistics and tedious narratives delivered in the monotonous voice that seemed to be the mark of official briefers. They revealed nothing nearly as newsworthy as the atrocity I had just witnessed in the Central Highlands.

It was hot and sticky in that press center, and many correspondents stared restlessly at their watches—especially the reporters of the lively Saigon press and Japanese and Korean correspondents whose deadlines were fast approaching. Then, just as we were readying ourselves to rush back to our typewriters, the daily Theatre of the Absurd commenced. One briefer mentioned a weird incident that had no real news value, but offered media cockalorums and lickspittles such as Joe, the neurotic big tabloid reporter, their 15 minutes of glory. Did I say 15 minutes? No, Andy Warhol said that. These were 30, 60, or 90 minutes of lunacy.

On that particular day, their mania was triggered thus: One briefer's deadpan voice announced that Buddhist monks in Central Vietnam had complained about American soldiers urinating against their rural pagoda. This set off a flurry of questions sounding roughly as follows:

"Did they urinate inside or outside the temple?"

"Are our soldiers not taught NEVER to expose themselves in public, especially not near a holy place?"

"Did they urinate while under the influence? If so, did this aggravate the situation, given that Buddhist monks shun liquor? Would they have urinated against a temple with just a Coke inside them?"

"What are the implications of this offense in Buddhist theology?"

"Given that Buddhists believe that all living things might be reincarnations of human beings, is not hitting an insect with urine the equivalent of peeing on a man?"

"What, if any, measures has MACV (the Military Assistance Command Vietnam) taken to wipe up this mess? Or did the monks have to do this themselves?"

"Has the U.S. command given any thought to building latrines for Americans in the vicinity of Buddhist temples?"

"Will these offenders be court-martialed for peeing against a temple, and what might the punishment be?"

The great scribes of the Theatre of the Absurd, Eugène Ionesco, Samuel Beckett, Jean Genet, Harold Pinter, Edward Albee or Friedrich Dürrenmatt, would have relished this moment, but even their imagination would not have equipped them for what came next: After a full hour of discussing urine, the lickspittles lost interest and fell silent. There was a blissful second of calm. We were exhausted, ready to go home. If we belonged to a select group of some 20 trusted correspondents, we could spend a little quality time at the *After-Follies*, a deep-background "no holds barred" briefing in the office of Barry Zorthian, the U.S. Government's chief press officer in Saigon.

But just as we were preparing to leave, Eberhard's act delayed our flight:

"AAARRRRRGH."

"*Ja, Herr Budelwitz,*" said the senior U.S. Embassy briefer who spoke German well, "*haben Sie noch eine Frage?*" Do you have an additional question?

"Vy don't you Amerrricans tell ze Buddhists to get zemselves a submarrrine?"

Everybody stared at Eberhard, stunned. Ronald Ross and I agreed that we should really have applauded him, because by associating in his drunken mind the runny nature of this incident with a naval vessel and a holy place, he brought the Theatre of the Absurd to an unforgettably crazy climax.

The Theatre of the Absurd is akin to Surrealism, the art movement that championed "a juxtaposition of two more or less distant realities," according to Pierre Reverdy. This inspired French poet wrote during World War I, "The more the relationship between the two juxtaposed realities is distant and true, the stronger the image will be—the greater its emotional power and poetic reality." One reason why I remember Eberhard so fondly is that his weird questions exposed the increasingly surrealistic features of the Vietnam War: distant realities were placed close together creating strong images of great emotional power despite the apparent absurdity.

Once I caught Eberhard before he finished his first screwdriver and asked him if his surrealistic questions were simply booze-driven or genuinely thoughtful in some eccentric way. Eberhard's answer reminded me of the neo-surrealist slogan of the international New Left: "All power to the imagination." Not that Eberhard himself subscribed to this concept, which seemed dangerously irrational, especially when it attempted to override the bloody realities of the Cold War that had turned hot in Indochina. No, Eberhard told me, his questions were no random scintillations; they were meant to reflect his reaction to the absurdity of what we were experiencing every day.

So what were the absurdities of this tragedy which to cover we had flown in from the most distant corners of the world? It was on that afternoon in the press room the absurd squandering of a second thought on whether or not a urinal misdemeanor could have taken place when night after night men, women and children in unprotected villages were being tortured to death at the command of a totalitarian fiend whose name student protesters began chanting around the Western world: "Ho-Ho-Ho-Chi-Minh." It was surreally ghoulish to measure the progress of the war in daily body counts amounting to statistical units with three-letter names—KIA, WIA and MIA (killed, wounded or missing in action)—as if this conflict was a sports event in which the good guys kept grisly scores.

It was—and here I am running ahead of my narrative—surreal in the most sickening way because while South Vietnamese, Americans, Australians, New Zealanders, South Koreans and Thais were dying in combat and terrorist attacks, a Hollywood film star, Jane Fonda, had herself photographed riding the gunner's seat of a Communist anti-aircraft canon, aiming it at her own country's pilots with a big idiotic grin on her face.

It was repugnantly absurd to hear visiting media stars make light of the Vietnamese war effort, portray these wounded people as crooked and incompetent cowards, ignore their daily sacrifice and overlook one incontrovertible fact: that of the millions of refugees this war and its French predecessor created, precious few sought safety in the Communist North or in the so-called "liberated zones" established by the Viet Cong in the South. Until the very end the majority fled into the shrinking regions controlled by Saigon and ARVN soldiers. Knowing that they had no hope and no longer any allies, still they fought valiantly for their lost cause.

I was appalled by the mindlessly surreal treatment self-centered baby boomers, parroting the inane slogan, "make love not war," meted out to America's returning soldiers. Every one of the veterans I ministered to in the late 1980s had been called a "baby killer" within the first 24 hours of his return from the war. To me, as an outside observer, it seemed that it was on college campuses and in public squares that "the ugly American" was much more in evidence than in the jungles of Southeast Asia where conscripts and professional soldiers gave their lives.

Perhaps the most surreal and reprehensible photograph of this entire conflict was taken 20 years after the Communist conquest of the South. It showed former Defense Secretary Robert McNamara sitting next to his old antagonist, Gen. Vo Nguyen Giap, laughing into the camera. Such hypocrisy made my blood boil: after all, Giap was the author of the carnage I had witnessed in the Central Highlands and, a few years later, in Huế. By Nuremberg standards Giap should have been tried for war crimes. Yet Mr. McNamara, one of John F. Kennedy's intellectual eggheads, honored his former adversary in a thigh slapping "good old fellow" manner, as if to say, "You won, we lost, but didn't we have a jolly good time fighting each other, ha ha ha?" I was scandalized by this mindless affront to the hundreds of thousands of South Vietnamese who had paid for their trust in the United States by being held for years in Giap's "reeducation camps," which were none other than concentration camps. This callous disregard for the men and women who, for the rest of their lives, had to suffer from the aftereffects of the torment inflicted upon them by Communist torturers filled me with bitter contempt.

All these were hideous aspects of the Theatre of the Absurd. They fit that motto of the New Left in the renaissance of surrealism in the 1960s: "All power to the imagination." In hindsight, Eberhard's eccentric behavior seemed eerily prophetic: in his boozy way, he drew a stingingly precise caricature of the future so many of us instinctively feared, including Sir Robert Thompson and Bernard Fall and those among us journalists who loved Vietnam and had read Vo Nguyen Giap's triumphant anticipation of the West's impending failure: "The enemy... does not possess ... the psychological and political means to fight a long, drawn-out war."

As far back as January 13, 1965, Stanley Karnow, one of the most vociferous critics in the American press of the Vietnam War, used this quote in his final installment of a syndicated series of newspaper articles titled "Inside the Viet Cong," Karnow inferred that by the term, "the enemy," Giap meant the succession of weak, faltering, and sometimes, repressive governments in Saigon. Yet Bernard Fall interpreted Giap's statement more accurately in a much larger context. In his masterpiece, *The Two Viet-Nams* (page 113), Fall refers to Giap's statement as an "estimate of the political-psychological shortcomings of a *democratic system* (my italics) when faced with an inconclusive military operation." Read this way, Giap's ominous words have huge implications for the viability of democracy.

As I am writing these lines forty years on, the Taliban in Afghanistan, a force as totalitarian and persevering as the Vietnamese Communists, has become the beneficiary of America's psychological and political inability to pursue a protracted war to its victorious end: Imprudently, the U.S. and its NATO allies have given the Taliban the date by which the Western forces will pull out. As in Vietnam, the enemies of freedom are brazenly displaying their inhumanity in anticipation of victory. Just the other day they beheaded 17 people for the "crime" of attending a mixed-sex party.

It is as if Washington has ignored the logical conclusion from Fall's dire warnings. He wrote:

"In all likelihood, Giap concludes, public opinion in the democracy will demand an end to the 'useless bloodshed,' or its legislature will insist on knowing for how long it will have to vote astronomical credits without a clear-cut victory in sight. This is what eternally compels the military leaders of democratic armies to promise a quick end to the war—to 'bring the boys home by Christmas'—or forces the democratic politicians to agree to almost any kind of humiliating compromise rather than to accept the idea of a semi-permanent anti-guerilla operation."

Ever since the Vietnam War, the media has been accused of having been the top villain in this Theatre of the Absurd, which future historians might well interpret in starker terms: as a requiem for democracy. But it would be unfair to blame the Saigon press corps for this tragic turn. When I first arrived in Saigon, most accredited journalists supported the war effort. Some did so in the finger-pointing style I have always found an irritating feature of American journalism: this display of a prosecutorial "gotcha" instinct in stories about blunders committed by their own side. Some of the lesser minds among them tended to overstress the "American angle" while showing scant interest in the people the war was all about: the Vietnamese. Correspondents of regional newspapers, such as my friend Ronald Ross, the *Minneapolis Tribune* correspondent, had the additional burden of having to produce their load of "hometowners;" but then these articles about soldiers and civilians from their papers' areas of circulation were an effective means of keeping readers focused on the war.

Even most of those 70 percent who, according to Richard Pyle, never went into combat, including the highly-strung Big Tabloid Joe, were no traitors, while the other 30 percent who did venture into the field were incredibly brave and often paid, for their courage, a high price in wounds, psychological trauma often resulting in divorce, and sometimes death. They included heroic friends of mine such as the legendary William Tuohy of the *Los Angeles Times*, R. W. Apple of the *New York Times*, Ron Nessen of *ABC* television who later became President Gerald Ford's White House press secretary, Kevin Buckley of *Newsweek*, the extraordinary AP photographer Horst Faas, an old German colleague of mine since the late 1950s; James Wilde of *Time*, and Peter R. Kann, the marvelously witty *Wall Street Journal* writer who rose to be CEO and chairman of the board at Dow Jones.

These were definitely not the ones who "lost Vietnam." Yet, as Gen. Giap told CBS correspondent Morley Safer in an interview in 1989: "Do not forget that the war was brought into the living rooms of the American people." Thus Giap acknowledged the media's role in his victory. Who, then, were these *de facto* allies of his if not the American reporters in the field? Here I may be permitted a brief excursus on media studies with the promise to return to my narrative after a few paragraphs. I have always resented the charge against war correspondents stationed in Saigon that their hearts were really in Hanoi or in Moscow, Hanoi's chief sponsor. To claim that we risked life and limb to betray the people whose daily sufferings many of us shared is a blatant calumny, which ignores the tectonic shift that occurred in American and ultimately Western journalism while we were doing our job the old-fashioned way.

Media celebrities of a new kind and their youthful wannabe acolytes had emerged in the newsrooms and boardrooms of broadcasting corporations and publishing houses in the 1960s. These were, on the one hand, luminaries such as Walter Cronkite, who had once been an admirable war reporter but long since acquired the aura of a superstar, and, on the other hand, products of increasingly ideological liberal arts colleges and universities.

They were driven not by the sense of wonderment that used to be the mark of the traditional journalist, but by a desire to "make this a better world," an aspiration most American journalism students offer to this day as a reason for choosing this career. This kind of rhetoric makes my generation of reporters cringe because we were trained to stay relentlessly curious, do our research properly and *inform* our readers accurately with well-written articles, rather than preach, pontificate and browbeat like the scribes of Joseph Goebbels' propaganda ministry in Nazi Germany or of the Soviet agitprop service. Publisher Rupert Murdoch would later contemptuously refer to this new breed as "self-serving pundits."

They followed a drift in journalism that became fashionable when the profession changed its character from a down-to-earth craft to another pseudo-academic ivory tower. As James Fallows wrote in his book, *Breaking the News* (New York: Pantheon, 1996), "The trend is... toward being a 'prominent' journalist without doing a reporter's work." Steven Cuozzo, the *New York Post's* former executive editor, recalls how the old, "rough, often heavy-drinking" blue-collar types in the Fourth Estate were being replaced by earnest and much better educated young men and women primarily interested in social issues. The former were capable of laughing about their beats—"later over a beer"; the latter's trademark was an "absence of a sense of humor." Cuozzo wrote this in his entertaining memoir *It's Alive!* (New York: Random House, 1996).

The traditional journalists, the craftsmen, were still on the job in my time in Vietnam. They had their stories published, albeit in many cases further and further in the back pages. The limelight was reserved for the new journalists, the pundits, stars who opined rather than reported. They flew in and out of Saigon on "special assignments" and, clad in freshly pressed fatigues, pontificated before millions of television viewers, not on the basis of what they had experienced in the jungles and villages, in the Mekong Delta or Central Highland, but on the basis of the stereotypical antiwar ideology they themselves were imposing on the American public square. And thus they brought about the situation Vo Nguyen Giap had anticipated when he wrote: "The enemy... does not possess... the psychological and political means to fight a long, drawn-out war."

That said, I will resume my sentimental journey back to my days as a charmed young reporter in what remained of Saigon as the Paris of the Orient; a journey back to the days when Tu Do Street still resembled the glamorous old Rue Catinat, before it evolved into a huge red-light district. I will return to an era when French was still the *lingua franca* of the educated classes, and where one could obtain access to one of the most powerful generals by listening to the discreetly whispered hint of his aide de camp: *"Aimez vous du champagne, Monsieur? Ah! Moi aussi, j'aime tant du Dom Pérignon"*—do you love champagne? Ah, me too! I so much love Dom Pérignon! I found three bottles in the PX and was promptly received by the general who remained my friend until I left Saigon for good. Not that the general drank the champagne; his poorly paid aide did. Chin-chin, *mon capitaine,* your tastes are noble.

That problem solved, I had to tackle an even more crucial one: how will I get my stories out? There was no Internet back then; there were neither emails nor fax machines. The wire services had their own telex systems, as did the *New York Times,* the *Washington Post-Los Angeles Times* news service, and some of the American correspondents could use those as well. But what about the rest of us? Airmail was slow and unreliable. I did have access to the U.S. military's trustworthy "APO postal service," but it would deliver letters only inside the United States. Sometimes I used airfreight, but this was an expensive and cumbersome way to get my copy out. Then there was an antebellum—in this case meaning, pre-World War II—institution: the *Postes, Téléphone et Télégraphe* (P.T.T.), a public corporation still owned and operated by its French parent company. To my knowledge, it only had one telephone line to Paris, perhaps two, but they were faulty. It took hours to get through to Hamburg, and, given the poor quality, the charges were outrageous. Telegrams were cheaper but only when sent to my newspaper's Paris bureau, where my texts arrived hopelessly garbled.

"What am I going to do?" I asked Lanh, the former Foreign Legion trombonist who was my occasional assistant.

"The problem is how to get around censorship," he suggested.

"I thought there was no censorship here," I protested.

"There's not supposed to be censorship, but there is, and the censors only know English or French. When you send a cable, I suspect that they will have to find an old foreign legionnaire who can read German. This delays everything, and I fear that some of your telegrams will never even go through. Let me see what I can do."

A few days later Lanh came to the *Continental Palace* in the company of an elderly and emaciated-looking gentleman whom he introduced as *"Monsieur le Sous-Directeur,"* or the deputy manager, of Saigon's Central Post office, an ornate palatial structure built in 1891, by Alfred Foulhoux and Henri Vildieu, two great architects of the French *Belle Époque*.

He presented himself as Monsieur Nguyen, a name as common in Vietnamese as Smith is in English, Dupont in French or Müller in German. Nguyen eagerly accepted my strong French *Gitanes* cigarettes, saying that they were infinitely better than the locally made *Bastos* brand he chain-smoked.

"Monsieur, I have come to you with an unusual request," he said. "You see, my nephew will die of tuberculosis unless some drastic steps are taken. None of the medicines available in Vietnam seem to have any effect. I hear that West Germany has developed a new drug that is not yet on the market but is still in the trial phase." Monsieur Nguyen handed me a slip of paper with a Latin name on it. "Could you possibly obtain it for us? I don't think we have much time left. I am happy to pay any reasonable price."

Looking at Nguyen, I strongly suspected that he was not really talking about a relative but himself.

"Let's see what we can do together," I answered as I went to my desk and typed out a telegram to Julius Hollos, my boss in Hamburg, urgently requesting him to ask Dr. Langsch, the chief physician of the *Axel Springer* corporation in Hamburg, to obtain that product from its manufacturer and put it on the next Air France plane to Saigon.

"Send this off to Hamburg today, please," I said to Nguyen. "Make sure it gets there before the weekend so that our company doctor can act immediately."

In a stunning exercise of German efficiency combined with the flexibility of a crisp and booming postwar publishing empire, Dr. Langsch managed to have the product delivered to me within three days. An elegant little note in the parcel informed Mr. Nguyen in French that this medicine was a gift from the *Axel Springer Verlag*, and would he please not hesitate to turn to me if he had any other health needs.

This solved my communications problems for the time being. From then on my telegrams reached our Paris bureau swiftly and were no longer garbled. When I ran into Monsieur Nguyen again several months later I could hardly recognize him. He looked much younger, full of health and well nourished. He had stopped smoking and advised me to do the same, which I did in Paris a decade later, in the month of Saigon's fall. He also said that his "nephew" was now cured, and would I please forward his heartfelt thanks to Hamburg.

Whenever I think of meeting the general's champagne-loving aide-de-camp and the emaciated P.T.T. *Sous-Directeur* with his saga about his tubercular "nephew" I feel pangs of nostalgia for the Saigon of my early days in Vietnam. It was amusing how differently my American and European colleagues reacted to these anecdotes. The Americans, especially the more earnest younger types, interpreted them as further evidence of how "corrupt" the South Vietnamese really were. The Europeans, notably visiting German television correspondents and my English friend Donald Wise, who had all been frontline officers in World War II, listened to my tales with knowing smiles. They found them enchanting because they showed the wholly civilized nature of our host country that made good use of human predicaments and harmless foibles just to get things done.

Reflection Four

The masquerade of evil

The great masquerade of evil has played havoc with all our ethical concepts. For evil to appear disguised as light, charity, historical necessity or social justice is quite bewildering to anyone brought up on our traditional ethical concepts, while for the Christian, who bases his life on the Bible, it merely confirms the fundamental wickedness of evil.

Dietrich Bonhoeffer,
Letters & Papers from Prison
(New York: Collier Books, 1953); p. 4

To Dietrich Bonhoeffer, evil appeared in Germany disguised as a system that called itself "national socialist." It pretended to end the disgrace resulting from defeat in World War I, the vindictiveness of the Versailles Treaty and the economic disaster that resulted from it. The system also provided millions of jobs.

To American soldiers fighting in Vietnam, evil came in a variety of disguises, some of which resembled those of the Nazis. The causes for which the North Vietnamese claimed to fight were national pride, unity and social justice. Like the Nazis, the North Vietnamese managed to camouflage the real purpose of their struggle, which was the imposition of their totalitarian system on the noncommunist part of their country as well as Laos and Cambodia.

In order to establish this totalitarian system, the highly disciplined North Vietnamese carried out unspeakable acts of cruelty. Americans, too, committed atrocities, such as the massacre of 347 to 504 unarmed civilians by a rogue task force of the U.S. Army in My Lai. Many journalists and other authors writing about Vietnam failed to stress sufficiently the difference between the two: what the North Vietnamese did was the execution of government doctrine and policy; by contrast, what happened in places such as My Lai occurred in direct violation of U.S. policy.

The resulting fallacies about America's military performance in Vietnam were largely responsible for the appalling way U.S. soldiers were treated when they came home.

Chapter Seven

Buffalo Đức

Early one morning, Lanh came to my room and said to me: "It's time for you to see the real Vietnam." To him, the "real Vietnam" was Huế, the former imperial capital, Lanh's hometown. He had a point. I had heard that, of all the major cities in this country, Huế was the most authentically Vietnamese. It was untouched by the more hideous features of Western culture, by urban blight and honky-tonk that had already begun to whittle away Saigon's charm.

Huế was a delightful city in ferment. It was home to the cauldron of militant Vietnamese nationalism: the *Lycée Quoc Hoc.* Emperor Thanh Thai founded it in 1896. President Ngo Dinh Diem's father, Ngo Dinh Kha, was the first headmaster of this élite high school, which offered the best of French and Asian education. Diem attended it, as did Ho Chi Minh and his Prime Minister Pham Van Dong, the son of the highest-ranking mandarin at the imperial court.

There was an additional incentive for a German reporter to visit Huế. German professors had founded its medical school. One of them, the psychiatrist Erich Wulff, had played a dubious role during the Buddhist uprising of 1963, which led to Diem's fall and ultimately his murder. Later it turned out that he was an outright Viet Cong supporter who would testify against the United States in Bertrand Russell's Vietnam Tribunal. He did this after the Vietnamese Communists had murdered his three colleagues, Alois Alteköster, Raimund Discher and Horst-Günther Krainick, as well as Krainick's wife Elisabetha, in the 1968 Têt Offensive. To his disgrace, Wulff blamed this atrocity on American-trained "liquidation units" operating in Viet Cong uniforms. That outrage happened three years after my first trip to Huế, which turned out to be one of the most instructive journeys in my five Vietnam years.

This time I didn't travel on a military C-123, but in a comfortable *Air Vietnam* DC-6A aircraft with wide seats and ample legroom. *Air Vietnam* was one of the gems of this war-torn nation: an airborne pocket of civilization doing justice to its motto, *The Airline with the Charming Tradition*. Our plane, propelled by four piston engines, felt almost pristine even though it was nearly 20 years old. Elegant stewardesses in alluring blue *Áo dài* robes served ham and cheese sandwiches of a quality that would make passengers on any present-day domestic flight in the United States envious.

Looking down through my large window, I saw how lovely Vietnam really was: how white its beaches were, how verdant its forests, how dramatic its mountains and valleys. Occasionally I could spot swarms of military helicopters a long way below us. Still, the landscape seemed so peaceful that I felt the urge to explore it by car or train, but I knew, of course, that it would be impossible to cross this country in my old *Citroën Traction* and that the railway lines were destroyed.

Next to me sat a young Indian Army captain in an immaculate British-style uniform. He introduced himself as a courier of the International Commission for Supervision and Control in Vietnam (ICSC), a force established in 1954 to oversee the implementation of the Geneva Accords that ended the first Indochina War. In every ICSC team the non-aligned Indians were the chairmen; the Canadians represented the West, and the Poles represented the Communist bloc.

"I am on my way to Gio Linh, the ICSC camp in the demilitarized zone," the captain announced. "Why don't you come along? As a journalist, you might find this interesting."

This was an offer I could not resist. The Control Commission had been difficult to approach for us correspondents, especially now that North Vietnam, in a brazen violation of the 1954 accords, was moving thousands of men across the Demilitarized Zone

(DMZ), which spanned 60 miles from the South China Sea in the east to the Annamite Cordilleras in the West. When I mentioned this to the captain he just shrugged: "We are powerless, Sir. What do you expect a small group of unarmed observers to do? We travel back and forth between Saigon and Hanoi on the Commission's almost 30 year-old Boeing 307, the only plane allowed to land in both capitals. But that's the extent of our work here: We look, listen, read—and do nothing."

Outside the terminal at Phú Bài, Huế's airport, a jeep of World War II vintage was waiting for us. It was painted white like all ICSC vehicles, including the ICSC's ancient airplane. There were sandbags on the floor of the car to protect the passengers against shrapnel from road mines. The driver was a wiry Vietnamese with piercing eyes and the weather-beaten features of a farmer. He greeted me without a smile and pretended not to understand when the Indian introduced me in English as a West German reporter.

"*Je suis un journaliste ouest-allemand,*" I explained in French. He stared at me, obviously puzzled by my presence.

"*Soyez la bienvenue!*" he said crisply—welcome! He did not give his name.

We drove north, crossed the River of Perfumes in Huế, allowing me a glimpse of the beautiful old city, and then continued on National Route 1 towards Quang Tri. The French called this highway "*La Rue Sans Joie,*" or Street Without Joy, because so many soldiers and civilians had died on it during the first Indochina War. *Street Without Joy* is also the title of a riveting book by Bernard Fall.

I never saw anybody drive the way our Vietnamese chauffeur did: lead-footed, his piercing eyes glued to the surface of the road, he yanked the steering wheel abruptly to the left, then to the right and left again in a seemingly erratic manner.

"Mines," he said deadpan. "You recognize mines by the way the dust on the road has changed its color. This is no job for blind people, Monsieur. Voilà, here's a landmine," he said as he jerked the steering wheel to the right, driving the jeep almost off the road.

"But why so fast?" I asked him.

"Snipers, Monsieur. These people have no regard for the white color identifying this jeep as a vehicle belonging to a neutral authority. The only way to avoid snipers is by putting your foot down and going as fast as you can."

We probably didn't travel any faster than 50 miles per hour. But the old jeep rattled and shook so wildly that it felt as if we were racing.

I thought it wise not to disturb him any further, except once when I remarked on the idyllic scene of children riding on the backs of long-horned water buffaloes in the fields on both sides of the road.

"Buffalo boys. All orphans. Very important in guerilla war," he remarked tersely as he continued his zigzag course north. The tense muscles at the back of his neck told me how much he was trying to concentrate on getting us safely to the ICSC camp located less than one mile south of the *Hiền Lương* Bridge. This log bridge built by the French spanned the Ben Hai River, which separated North and South Vietnam.

I looked warily to the left. The sun was low in the sky and would soon disappear behind the mountain range where I knew that large North Vietnamese units were holed up in chalk caves. We had to reach the Gio Linh camp before dark, and we did, though only just. But the sentry at the gate would not let me in. He informed me that my American and South Vietnamese press cards did not qualify me to enter the Control Commission's neutral grounds. In the end, the young captain persuaded the sentry to call Gio Linh's commanding officer, an Indian lieutenant colonel.

"You can't come in, Sir," he said.

"But Sir," objected the captain in an astonishing display of guts. "Sir, all this is not this gentleman's fault. It was my mistake, Sir. I should not have invited him. I didn't realize the international implications. We can't let him wander around in the dark. There is a war on out there, Sir! Please, grant him hospitality."

I was impressed by this young officer's civil courage, and so obviously was the colonel.

"You have a point, Captain. Please come in, Sir. Consider yourself a guest of the Indian contingent tonight. You'll stay at our quarters and eat at my table. I'll inform the Canadians, but let's not tell the Poles who you are—a *West German*, goodness gracious me! If you were Swiss or Dutch, perhaps... but a *German?* They wouldn't like that at all, given that they consider the West Germans their archenemies. Better not have an international incident, what, what?"

And so I was allowed to enter neutral grounds. I was assigned a bed in the young captain's room, took a shower and accompanied him to the strangest mess hall I had ever seen. It featured three identical dining tables: one for the Indians, one for the Canadians and one for the Poles. The lieutenant colonel invited me to sit on his left where my back was turned to the Poles though I could see the Canadians who took no apparent interest in my presence.

The three groups were also segregated by cuisine. At my table a spicy Indian curry was served, which I loved. I saw what the Canadians were eating: standard North American fare. But what the Poles were getting I could only smell. The mouthwatering scent of sausages and sauerkraut came wafting over to us, reminding me of my grandmother's home cooking.

While the Indians and Canadians were conducting discreet dinner conversations, the Poles were getting gradually more boisterous. The lieutenant colonel, finishing his tea, remarked with some displeasure that our neighbors were now passing the vodka bottle around. Suddenly he stared at me with alarm, as did the other Indian officers. Next I felt a heavy hand on my left shoulder. I looked up and saw the bandaged face of a Polish major.

"*Sprechen Sie Deutsch?*" he asked me—do you speak German?

"*Ja*," I answered.

"*...und Französisch?*" he went on—and French?

"*Auch Französisch*," I replied—French too.

He grinned and asked me, in German, if I could do him a favor. He had suffered a bad injury, not as a result of war but in a volleyball game.

"Tomorrow I will have my stitches pulled at the Vietnamese hospital in Quang Tri. I have some other health issues to discuss with the doctor, but he only speaks French. Would you please be my interpreter?"

"By all means," I answered, "But I will have to ask the colonel for his permission. After all, I am his guest."

I translated our conversation into English. The lieutenant colonel nodded warily.

"It's okay," I told the Pole, adding wickedly, "However, you'll have to pay me for that. The price will be one of your sausages and a little sauerkraut. They smell so good."

"Only if you join our table."

I took leave from the lieutenant colonel, who did not seem pleased! The Poles served me a huge portion of sausages and filled a water glass to the top with *Zubrówka* Vodka. All spoke at least some German. After a while we were gloriously inebriated.

A middle-aged civilian introduced himself as a minister-counselor attached to the Polish embassy in Hanoi, but seconded to the ICSC. He asked me:

"How come an Englishman speaks German so well?"

"I am not English. I am German."

The tipsy Poles burst into uproarious laughter, including the minister-counselor who would later become a fascinating contact. It turned out that he also maintained a permanent room in the *Continental Palace* in Saigon. We sometimes met for an Alsatian meal of sausages and sauerkraut at the *Guillaume Tell* restaurant or just for Polish vodka and German *Löwenbräu* beer I purchased at the PX. We carefully avoided discussing politics or the war. But we enjoyed each other's company as two old-fashioned Central

Europeans in an exotic part of the world. Moreover, as he commuted regularly on the ICSC's ancient Boeing 307 between Saigon and Hanoi, he turned out to be a reliable source of information about daily life in North Vietnam, a country that never granted me a visa.

The Indian lieutenant colonel banged with a spoon against his tea glass and shouted: "Gentlemen! Cinema time!"

We moved next door into a makeshift leisure room to watch an American black-and-white movie displayed on a primitive screen. I took my place next to the lieutenant colonel, who by then had regained his *bonhomie*. He slapped my right thigh and said, "You are a funny German, old boy, very, very funny, what what!"

Vietnamese children squatted on the ground along the leisure room's bamboo walls.

"Who are they?" I asked the colonel.

"Kids from Vinh Thanh village."

"How come some of them are blond and blue-eyed?"

"Don't look at me, Sir," said the colonel, "Indians don't come blond and blue-eyed, what, what!"

I looked at the Canadians. They shook their heads indignantly. I looked at my vodka-happy Polish friends. "Not us," said the major with the bandaged head. Later I learned to my amusement that these children were the offspring of former German soldiers in the French Foreign Legion.

Early in the morning, the Polish major, the Vietnamese driver with piercing eyes and I set off to the old French *Hôpital de Quang-Tri* where, during the first Indochina War, hundreds of wounded soldiers had died, including many German legionnaires. I did my duty as interpreter. On the way back, the major came up with what seemed a nutty idea:

"You know what our job is, don't you?" he asked.

"Not really."

"Well, although our group is based in South Vietnam it patrols the DMZ on the North Vietnamese side. Why don't you join us? It will be fun. We'll cross the Ben Hai River early in the morning.

There will be bicycles waiting for us on the other side. We'll ride to the beach. No Viet Cong snipers there. We swim and then pedal back. That's good exercise. In the evening we'll return to camp."

"Do you really believe the North Vietnamese will let a West German in?" I asked.

"They will if you wear a Polish officer's uniform and don't show your German passport. We are about the same size. I'll lend you one of mine. You will just have to remember to talk to us in German. The North Vietnamese won't know the difference."

Piercing Eyes turned around and for a split second gave me a warning gaze. What a mysterious man Piercing Eyes was; he had understood our German conversation!

In Gio Linh, we presented the Indian lieutenant colonel with the Polish major's idea, but the Indian wasn't having any of this:

"Come to your senses, gentlemen! I am not going to risk an international incident over this sort of nonsense, what, what!" Pointing his forefinger at me, he went on: "You, Sir, may accompany us to the Hiền Lương Bridge and wave us a fond goodbye as we cross it. Then our driver, here, will take you back to Huế. Is that clear?"

Thus ended one of my strangest episodes in Vietnam, or so I thought.

On the following morning, I watched my Indian, Polish and Canadian friends walk across the French log bridge to North Vietnam. The young captain had already returned the day before. Piercing Eyes and I were alone in the jeep as we rattled south on the Street Without Joy. What happened next would remain dormant in my memory for 47 years. It only came back to me when I rummaged through my badly organized files in preparation for this book. There I found a draft of a novel I had written during a sabbatical in England in my father-in-law's office for a publishing house in Vienna. It was meant to be a work of fiction based on fact about the buffalo boys along the Street Without Joy.

I never finished the draft because a major crisis erupted in the Middle East, culminating in the Six-Day War of 1967, which I was assigned to cover on the Arab side, primarily reporting from Jordan and the Lebanon. Following that I returned to the Far East, where I had by now two huge topics to report about: Vietnam and Mao's Cultural Revolution in China. Not once did I waste a moment's thought on my novel until I discovered my yellowed manuscript in my library in France.

As I continue my narrative, I must advise my readers that it is reconstituted material based on that draft, which contained detailed information given to me by the ICSC driver Piercing Eyes on our way from the Ben Hai River to Huế. I now recall it with geriatric clarity.

"On our way up you mentioned these children," said Piercing Eyes, pointing at the buffalo boys who were waving at us.

"Yes?"

"As I said, all of these are orphans, and they are playing a very important role in this war. They are organized in gangs or guilds. Some are loyal to the Viet Cong, others to the Saigon government. This depends on which territory we are driving through. These boys here are waving at us because they know that this jeep belongs to a neutral organization. If this were an American or South Vietnamese military vehicle, they might just pretend to ignore us."

"Please explain."

"Many of these gangs constitute early warning systems stretching over many kilometers. Right now I am certain that these boys are giving signals to each other that a neutral jeep is passing through. That's good for us. If they were pro-Viet Cong and saw an ARVN convoy coming their signals might well lead to a Communist ambush."

"Why are some on the Communist side and why do others sympathize with the government?"

"Let me tell you a story," said Piercing Eyes. "It's the story about a former buffalo boy by the name of Đức."

"I have a friend called Đức," I interrupted him. "He heads a gang of street urchins selling newspapers outside my hotel in Saigon."

"Đức is a very common name in Vietnam. The Đức in my story is your Đức's rural counterpart."

Piercing Eyes' narrative began with the description of a massacre similar to the atrocity I described in Chapter Five, except that it occurred in the first Indochina War in the early 1950s. One winter's night, the Communist Viet Minh invaded a predominantly Catholic village close to the Street Without Joy intent on murdering the mayor, his wife and their eight children because the mayor had been loyal to the French. They made every inhabitant watch as they hanged the mayor by his hands, cut off his genitals and stuffed them into his mouth in the way they often dealt with captured French soldiers. Then they strung up his wife and cut her breasts off. The children were to be next but the Viet Minh didn't notice that Đức had dropped to the ground. Two brave onlookers quietly stepped in front of him so that the guerillas could no longer see him. He crept away, disappearing into the surrounding countryside. Once he had gained a fair distance from the village he ran through muddy fields until he collapsed, exhausted. When he woke, he felt something warm and heavy on top of him. It was a water buffalo.

Đức was eight years old then, according to Piercing Eyes. When he crawled out from under the buffalo's belly, a 14-year old boy stood in front of him, saying, "You are an orphan, aren't you? So are we all." He pointed to a group of children standing around. "We are a family now, and you are part of our family." There were 38 boys and girls of all ages, the older ones not only herded the buffaloes but also took care of the younger children. They would spend all day riding and minding the animals belonging to local farmers; at night they slept under the warm bovine bellies. The older children taught the young ones to read and write; as they had no books, paper or pens, they used road signs to copy and drew letters and numbers with their fingers in the mud during the wet season or the dust when it was dry. They shared the rice, fruit and vegetables farmers gave them, and the fish and shellfish they caught in brooks or ponds.

One day, Đức told the older ones, "We should really go to school. I remember a French missionary who ministered to our village. He has a little schoolhouse. Maybe he can take in half of us, and those children will teach the other half at night, and we'll take turns between those who mind the buffaloes and those who go to class." So the kids sent Đức off to see the priest, a Jesuit by the name of Père Alexandre. The missionary agreed to the arrangement, but he didn't have enough money to buy pencils, paper and textbooks for all 38 buffalo children. Then his little school was destroyed in a battle and his bishop refused to give money for its reconstruction or to finance pencils, papers and textbooks for the other pupils. Eventually the Viet Minh killed Père Alexandre, and the children were back to teaching each other the way they had before: by writing with their forefingers in mud.

Eventually some boys from Đức's gang met other orphans minding buffaloes in a neighboring district that was controlled by the Viet Minh. They said the Communists were building a brand-new school and invited Đức and his friends to attend it.

"To cut a long story short, this is how Đức and his crew were recruited into the Viet Minh," said Piercing Eyes. "At school they were taught how to read and write. They were instructed in algebra, chemistry, basic physics and geography. But they were also indoctrinated. They were made to read Communist propaganda and trained to pass signals to each other, neighboring gangs and ultimately Viet Minh scouts when they saw French troop movements along the Street Without Joy."

According to Piercing Eyes, Đức was made a cadre of the Viet Minh's successor organization, which became known as the Viet Cong. It was the fighting arm of the "National Liberation Front of South Vietnam," which was officially founded six years after the ceasefire following the 1954 Geneva Accords. Like the Viet Minh, the Viet Cong massacred their political opponents and their families, in line with Gen. Vo Nguyen Giap's formula for a "People's War." However, Đức recalled the slaughter of his family when he was a child, and when he was ordered to take command of a mass execution, he defected to the French.

Piercing Eyes reached this part of his story as we were having lunch in a village between Quang Tri and Huế. He stared at me as if to discern my emotions. I was shaken, thinking back to the murder scene I had seen a few weeks early near Nhat Trang. Gulping down a whole bottle of *Bière 33*, I spotted a crucifix on a chain half-hidden in his shirt, and remembered that Đức was a Christian.

"*Đức—c'est bien vous!* I burst out—Đức, that's you!

For the first time he smiled: "*Non, Monsieur, mais je le connais bien ce Đức,*" he answered quietly—no, but I know him well, that Đức. He assured me that Đức was "safe." With that he fell silent.

"One more question," I said. "Yesterday it was obvious to me that you understood German."

"I know German well enough to understand the Polish major's demented scheme, which you Germans would call *eine Schnapsidee* (a crazy, booze-driven thought). I was glad that you read my eyes, and I am much relieved that the Indian colonel stopped this nonsense."

"Where did you learn German?"

"From German soldiers in the Foreign Legion. There were many around here in the French days, and they were very kind to us children. We loved being around them, especially at Christmas time. They sang such beautiful carols: I still have some of these hymns in my ears: '*Tochter Zion, freue dich*' in the Advent season, and '*Stille Nacht, Heilige Nacht*' on Christmas Eve."

"So did you spend Christmas with them?"

"Yes, if the security situation permitted. They invited us for Christmas to their compound. '*Weihnachten ohne Kinder ist kein Weihnachten,*' they told us"—Christmas without children is no Christmas.

"Did you eat Christmas goose?"

"Oh yes, and red cabbage and potato dumplings. They had a fantastic *Küchenbulle* (cook). The French loved his cuisine, too. Everybody wanted to spend Christmas with the Germans."

"Did you know how they became foreign legionnaires?"

"We knew that most of them had been recruited in French POW camps after World War II. They were given a choice between starving to death or taking their chance in another war; so they chose the latter. Some were very *vornehm*, as you say in German, very gentlemanly. We were told that they had been *Wehrmacht* officers, including submarine captains, but in the Legion they were simple privates."

"What did they do for you?"

"They tried to protect us when they could. They gave us food, sweets and other presents. They were homesick and spoke a lot about their lost homeland. They taught us music."

"A friend of mine, Lanh, is from Huế. He learned to play the trombone in a Foreign Legion band," I interjected.

"Yes, and one legionnaire gave me his harmonica and taught me how to play it. I still have it at home. They also taught us their language and their poetry. We enjoyed listening to them when they spoke. I have good memories of these Germans, but they are also sad memories because so many lost their lives here."

We continued our journey to Huế in silence. As we approached the city, he asked me:

"Where would you like me to drop you off?"

"The *Cité Universitaire*," I said, meaning the hideous French-style housing estate by the Phu Cam Canal where the German and other professors were lodged.

"Don't go there just yet," Piercing Eyes advised me. "You have just heard an authentically Vietnamese story. Indulge in an authentically Vietnamese evening before joining your German compatriots."

"I am in your hands. What do you suggest?"

"Let me show you." We drove into the Old City of Huế and on to the northwest bank of the River of Perfumes. And there, within sight of the Citadel and Imperial City, we stopped at a landing for floating hotels.

"This is where you will sleep," said Piercing Eyes pointing to a sampan. "You'll be comfortable and in safe hands. I know the boatman."

He slipped the boatman a few piaster notes, told him who I was, and bid me farewell.

"*Au revoir*, Monsieur, tonight you will be my guest. Please keep us in your prayers."

With that, Piercing Eyes drove off to Phú Bài Airport to pick up another visitor from Saigon.

The boatman guided me to the sampan's simple cabin where a plain, impeccably clean bed was made up for me. There was a little basket filled with mangosteen fruit, bananas and oranges and a bottle of mineral water, the dual purpose of which the boatman explained to me in sign language: it was good to drink and to clean my teeth with. He lit joss sticks against mosquitoes and took me outside to show me a bucket on a rope indicating that I could use it later for a good shower in mid-stream.

Just before he punted the sampan from its mooring, a pretty young girl with a long mane of shiny black hair came on board. She was at most 16 years old. I assumed that she was the boatman's daughter. The girl carried a trapeze-shaped instrument with three strings and a long wooden neck studded by ten frets. Later I found out that this was a lute indigenous to central and northern Vietnam called *Đàn Đáy*.

She slipped to the bow of the sampan as we were gliding toward mid-stream, where a delicious breeze embraced me while I was stretched out on my bunk. The sun set in the mountains to the west of Huế reflecting on the surface of the River of Perfumes like a well-defined stream of lava; this fiery stream seemed flanked on both sides by a huge body of molten gold. At that point the girl on the sampan's bow began to sing, accompanying herself on her three-stringed *Đàn Đáy*. To my German ears, her indescribably beautiful songs were hauntingly sensuous and noble. I was later told that some of this ancient music descended from the imperial court of Annam.

The girl sang on as the sun disappeared behind the mountains and the river altered its color from red-gold to dark blue and then with the rising moon to silver. She seemed to choose her exotic melodies to match the change of colors. As I listened to her, I thought of Piercing Eyes, the crucifix half-hidden in his shirt and his story of Đức; I thought of Đức, my street urchin friend in Saigon, of Capt. Ngu in Long Khốt, of the massacre near Nha Trang, and of my assistant Lanh in Saigon. Before drifting off to sleep I was overcome by the ghastly premonition that this sampan transformed itself into a troop-carrying landing craft with armored sidings, and that the discordant rat-tat-tat of thousands of machine gun rounds bounced off the steel, drowning out the royal chants of the boatman's beautiful daughter.

When I woke early in the morning I saw the girl curled up under a canvas cover and felt a deep sense of impending loss as the boatman punted his sampan back to shore. I had no desire to visit the German doctors, but in retrospect I am glad I did. I had dinner with Dr. Krainick and his wife Elisabetha, two humble Catholic Christians who had given up the comforts of academic life at Freiburg University to teach medicine in this dangerous country for less than a third of a German professor's salary. I sat in their dining room and admired Krainick's beloved collection of behind-the-glass paintings and listened to his stories about clinics he had set up at his own expense in contested villages outside Huế where he treated the sick regardless of whether their loyalties lay with the Saigon government or the Communists.

Then over a nightcap in Erich Wulff's apartment next door, where I spent the night, I had to contain myself as this agitated leftwing psychiatrist ranted about Elisabetha Krainick's "elitist" habit of swimming and playing tennis in the old French *Cercle Sportif* off Le Loi Boulevard on the southeast bank of the River of Perfumes; I could have strangled him when he declared Krainick an "insensitive fool" for occasionally accepting helicopter rides from the Americans in order to reach his rural clinics quickly.

That night, my dark premonitions returned with a vengeance. I decided to return to Saigon the next morning.

On the *Air Vietnam* DC-6A I remembered gratefully Lanh's admonition: "It is time for you to see the authentic Vietnam."

I saw the authentic Vietnam, my friend Lanh. But then I had two frightening nightmares that would become reality three years later.

Chapter Eight

Boys vs. boys

My journey to Huế and the Demilitarized Zone marked the end of my first tour in Vietnam and also, in my mind, of a chapter in the Vietnam War. When I left Saigon in the spring of 1965, it still had the flair of a French city, and the conflict consisted primarily of guerrilla action, which was characteristic of phase II of a "People's War," according Gen. Vo Nguyen Giap's textbook. When I returned in the summer, the center of Saigon reminded me more of the area around the central train station at Frankfurt in Germany than of a glamorous metropolis in France. Following the arrival of large U.S. ground forces, a red light district was metastasizing in the city center, and the conflict was in the process of entering phase III: conventional warfare.

I flew to New York via Hamburg where evidence of an embryonic antiwar movement was awaiting me at the head office: piles of letters from leftwing student groups in Frankfurt and West Berlin, and an article in the radical magazine, *konkret*, accusing me of glorifying war and being, "insensitive to the aspirations of an oppressed people." The editor-in-chief of this publication was Ulrike Meinhof who, three years later, became the leader of the *Red Army Faction*, a murderous terrorist organization. The article carried no byline, but I discovered later that its author was a former classmate of mine at boarding school; we actually had once been friends.

For dramaturgical reasons, I will now fast-forward briefly by more than two decades to the summer of 1987. I had interrupted my career as a journalist to work as chaplain intern at the VA Medical Center in Saint Cloud, Minnesota. My job was to provide pastoral care to Vietnam veterans suffering from Post-Traumatic Stress Disorder and other war-related illnesses.

One hot Saturday, when I was off duty, I drove to Duluth on the "Scandinavian Riviera" along Lake Superior and stopped *en route* for a beer at a country tavern. Only one other guest stood at the bar: a lean and wiry man in his late thirties dressed in shorts. I had no trouble identifying him as a Vietnam vet, for his body language and facial expression bespoke defiance, which was the mark of Vietnam veterans then.

"What brought you here?" he asked me.

"Just passing through," I replied, "I am a chaplain working with Vietnam veterans in St. Cloud."

"You are looking at a Vietnam vet," said the stranger introducing himself as—let's say—Kurt.

"I can see that."

"So you think I look like a baby killer!"

"Why would you say that, Kurt?" I asked.

"Everybody calls us baby killers. In my case this is actually true. I shot an eight-year old boy the day I arrived over there. Do you know what I am going through every night? For over 20 years I have been seeing in my nightmares the face of that dying child."

"How did this happen?"

"I was only 18 then, a conscript," Kurt went on. "I was riding shotgun on the back of a truck that was taking my platoon to a forward position. The child stood close to our convoy with a basket full of mangoes. He was smiling and waving at us, and we waved back." Kurt continued, mimicking the boy's movements:

"He reached into his basket, took out a hand grenade from under the fruit and pulled the pin, ready to throw the grenade on our truck. My whole platoon would have been wiped out had I not blown him away with my M-16. Now, in my sleep, I see his face as he lay dying and as the explosion of the grenade in his hand ripped him to pieces."

"These flashbacks are common among combat veterans," I said. "I hear about them every day in my work."

"I know," Kurt replied. "But my flashbacks have become even crueler lately. You see, I have twins now: two eight-year old boys.

In my daily nightmares, the dying kid's contorted face takes on the features of my own two boys."

He told me that he had been working as a baker in St. Paul, but because of his mental condition he found it impossible to be around other people, including his wife. Like other ex-soldiers living in self-imposed isolation in Minnesota, he had bought a sizeable plot of land deep inside the forest. There he created for himself a habitat resembling the forward encampments he had known in the jungles of Vietnam. It was protected against intruders by concertina wires and sandbags.

"Against whom are you protecting yourself?" I asked.

"Them," Kurt replied elusively. "Let the bastards come; I am ready for them. I have dug trenches and have plenty of arms and ammo."

"Do you live like this by yourself and all year around?"

"Yes, except for the summer months. Then I drive down to St. Paul to pick up my boys who will spend their vacations with me in my camp. They are there now. Why don't you come and meet them?"

Journalistic curiosity trumping prudence, I agreed to spend the rest of the weekend with Kurt and his children in the forest. He had a four-wheel off-road scooter parked outside the tavern and invited me to follow him in my *Volkswagen Rabbit*.

We drove into a wooded area northwest of Duluth, left the paved road, and continued on a dirt track deep into the thick forest. The ground became muddier, and eventually my little car got stuck.

"Not to worry," said Kurt. "We are not far from my camp. I have a jeep and will be back in half an hour to pull you out."

I waited thirty minutes sitting in my car with the window on the driver's side down. Suddenly I felt cold metal pressing against my left temple: the nozzle of a 0.45 Colt!

"I want you to get the f..k out of here," Kurt said agitatedly. "I don't want you to come to our tent because I don't want my kids to find out that I am a killer."

If there is one useful trait I discovered about myself as a child during the bombing nights of World War II, it is this: in moments of danger I turn insensate—I go stone-cold. I am taking no personal pride in this; it is no accomplishment of mine, but a gift for which I have had occasion to be grateful many times in my life. With Kurt's gun pressed against my head, I spoke to him patiently for at least twenty minutes, persuading him to hand me his weapon.

"If you shoot me now or return to camp toting your gun, your sons will indeed see you as a killer," I remember telling him. In the end, he gave me his Colt. I secured it, took out the magazine, returned the gun to him and suggested he hide it from his children. He fell to his knees, weeping. After a while he got up, went to his jeep quietly, came back with a rope, attached it to my *Volkswagen*, gunned his engine and pulled me out of the mud. He unhooked the rope and shook my hand. I managed to slip the magazine into his trouser pocket before he ran to his jeep and disappeared into the woods.

My hands were trembling wildly as I raced back to the tavern. No longer insensate, I ordered a treble Scotch.

"Did Kurt give you a hard time?" asked the barman who had overheard our conversation earlier that day.

"Phew!"

"I know. I know. This is not the first time."

"What do you make of him?" I asked the barman.

"Poor guy. He has never harmed anybody, as far as I know. But I feel so sorry for him. He is a broken man, and he is not the only one around here."

"You mean there are others like Kurt out there in the woods?"

"Oh yes, quite a few, all holed up by themselves behind concertina wires and sandbags in their own jungle compounds; all angry; all saying that America had dumped them like junk; all convinced that God had condemned them for eternity, which is why they are now creating their own private hells in the forest.

Very, very sad, Sir! Some are in worse shape than Kurt. They won't talk to outsiders."

It wasn't until early in the evening that I had regained my composure enough to continue my journey up the "Scandinavian Riviera," still shaken by the realization that I had just been thrust back 22 years to when I saw the first American teenagers stumble bewildered through the Central Highlands of Vietnam. I remembered how moved I was by their innocence. They were too young to vote or to have a beer, but old enough to kill and be killed. Kurt was part of this tragic group of young Americans.

When I returned to St. Cloud, I told the men in my pastoral care groups about my experience with Kurt. Some of these former warriors knew Kurt and volunteered to invite him to join us. He declined, but asked them to tell me how sorry he was about his erratic behavior. We discussed Kurt's case for several weeks because it seemed typical of what many veterans had experienced. We calculated that in 1965 Kurt was one of those 18-year old conscripts who lacked the academic credentials or financial means to attend college, which would have delayed their enlistment, if indeed they desired to dodge the draft in the first place. I suspect that Kurt was too patriotic for that. His torment over his rejection by other Americans struck a raw nerve with members of our groups, but it reflected the quintessential homecoming experience of Vietnam veterans.

Most of the men in my St. Cloud groups told haunting tales explaining why they felt so alienated and alone. One of the most scandalous of these was the story of one veteran who had completed his twelve-month tour in Vietnam. He arrived home on a Saturday evening. The next morning he accompanied his parents to the church where he had been confirmed five years earlier. In the pulpit stood a new pastor: a young, longhaired pacifist. He spotted the returning young warrior wearing a crew cut and a freshly pressed uniform, and scolded him: "Don't you come back here until your hair has grown and you've got yourself some decent clothes!" The veteran never set foot in a church again.

Kurt never overcame his shame over having shot a child, although the boy had been trained as a killer by a ruthless enemy, and having to fight North Vietnamese soldiers three years younger than he. In this he was not alone. Nothing in their upbringing had prepared these American draftees for a confrontation with the abject evil emblematic of totalitarian rulers who have no qualms about sacrificing children for their twisted ideological purposes. The Nazis put the lives of child-soldiers at risk by assigning them to anti-aircraft batteries; one of these boys was one Joseph Ratzinger, later Pope Benedict XVI. In Mao's Great Cultural Revolution in China, which I covered concurrently with the Vietnam War, children were made to commit some of the most gruesome atrocities, and the same was true later during the Cambodian holocaust.

The Communists' fiendish use of children in the two Indochina wars of the twentieth century was the cynical handiwork of a former schoolteacher: Gen. Vo Nguyen Giap. After Hanoi's victory in 1975, the party placed him in charge of the destruction of an even larger number of even younger lives. It made him chairman of the National Committee on Population and Family Planning. This Committee's tasks included formulating and enforcing Vietnam's abortion policies. Outlawed in South Vietnam, abortions were legalized throughout the country when it was reunified in 1975. Under Giap, Vietnam became the leading power in the worldwide Culture of Death, terminating more than 1.5 million pregnancies annually. With 83.3 abortions per 1,000 women every year, Vietnam is outdistancing Romania, Cuba, and the Russian Federation, according to the New York-based Alan Guttmacher Institute. As I am writing this, Giap is 101 years old and enjoying his retirement in Hanoi.

On the American and South Vietnamese side, most soldiers had barely outgrown adolescence, but the same could be said for almost any country at war; like elsewhere in the world, the draft age in the U.S. was 18. When I first saw the GIs in action in Vietnam I was touched by their childlike demeanor. These soldiers were part of the First Cavalry Division that had landed in the Central Highlands in mid-1965; they became immortalized in the book, *We Were Soldiers Once... And Young* by Lt. Gen. Harold G. Moore and the journalist Joseph L. Galloway. Nicknamed Air Cav because it went into battle with 434 helicopters rather than on horses or in armored vehicles, this 17,000-man unit impressed me as a curious cross between high-tech progress and personal immaturity when I first visited its base in An Khe, though its immaturity evaporated quickly in bloody battles.

I landed in An Khe in the company of my friend Donald Wise, an English correspondent and former counterinsurgency officer in Malaya. Twirling his David Niven-style moustache, he scrutinized the base asking wryly, "Have you noticed that they installed an ice cream machine before securing their defense perimeter? What are we to think of that order of priorities?"

When we went on our first patrol with one of the First Cav companies the next day, Donald observed, "These people are not combat-ready. Look how they cluster together like scared boys when they are supposed to march single file! This is extremely dangerous. Let one soldier step on a mine, and a whole bunch of them will get maimed. They should keep a distance of at least ten meters from each other to minimize the risk of casualties."

A staff sergeant overheard us and growled: "That's what I keep trying to get into their thick heads. They won't take the most basic precautions. They don't wear their helmets, not realizing that this would protect them against enemy fire and also shield them from the sun. Look at their scalps. They look like boiled lobsters transplanted into the bush. They don't drink nearly enough water either. Yesterday one of our companies was practically wiped out due to heat casualties."

Donald continued: "It doesn't help in this climate that so many of your men are overweight from too many hamburgers, sodas and ice cream."

In a guerrilla war, a reporter can rarely predict where the action is and where he will find a story. Donald suggested that we stay close to medical evacuation helicopters, because where they flew there was combat as their job was to rescue wounded men.

We stretched out in the shadow of a UH1-B *Medevac* chopper, which was marked with large red crosses that were supposed to protect the aircraft against enemy fire. A CBS television team joined us. The pilots said: "Gentlemen, you are welcome to ride with us *into* battle but not out of it because the helicopter will be loaded with dead or wounded men."

It didn't take long before the chopper was ordered to rescue a casualty of one of the first major skirmishes involving American troops in the Vietnam War. As we approached the landing zone, enemy fire knocked out our engine, forcing the pilots to come down fast with the help of autorotation. I survived the crash almost unharmed because I was a skinny and supple young man in those days, weighing merely 140 pounds. The impact felt like a jump from a five-meter wall. It compacted my spine, but I did not discover this until much later when I was a middle-aged man.

We journalists, pilots and crewmembers jumped out of the chopper's wreck immediately and ran for cover because we had landed in the middle of an intense firefight. Seconds later, a mortar round demolished our damaged aircraft altogether. None of us was injured, but the wounded soldier we had come to evacuate died. He was a 17-year old boy who had lied about his age when volunteering for military service. A Kalashnikov round had hit him in the lung. In his last seconds he cried out, like a child, first to his mother and then to God. He was the first American I saw killed in action. Soon there would be hundreds more, almost all calling to their distant mothers and then to God, and always in that order.

One of the great personalities I met when visiting the First Cav was Charlie Black, a fellow journalist. He was the military writer for the *Ledger Enquirer*, the long-established newspaper of Columbus, Georgia, which lies nine miles north of Fort Benning, the division's home base. Black was unlike any member of the Saigon press corps. He did not arrive in Vietnam with a fancy expense account. He didn't stay in colonial style grand hotels, nor did he dine in fine French restaurants. He was not concerned with the byzantine politics in Saigon or salacious homicide cases; neither did he drive to a seaside resort in the company of glamorous women. Aircraft carriers, self-immolating Buddhist monks or the imperial family of Vietnam were not part of his assignment.

No, Charlie Black was a simple newsman with a simple task. He was on orders to cover the 17,000 men in the First Cav in the way a solid small town newspaperman would cover his local beat. Charlie was a former Marine who had seen combat as a sniper in the Pacific theater in World War II and as a gunnery sergeant in Korea. He arrived in 1965 with a meager expense advance of $430 in his pocket and his publisher's advice to cash in the return portion of his airline ticket should he run out of money. His boss had given him stamps and onionskin paper, and told him to type his stories single-spaced on both sides of the page in order to keep the postage down. Charlie was not allowed to cable his stories home but rather to file them via APO, the Armed Forces Postal System. His orders were to garnish his texts with as many names as possible for the benefit of military families living at Fort Benning. The family then clipped his stories from the *Enquirer* and sent them back to their men in the field.

Charlie was billeted with the troops, ate in their mess hall and shared their combat rations ("C" rations) when in the field. He rarely set foot at the officer's club where other correspondents liked to relax in the evening, picking up bits of information from casual conversations. He preferred the company of the enlisted men with whom he also spent many nights manning the perimeter and many days in battle.

War reporters rarely bear arms, but Charlie Black always carried an M-16 and often used it, mostly against the Viet Cong and sometimes against wild beasts. One dark night he heard a rustling noise in the bushes, assumed that it was caused by Viet Cong guerrillas and opened fire. Suddenly, Charlie saw a bleeding tiger leaping towards him, or so First Cav legend went. Charlie fired again, the big cat dropped dead at his feet, and he wondered where to get the animal's skin cured and how to send it home to Georgia as a souvenir.

When Charlie Black, a high school dropout, died in 1982 at age 59, an obituary in the *New York Times* noted snootily, "His reports were more like letters than traditional journalism." I remember one of these "letters" as one of the most gripping stories ever about the Vietnam conflict. What made this piece so powerful was its stark simplicity. It needed no embellishment. I am citing it here because it relates to the main theme of this chapter, which concerns Gen. Giap's callous deployment of children in his so-called war of national liberation.

The article's protagonist was Private First Class Toby Braveboy, a soldier of Creek Indian origin who hailed from a town with the unlikely name of Coward, North Carolina. Here are excerpts from what Black wrote about Braveboy in the December 7, 1965, issue of the *Ledger Enquirer*:

> On Nov. 17, Braveboy... was walking on point... when a shattering North Vietnamese attack struck the unit. When darkness fell, Braveboy was wounded in his left hand, his arm and leg. His only companions were other wounded Americans. The rest of the battalion had pulled into a fighting perimeter and was embroiled in one of the bitterest battles... "I wanted to get help for my three buddies who were with me," Braveboy said. "They were all hit... I tried to crawl for help..."
>
> He crawled toward the sound of the fighting... A group of [North] Vietnamese soldiers came toward him and he feigned death. They executed wounded [Americans], blood spraying him once when they decapitated a wounded American... At night he crawled into the brush... and huddled beside a bank of earth... "I heard footsteps, then four North Vietnamese soldiers went by

me," he said. "Three... didn't see me, but the fourth... looked me right in the eye."

"He stopped and pointed his rifle at me. I raised my wounded hand and shook my head 'no'... I don't know why, but he lowered his rifle and walked away. He was so young, just a boy, no more than 16 or 17."

This happened in the battle of the Ia Drang Valley, which I covered. There is no need to replicate Joe Galloway's and Harold Moore's magnificent description of this historic event in *We Were Soldiers Once... And Young*. However, Braveboy's stirring words, "He was so young, just a boy," at the end of Charlie Black's report brought back my most powerful emotions during all of this bloodbath: As one who had seen so many children and adolescents die in World War II, watching the sacrifice of these young soldiers sickened me, regardless of their nationality. This was reflected in my article about this event published in *Die Welt* on December 13, 1965.

Titled, *Und das Gras ist rot* (And the Grass is Red), this story described my arrival in a small clearing that had just been the site of a frightening clash between a large North Vietnamese formation and units of the First Cav. I depicted it as a human wave attack by the Communists, even though military historians later voiced doubt that this term was applicable. From what I saw and from the position of the dead North Vietnamese warriors on the ground, this was precisely what had happened here: wave after wave of fresh troops surging toward American positions in a style emulating the charge of young and badly trained Red Army soldiers against the *Wehrmacht* on Germany's Eastern Front.

I wrote that the massive bloodshed had colored the clearing's three-foot elephant grass red. Our chopper hovered above ground for a while so as not to land on the fallen *Bo Doi*, as the North Vietnamese soldiers were called. They lay there, their arms stretched forward as if they were still surging toward the U.S.

perimeter. We could finally touch down after American soldiers had cleared away some of the dead.

The American dead and wounded had already been flown out, but some North Vietnamese POWs were still there, squatting blindfolded and tied together under trees. Some giggled nervously, infuriating a First Cav sergeant. "So you (expletive deleted) think this is funny?" he screamed. We had to restrain him lest he mow them down with his M-16. Nobody had told him that in Asia this kind of a giggle was an expression of embarrassment, not hilarity.

It was ironic that the dead North Vietnamese seemed better clad than the Americans. Their khakis looked new compared with the GIs' shabby and torn fatigues, the state of which bespoke the scandalous failure of the U.S. Defense Logistics Agency to provide the division with uniforms and boots fit for jungle warfare, although there was no shortage of those on Saigon's black market.

"What are you going to do with all the dead North Vietnamese?" I asked an officer who seemed to be in charge of this clearing.

"We can't bury them. There are too many," he said. "I guess the Air Force will napalm them as soon as we are gone."

Some GIs collected the backpacks and wallets from the North Vietnamese bodies and loaded some of them on helicopters, including ours. On the flight back to the First Cav's forward base at Plei Ku we rifled through these bags and found that they contained changes of fatigues and underwear, all freshly pressed by somebody's mother or wife in Vinh, Haiphong or Hanoi.

Reading the documents found in the soldiers' wallets gave us a jolt: they revealed that many of their bearers were 15-year old boys. On many of these dead child-soldiers American leaflets were found urging them to desert. Later it turned out that at least one quarter of these adolescents carried these flyers on them and were probably waiting for an opportunity to switch sides. The ferociousness of the battle deprived them of their chance. Had they attempted to break from their units while charging American positions, their comrades would have shot them in the back; such is the nature of a human wave attack.

The next morning, a U.S. Air Force *Hercules C-130* landed in Plei Ku depositing much of the Saigon press corps who had not covered the Ia Drang Valley battle. Among them was Joe the highly-strung tabloid correspondent who ordinarily never left town. The large cargo plane was meant to take those of us who had been in battle for days back to the capital, along with military personnel, including several wounded soldiers. The other journalists were told to wait for a later flight, but Joe would have none of that; after a short press briefing on the tarmac he jumped the line, making the burly loadmaster very angry. "Just you wait your turn, Mister," he snarled. "You are not on the manifest for this flight."

My *Schadenfreude* was, alas, too feeble to trump my grief over what I had seen the previous days. I returned to the *Continental Palace*, had a long shower and met Donald for a drink on the terrace.

"You look terrible, old boy," he said.

"Donald, I don't think I'll ever get used to the sight of dead and wounded young people, and I don't care whether they are American, South Vietnamese, North Vietnamese or Viet Cong."

"Neither do I, old boy, neither do I, and I have seen lots of that in my life. But I have something for you that might lighten you up a little. Let's have dinner tonight at my *Stammtisch*."

Donald had borrowed a term he had learned in Germany. A *Stammtisch* is popular institution in our public houses and restaurants: a weekly regulars' table where members discuss their favorite topic, usually politics. By contrast, Donald Wise's *Stammtisch* was a dinner party of European journalists designed to protect the mental sanity of its participants by eschewing anything remotely related to Vietnam: the war, political intrigues, the war in Laos, Soviet and Chinese designs on Indochina, plus American foreign policy of any kind.

The rule was that none of these topics was to be mentioned, and if any member was foolish enough to do so, he had to pay for the entire tab, which was prohibitively expensive because these dinners took place at *Aterbéa's*, Saigon's finest French restaurant. Donald Wise told me that he had come up with this idea while trying to wash the stench of death out of his moustache three times after covering the annihilation of an ARVN battalion.

"I soaped myself up and still stank," he said. "I felt so uncivilized. Yet we were supposed to be cultured people. And so I returned to a thought I had had as a Japanese prisoner of war in World War II: Surely a way can be found to live like a civilized human being, at least once a week."

Aterbéa's was the way. There were nine of us that evening: five Englishmen, two Australians, one Frenchman and I, a German. All of us wore suits or at least blazers. We ordered good wines and discussed music, the arts, literature and history and, yes, women, but those without discussing their nationality lest the mention of a local beauty might cause any of us to blow away his budget for an entire month. After a while, though, we were out of topics for discussion and fell silent.

"Let's compose a limerick," suggested Donald. One off-color poem we rhymed on the evening of my return from the Ia Drang Valley seems to have gained some notoriety, for I found some inelegant variants of it on the Internet. But unless senility has got the better of me, I am here to state categorically that it was our work. It ran thus:

There was a young fellow named Yorrick,
Who could, in his moments euphoric,
Produce for selection
Three kinds of erection:
Ionic,
Corinthian,
and Doric.

We staggered back to our hotels, laughing the most liberating laugh I can remember from my entire Vietnam experience. For once we felt that we were back in what we thought of as the real world. Full of red wine from France I fell into my bed, mumbling, "Doric, Doric," knowing all too well that the images of the Ia Drang Valley would return to me on the following day. They did.

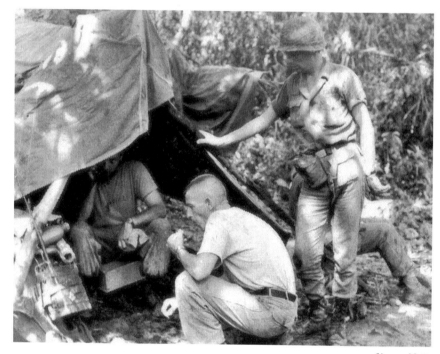

The author (r) in the Ia Drang Valley battle, 1965.

Reflection Five

Isolated from the Vietnamese

The press was instinctively "agin [sic] the Government"—and, at least reflexively, for Saigon's enemies. During the latter half of the 15-year American involvement the media became the primary battlefield. Illusory events reported by the press as well as real events within the press corps were more decisive than the clash of arms or the contention of ideologies. For the first time in modern history, the outcome of the war was determined not on the battlefield but on the printed page and, above all, on the television screen. Looking back coolly, I believe it can be said... that American and South Vietnamese forces actually won the limited military struggle.

Most correspondents were isolated from the Vietnamese by ignorance of their language and culture, as well as by a measure of race estrangement. Most were isolated from the quixotic American Army establishment, itself often as confused as they themselves were by their moralistic attitudes and their political prejudices. It was inevitable, in the circumstances, that they came to write, in the first instance, for each other.

I recall with chagrin my rather condescending amusement when a television producer argued in the mid-1960s: "We shouldn't be in Indo-China because the American people can't understand the war—and the people won't support a war they don't understand." He was, of course, right (even if the American press helped to prevent any proper understanding).

The Western press appears either unaware of the direct connection between cause (its reporting) and effect (the Western defeat in Vietnam), or strangely reluctant to proclaim that the pen and the camera proved decisively mightier than the bayonet and ultra-modern weapons.

Robert Elegant in "How to Lose a War."
The Encounter, Vol. LVII., No. 2.
August 1981, pp. 73–90

Chapter Nine

Qui? Gie, Ky

Of all German dialects, none is as grotesque as the argot of Saxony, my native land; I mentioned this in an earlier chapter where I described my encounter with a Saxon-speaking North Vietnamese army doctor in a POW camp on the island of Phú Quốc. Spoken with a grin in a spirit of self-mockery, this bizarre twang is amusing; shrieked in an Oriental environment by a female philistine from Dresden, it is a frightening sound.

Imagine, therefore, my consternation when I found myself acoustically catapulted back to my childhood in the most improbable setting. Early one summer morning, I was savoring an hour of solitary bliss in Suite 214, my French colonial refuge in the *Continental Palace*. It was still cool outside, and so I had the windows open. I sat in my leather armchair having breakfast and watching, as usual, the enthralling *Áo dài* parade on the sidewalks of Tu Do Street.

Out of the blue, a jarring voice from across the road filled my room, and presumably the entire neighborhood, with a discordant string of consonants and vowels, sounding like this:

"Awwr, awwr, meinä Gudsdä: där Gie, där Gie! Nää wärglich! Ich gann Ihn'n saach'n: im Bädde issr cha guud, awwr als Brämchähminisd'r?" In English: "But, my dear! That Ky, that Ky! Really now! He's good in bed, but [how good will he be] as prime minister?"

This is how I first found out about Air Vice Marshal Nguyen Cao Ky's elevation to the position of prime minister after a succession of demented coups and counter-coups had given the governments of South Vietnam an average life span of 70 days.

I had no trouble identifying the voice as that of Frau L., the flaccid wife of an attaché at the West German embassy, although I was mystified by her alleged familiarity with Ky's libidinous talents. Frau L.'s propensity for gaffes was legendary. Only a few nights ago she had mortified Saigon's otherwise mannerly German colony by warning my friend Fabian Fuchs at the top of her voice during a diplomatic reception in Ambassador Wilhelm Kopf's residence against marrying into Saigon high society: "*Vorsichd, Vorsichd! Die Fietnamäs'n sinn änne ganz verschlaachene Rasse*" — careful, careful, now! The Vietnamese are a very shifty race.

This *faux pas* caused discomfited silence in the ambassador's salon; for minutes all one could hear were the takeoffs and landings of planes at nearby Tan Son Nhut airport. Embarrassed, guests took pains not to stare at the German-born Jews in their midst, many of whom served as senior U.S. officials in Saigon; surely this was not the kind of rhetoric they liked to hear from a West German diplomat's wife a mere twenty years after World War II.

"Ahem," said Ambassador Kopf to all of us, "Have you already seen my cheetahs? Nice big tame cats! Come and meet them." Whereupon nearly everybody, minus Frau L. (but including her husband), followed Mr. Kopf into the garden to admire two magnificent felines known for their Ferrari-like ability to reach speeds of 62 miles per hour in three seconds; they were a farewell gift from King Faisal of Saudi Arabia where Kopf had been previously posted.

Frau L. was not the only foreigner to find fault with the dashing 35-year old pilot Nguyen Cao Ky who was often seen cruising in a convertible with his exquisite wife, Tuyet Mai, through the streets of Saigon; or pivoting his hips to the beat of the Twist in *Le Moulin Rouge*, a trendy nightclub in Cholon, Saigon's Chinatown; or reciting French love poems into the microphone at a fashionable downtown bar. Liberal American journalists disliked the flashy ways of this richly perfumed general whose trademark was a lilac-colored scarf draped around his neck. Stanley Karnow dismissed him as "a flamboyant character in a gaudy uniform and a sinister moustache." Neil Sheehan of the *New York Times* went apoplectic when Ky called for the liberation of North Vietnam: "That little bastard... goddamn little fool!" he cursed.

I liked Ky. This is not meant to be a partisan testimonial nor an indication of my approval of his breathtakingly imprudent statements and acts; for instance, severing diplomatic relations with France—a folly that prompted President Charles de Gaulle to coin an aphorism that has since attained an indelible place in the annals of political putdowns: *"Qui est Ky?"* (Who is Ky?). It is not my place to take sides in past fights between him and President Nguyen Van Thieu, or in the enduring quarrels among Ky's admirers and detractors in the Vietnamese exile community. Neither is this a reflection on Ky's foolhardy power struggle with his equally flamboyant lookalike, Lt. Gen. Nguyen Chanh Thi, the commander of I. Corps in the northernmost part of South Vietnam.

Finally, it is not for me to judge whether he betrayed the cause of Vietnam's freedom by returning to his Communist-controlled homeland in 2004. Having myself been driven into exile by Communists as a child, I know this much: homesickness is a disease that can crush one, especially in one's advancing years; who can condemn a man thus stricken?

Ky died in Malaysia in 2012, and when his ashes arrived in America to be buried in the Buddhist columbarium at Rose Hills Memorial Park in Whittier, California, Neil Sheehan denounced him posthumously as, "one of those corrupt young Turks." I thought this an unnecessary offense against a tenet of social behavior going back to Roman days: *de mortuis nihil nisi bonum*, of the dead, nothing unless good [should be spoken]. Moreover, if personal gain had motivated Ky while in office, how was he reduced to running a liquor store in Huntington Beach after his escape by helicopter from Vietnam in 1975? Had he really squirreled away millions of dollars abroad during his tenures as prime minister and vice president of South Vietnam, he would surely have done better as a political refugee later.

The Nguyen Cao Ky I was introduced to by a champagne-loving aide-de-camp in 1965 was a peacock; this is true. But he was certainly not the first and only peacock in military history. One could fill a museum of *Louvre* proportions with portraits of vain and colorfully clad officers of every period of history and all nations: Greek, Roman, French, Italian, British, German, American, Soviet and even North Vietnamese, to wit recent photographs of the centenarian ex-school teacher and jungle fighter Vo Nguyen Giap in a white dress uniform with gold epaulettes studded with four pips. Granted, Ky was perhaps the only peacock flying into combat in a tailor-made black flight suit and patent leather shoes. He wore this combination when, at the controls of an *A-1 Skyraider* fighter-bomber, he led the only South Vietnamese airborne raid against the North, and even made his wife, Tuyet Mai, wear this extraordinary attire when the two of them appeared at military functions together. Tsk, tsk, tsk: flyboy and flygirl synchronized in black! Some of my American colleagues found this in bad taste.

As for me, it made me smile, just as I found it amusing that, when he was still courting this former *Air Vietnam* stewardess, he saluted her upon his return from a bombing mission by having his entire squadron "treetop" her neighborhood; what a splendid gesture of old-fashioned chivalry! On the other hand, I admit that seeing a wire service picture of Ky, attired in a white Filipino *barong tegalog* shirt with his hair held in place presumably by half a pound of brilliantine, whirling Ladybird Johnson nimbly around the dance floor at a ball on the occasion of a summit conference gave me pause: How, I wondered, would Vietnamese sophisticates with their highly developed sense of form react to this image of their prime minister playing gigolo to the American president's wife?

That said, Nguyen Cao Ky was at least colorful; he and Tuyet Mai made "good copy," as we journalists say, which is why he is given more space in this book than his rival, the reserved, circumspect and statesmanlike President Nguyen Van Thieu, a lieutenant-general. I met Thieu several times. Our interviews were always agreeable and informative but never resulted in catchy headlines; they never made the front page of the newspapers that had sent me to Vietnam, and never led "page three," which, in the German press, is traditionally reserved for major political feature articles.

Thieu, too, had a beautiful wife, the regal and elegant Nguyen Thi Mai Anh. She did not possess Madame Ky's star-like glamour but fit more readily in the mould of the proverbial Vietnamese power woman. European journalists in Saigon liked to jest that the important political decisions in Saigon were not so much made in Thieu's cabinet meetings as at his wife's tea parties in the garden of the Presidential Palace. I encountered Madame Ky more frequently than Madame Thieu and once sat next to her for many hours on an *Air France* journey from Paris to Saigon. I found her alluring and quietly flirtatious yet oddly shy. None of these attributes applied to Madame Thieu. For all her graciousness, she left visitors in no doubt that they were in the presence of a formidable and determined personality.

Let us return to Nguyen Cao Ky though, because he, rather than Thieu, was in a sense paradigmatic of South Vietnam's dilemma: the Nguyen Cao Ky as he was perceived by many Westerners seemed at odds with the real Nguyen Cao Ky who could only be discovered if one disregarded his outward demeanor.

One day Ky invited me to his home, where I was surprised by its simplicity. He had eschewed the Prime Minister's official residence in the city center and lived with his family in two sparsely furnished Quonset huts on Tan Son Nhut military airbase while his modest bungalow nearby was being refurbished. Outside this bleak abode grazed two does, a gift from soldiers. Once he had moved into this bungalow, he invited guests to his porch to shoot wild pigs, which a servant released from a sty in the garden, a form of entertainment I deemed unexciting but inoffensive.

Strangely, in the years since leaving Vietnam I have thought about Ky more often than about any politician I ever met, precisely because he seemed so contradictory. At his home, his buffoonery evaporated; the wannabe playboy doing the twist in *Le Moulin Rouge* or reciting love poems in a bar turned out to be a plain lansquenet with a recurring reverie of taking up the weapon of his choice again soon: the controls of fighter bombers he had learned to pilot first with the French Air Force in Morocco and then in the United States; this became his favorite subject in all our interviews.

Recently in my archives I discovered my first big story about Ky. It was published as a four-page spread in *Bild am Sonntag*, a large-circulation Sunday paper, of August 22, 1965. Its headline read, *Der Tänzer auf dem Pulverfaß*—the Dancer on the Powder Keg. Reading this article again after nearly five decades was perplexing given that Neil Sheehan had vilified Ky as a "corrupt young Turk" following his death. In my report, as in all my subsequent pieces about Ky, his preoccupation with the decay in South Vietnamese society was paramount: his anger over civil servants enriching themselves by extorting big bribes for draft deferments and passports, and his fury directed against wholesale merchants hoarding rice, flour, salt, sugar and concentrated milk in order to drive up prices.

"This is causing civil unrest," he thundered. "It is undermining our war effort. These people are traitors and must be shot. If need be I'll shoot 10,000 of these swine in order to save 14 million Vietnamese."

Remembering the hated profiteers and black marketers in my own country during and after the last war—they were the only obese Germans then—I shared his feelings. But then Ky repeated to me what he had said to my friend Donald Wise of the London *Daily Mirror* one month earlier, a moronic statement doing much damage to the reputation of South Vietnam as it was fighting for its survival. He said,

"I admire Hitler because he pulled your country together when it was in a terrible state in the early thirties. Our situation here in Vietnam is so desperate that we need four or five Hitlers."

"Please, Prime Minister, don't keep saying this!" I begged him. "This is not what a young German wants to hear. I remember Nazi Germany. I know what Hitler has brought upon us: the murder of millions of innocent people, national shame, the destruction of our cities and the division of my country!"

"Well, that's not why I think we need a Hitler. I mean, we need somebody to restore order," said Ky.

"Then you definitely do not need Hitler, because he didn't establish order in Germany; he rather destroyed civilized order."

"Monsieur, I was speaking euphemistically…"

"This is not a working euphemism if you don't mind my saying so, *Monsieur le Premier Ministre*, especially if you consider how many Jewish refugees from Germany are serving in your country as senior American diplomats and intelligence officers. Why would you want to hurt these friends?"

"I don't want to hurt them. Perhaps you are right: let's drop Hitler."

That was vintage Ky. He never held my censure against me, and we remained on good terms. Sadly, he did not drop Hitler for good; he didn't erase his ill-informed empathy for the Nazis from his mind. A few years before his death, he gave an interview to *Stormfront,* an American White Power publication, again praising Hitler and especially Hermann Goering, the commander-in-chief of the German *Luftwaffe*. I am sorry I wasn't there to tell him that Goering, a flying ace who had earned the *Pour Le Mérite*, the highest German decoration in World War I, was also the most corrupt of all Nazi leaders, an art thief and a genocidal fiend.

Next I saw Ky in court. Having made good on his promise of cutting the salaries of indolent civil servants in half, he now turned up at a trial of the kind he had pledged to introduce in an effort to fight corruption. The defendant was a Chinese-Vietnamese millionaire by the name of Ta Vinh. Like Ky, he was 35 years old, but unlike the trim air force general, Ta Vinh was stout and pudgy, thus fitting the international stereotype of profiteers as the only fat people in times of war.

Ta Vinh was charged with embezzling $104,000 in public funds, of hoarding, illegal speculation, and the attempted bribery of a policeman. A panel of three military judges sentenced him to be executed by firing squad for the crime of "economic sabotage." His plea for leniency was rejected. So in the early hours of March 14, 1966, a battalion of South Vietnamese paratroopers secured the floodlighted execution site at Saigon's Central Market. At dawn, the prisoner, accompanied by a Catholic military chaplain, was led to a stake in front of a wall of sandbags. Among the spectators were Ta Vinh's wife and seven of his eight children. Wailing, she pleaded for his life in English, Vietnamese and Cantonese, but to no avail. Ta Vinh was tied to the stake, and then a 10-man execution squad fired off a salvo but botched the job, only wounding him! Their commanding officer gave Ta Vinh the *coup de grace* with his service pistol. On the same day, one of Ky's special anti-corruption tribunals sentenced the former Treasury Service chief in the mountain resort of Dalat to death for graft.

I am no fervent supporter of capital punishment but could not quite bring myself to bristle at this verdict in the way Walt Friedenberg, a Scripps Howard correspondent, did in his report. Friedenberg led his story thus: "The South Vietnamese government has just pushed itself further away from the people it is supposed to win over as ardent followers." Then followed the stereotypical string of "man in the street" interviews with taxi drivers, shopkeepers, domestic servants and other unnamed people all allegedly outraged by the public killing of a man who, in Friedenberg's own words, was "as crooked as a horseshoe."

I wondered where he found all these furious critics, because everybody I spoke to after Ta Vinh's execution said it was high time that the government did something about the rampant wave of economic crimes which threatened to result in an insurrection. Again I suspected that certain American correspondents in Saigon were moving into a different professional universe.

Outside the *Continental Palace,* I ran into my impish friend Đức, tenant and minder of my old *Citroën.*

"Hee hee," he said, "Ta Vinh, he no dead."

"Nonsense," I answered, "I heard his wife wail as he died at the stake."

"Hee hee, yes, Ta Vinh wife wail but Ta Vinh, he no dead."

"Come on, Đức, this is downright nonsense. Who was it that died, then?"

"Other prisoner, poor Vietnamese man, paid off in prison to die in Ta Vinh place."

"Đức, come to your senses. Who would agree to such a deal?"

"Poor man, he would die in prison anyway, leave family behind with no money. But now family rich and Ta Vinh go to Hong Kong."

"But Đức," I argued. "A fat man died at the stake. Surely Ta Vinh must have been the only fat man in jail."

"Other man fat because Ta Vinh family give him beaucoup rice in prison to make him look like Ta Vinh."

"Says who?"

"Everybody," said Đức, pointing up and down Tu Do Street, "You no trust me. Everybody say. Go ask!"

To this day I am convinced that what Đức gave me was a cockamamie story of the sort one could hear in Saigon daily. I am telling it here not because I believe it to be true, but merely because it illustrates so well the mood in this former *Paris of the Orient* that had lost its luster and been sliding deeper and deeper into decay by the time Nguyen Cao Ky, once acclaimed as a "flyboy with bedroom eyes," rose to power for a short period in Vietnamese history.

A South Vietnamese hero: Prime Minister Nguyen Cao Ky awards his country's Medal of Honor to a paratroop major in 1966.

Chapter Ten

Taxi girls and white scalps

In 1966, I spent a total of eight months in Vietnam, but not all in one stretch. I commuted back and forth between Saigon and New York covering two sides of the war: the military and political actions on the spot and troubling developments on the home front in the U.S. Almost every time I returned to Vietnam I was treated to an unusual luxury for a young war reporter. I was met at Tan Son Nhut Airport by an air-conditioned Mercedes-Benz with diplomatic license plates and a German lieutenant colonel at its wheel. This officer was my friend Joachim Tzschaschel, the West German defense attaché and only official at our embassy voicing doubts that America and its South Vietnamese allies would ultimately prevail. He told American officers point-blank as early as 1966: "The U.S. can no longer win this war."

Not that Lt. Col. Tzschaschel wished for the Viet Cong to succeed. On the contrary, given that Germany and Vietnam suffered the common fate of being divided into a free and a Communist part, he was desperately hoping that his pessimistic gut feelings would prove wrong in the end. But Tzschaschel was a realist. He had studied the enemy's writings and knew that Gen. Vo Nguyen Giap's assessment that the United States was psychologically not equipped to win a protracted "war of national liberation" was correct. Therefore this German officer shared the misgivings of Sir Robert Thompson, the British expert on insurgencies, and Bernard Fall, the French historian.

There was one especially chilling remark made by Mao Zedong which Tzschaschel, Thompson and Fall kept quoting to friends in the U.S. military: "He who does not win in a people's war or in a guerilla struggle, loses. He who does not lose, wins."

Tzschaschel once told me, "Many of my American military friends were familiar with this remark, and it made them very pensive, because they were aware that much of their own country's élite and leadership lacked the determination to succeed in Vietnam."

Another skeptic of similar persuasion was Tzschaschel's friend Adelbert Weinstein, the superb military analyst of the prestigious *Frankfurter Allgemeine Zeitung*, who had served as a G-1 chief of staff of a German infantry division in World War II and was a colonel, later brigadier general, in the West German army reserves. Weinstein had covered both Indochina wars. In 1975 he wrote a moving commentary on the Fall of Saigon, ending with this elegiac punch line: "America couldn't wait." In other words, America did not have the patience to conclude this conflict victoriously, a thought unsettling for West Germans aware of their total dependence on U.S. protection against the threat of Soviet military might.

This is why Lt. Col. Tzschaschel, whenever he drove me from the airport to the *Continental Palace,* eagerly grilled me about the mood in the United States: was the peace movement growing? Were there already signs of increasing war weariness? How, for example, did Americans react to the seemingly absurd power struggle between prime minister Ky and his nemesis, Lt. Gen. Nguyen Chanh Thi, whom Ky had just ousted as commander of I. Corps in the northernmost part of South Vietnam involving armed clashes between units of the South Vietnamese military? What impact, if any, did the new Buddhist upheaval, resulting from this power struggle, have on public opinion in the United States? Did the American man in the street interpret the increasingly violent riots as evidence of the unpopularity of the Ky government, which consequently was not worth shedding American blood for?

Tzschaschel did, of course, read American press reports and dispatches from our embassy in Washington, but he wanted to learn more. Knowing that I never confined my research in America to Washington and New York, but that I traveled around the country focusing on the mood in the hinterland and on university campuses, he questioned me like a seasoned reporter about what "Joe Blow" had to say.

Once, though, at the height of the 1966 Buddhist crisis, our arrangement faltered. As usual, I wired the date and time of my arrival to his cable address, *Diplogerma Saigon*, but received no answer. I had a hunch that he was annoyed with me, and suspected the reason: during my absence from Saigon a roving reporter of the tabloid *Bild am Sonntag*, Germany's biggest Sunday paper belonging to the *Axel Springer* group, visited Vietnam. Before leaving Hamburg, he had sent me a telex asking for a list of useful contacts, which I supplied. Foolishly I included Tzschaschel's name, impressing upon this reporter never to quote the colonel "on the record." This meant that Tzschaschel only spoke "on background" without allowing his identity to be divulged. Back then protecting one's source was a firm tenet of journalistic ethics, a point of honor that today is often violated by hubristic media luminaries. I expected my German colleague to honor this rule.

When I read his article from Saigon a fortnight later, I became apoplectic. Pompously labeled an "exclusive report," it was unadulterated pamphleteering detailing dire prognostications by "Lt. Col. Joachim Tzschaschel, the German defense attaché." I feared that this brainless feature story would jeopardize my friend's professional effectiveness and possibly his career. Luckily, it contained so many factual errors that the colonel's superiors in Germany would have immediately recognized the root cause of these glitches: the man I had sent to Tzschaschel turned out to be a blithering amateur.

Thank God I had withheld from him one vital bit of information about Joachim Tzschaschel! In reality he was more than a run-of-the-mill light colonel in the tropics but rather one of Germany's star spooks. He was the Saigon station chief of the BND, the German equivalent of the CIA. Six years earlier, as a major on the military attaché's staff at the West German embassy in Paris, he had been one of the BND's liaison officers to Israel's

Mossad in "Operation Eichmann," which resulted in the capture and ultimate death by hanging of this holocaust organizer. Years later, as a brigadier general, Tzschaschel became the BND's senior briefer of Chancellor Helmut Schmidt.

I worried that I might have lost the confidence of one of the best strategic analysts in the field and, more importantly, the friendship of this unusually sharp and humorous officer. It turned out that I was "rewarded" instead with a fascinating glimpse into his world of skullduggery. When my Pan Am plane landed in Tan Son Nhut, Lt. Col. Tzschaschel wasn't there but Sgt. Maj. Abraham, his senior NCO, waited for me at customs controls. Abraham grabbed my suitcases and took me outside the terminal to an olive drab *DKW Munga*, a peculiarly underpowered all-terrain vehicle with a two-stroke engine throwing out blue fumes. This jeep-like vehicle sported black-on-white German army license plates showing the German national colors, black, red and gold, and looked and sounded hilariously exotic as it sputtered through Saigon's chaotic streets, attracting bemused stares.

"The colonel is displeased," said Abraham.

"I know. I made an idiotic mistake giving his name to that moron from Hamburg. As they say here in Saigon: So sorry 'bout that."

"It will cost you," Sgt. Maj. Abraham warned, pokerfaced.

"In what way?"

"You will find out," said Abraham. "The colonel would like you to shower and change quickly and then meet him in a restaurant. I will drive you. He has taken your car."

"What about his Mercedes?"

"It's being serviced."

The restaurant Sgt. Maj. Abraham drove me to in the early evening was one of those marvelously quaint places that were typical for Saigon. It was an old-time ballroom featuring passable French cooking, a big band and a crooner emitting tunes of the 1950s: tangos, waltzes, Cha-Cha-Cha, soft Rock 'n' Roll, and the occasional Twist. It also offered throngs of taxi girls—not prostitutes but pretty women costing guests 200 piasters a whirl, to be paid in advance to a cashier before entering the dance floor.

This was no sleazy bar for GIs, but a refuge for Vietnamese and European "squares" nostalgic for happier times; it was also the type of place where war correspondents could rendezvous secretly with representatives of the National Liberation Front, the political organization of the Viet Cong. In one such case, a very hungry trio of Communists showed up, consisting of a burly trade unionist, a tough military type, and a typical Asian intellectual with wire-rimmed spectacles; one had a raincoat slung over his arm; this was their agreed identification mark.

I wasn't surprised to find Tzschaschel in this ballroom for it was just the kind of anonymous venue in which spooks liked to do business: its lights were dim, the *maître d'hôtel* discreet, the waiters efficient, and the patrons an eclectic crowd wholly disinterested in the middle aged and balding European of medium build flanked by two comely Vietnamese women in Western dress. Although at closer inspection, all three of them would have seemed oddly out of place here. The women were probably in their mid or late thirties, spoke the elegant French of Sorbonne graduates and had the demeanor of senior officers' wives or perhaps widows.

"This is Mai," said Tzschaschel touching the lower arm of the woman on his left. "I thought you might enjoy her company this evening," he added with a malicious grin. "And of course you realize, Uwe, that this *is your* dinner, Uwe, *yours!* You owe me."

"I know, colonel, I know!" I answered.

I don't believe he ever mentioned his other companion's name, but I remember her striking looks. Her eyes were bright, inquisitive and smiling, but reservedly so, and she immediately engaged me in a conversation about the media's role in Vietnam.

"Do you know Thich Tam Chau?" she wanted to know.

"Yes, I do. He is the moderate Buddhist leader here in Saigon," I replied. "I have quite a good rapport with him. Recently he asked me if I would teach German classes at the Buddhist University."

"Really! Why German?" she asked.

"For reasons of good scholarship. All the essential sacred texts of Hinduism and Buddhism were first compiled in German by the philologist Max Müller [1823–1900]."

"In that case it would make sense for Buddhist scholars to study German. Did you know that Thich Tam Chau has ordered his followers to end their hunger strike against the Ky government and forget about suicide by self-immolation?" she inquired.

"Yes."

"But the American media don't seem to have reported this. What's the matter with them?"

"They have mentioned it but most are playing this fact down. They prefer to emphasize the specter of combat troops with fixed bayonets laying siege on the Vien Hoa Dao compound where hundreds are allegedly threatened by an outbreak of cholera." The Vien Hoa Dao, or Institute for the Propagation of the Dharma, was the staging area of violent street demonstrations against Ky and his American allies.

"This violence is un-Buddhist," she pressed on. "Don't American journalists understand this? Why are they so one-sided?"

"There are many excellent American journalists here who are not one-sided, but many are biased, you are right! Why are they like that? I guess they are only writing for each other, not really for the public. It is so facile to depict this conflict as a clash between Vietnam's Buddhist culture and an oppressive military regime. I know this is a stupid cliché. But if you are career-minded it's safer not to deviate from the stereotypes of the *Zeitgeist*," I explained.

"Well, to hell with the *Zeitgeist*, go look for yourself! It will be interesting to see what you'll make of these so-called 'Buddhist monks' armed with clubs and bicycle chains," she said, concluding our conversation.

The unnamed woman and Tzschaschel rose. "We have to go," he said. "Why don't you stay here for a little longer, have a few dances with Mai, and then drive her home? She lives opposite the Vien Hoa Dao in a neighborhood that is blocked off by combat troops. No taxis, *cyclo-pousses* (tricycle rickshaws or pedicabs) or private vehicles are allowed in and out after dark, unless they have special *laissez-passers*."

Chuckling, Tzschaschel continued: "Of course Sgt. Maj. Abraham could take us there, but it would raise eyebrows if we showed up at the checkpoints in a German Army *Munga*. You'll be fine with your press passes and the embassy sticker on your windscreen. That's why I brought your old *Citroën* here tonight. It's right outside."

Tzschaschel laughed as the two of them sauntered toward the exit to the sound of a rumba. As instructed, I danced a few rounds with Mai and then drove her home through angry crowds of demonstrators and past a series of military controls.

The inside of Mai's modest apartment above a shop directly across from the Vien Hoa Dao surprised me because it seemed antiseptic and curiously un-Vietnamese. The living room was sparsely equipped with a 'fifties-style furniture set including a sofa and a kidney-shaped coffee table covered with neat stacks of newspaper clippings. However, the most fascinating feature of this place was a telephone on a stand by the window. It was very state-of-the-art and marked with the letters T and N in a rhombus: the company logo of Frankfurt-based manufacturer *Telefonbau und Normalzeit GmbH*. The only other place where I had seen this in Saigon was at the German embassy.

Mai offered me a bottle of *Löwenbräu* beer, suggesting: "Don't return to your hotel tonight. It's too dangerous out there at this hour. Stay here. You can sleep on the sofa." By her body language she also made it obvious that lust was not part of that evening's program. She brought me a fresh toothbrush, two towels, a pillow and sheets and then withdrew to her bedroom.

The ping of a German telephone woke me early in the morning. It was Tzschaschel.

"Had a good night?" he asked.

"Surprisingly so, considering my jetlag."

"It seems so," he said with a chortle. "Otherwise you would have been awakened by the racket outside your window. Take a look."

Below Mai's window I saw a large, noisy crowd facing a contingent of combat troops with fixed bayonets. Most of the demonstrators were young monks, many equipped with bicycle chains and clubs.

They were wielding their weapons at random, even against journalists who had rushed to the Vien Hoa Dao expecting another fiery suicide by a Buddhist cleric. Almost immediately below, I made out Horst Faas, the Pulitzer prize-winning photographer of the Associated Press (AP). Horst and I had been friends since our time together with the AP in Germany in the late 1950s. He was a burly, brave, but very gentle reporter who would never attack an innocent man. But here he was furiously thumping his heavy camera on the shaved heads of angry young monks trying to yank his equipment away from him. I described this scene to Tzschaschel.

"What color are the monks' scalps?" he asked.

"Mostly gleaming white."

"What does that tell you?" he quizzed me.

"That these heads are freshly shaved."

"And...?"

"That they hadn't been shaved before."

"So?"

"These are probably not real monks. They look like Viet Cong fighters in cassocks."

"Bravo, Uwe! That's what I suspect," Tzschaschel told me. "This has all the marks of a bogus show staged for public

132

consumption in the United States, and many American reporters seem complicit in this scam."

"Very sad," I replied.

"Yes, very sad, and here is some interesting news for you. Yesterday evening, a young monk was taken to the *Hôpital Grall* with third-degree burns all over his body. The strange thing is that he belongs to the minority *Hinayana* (lesser vehicle) branch of Buddhism, which you find in the Mekong Delta and which has stayed aloof from the uprising staged by *Mahayana* (greater vehicle) Buddhists of Huế and Saigon. I understand he is awake and talking."

"I'll try to interview him. Mai can interpret."

By noontime, the South Vietnamese Army had brought the situation outside the Vien Hoa Dao sufficiently under control for us to drive to the venerable French hospital founded in 1861.

It was easy to find the burned monk. All we had to do was follow the steady stream of police officers, interrogators, doctors and Buddhist clerics heading toward his room. To my surprise, we were allowed to talk to him briefly. His voice was so weak that I did not get a word, but bending close to his face Mai managed to get his story.

He was from a monastery near My Tho in the Delta. His seniors had sent him on some errand to Saigon. The saffron-robed monk took an *Air Vietnam* flight to Tan Son Nhut Airport and proceeded on foot to a small temple of his branch of Buddhism.

"A *cyclo-pousse* (pedicab) carrying a monk in a brown robe stopped by my side and the monk asked me if I wanted a ride," he told Mai. "So I squeezed next to him in the passenger seat of the *cyclo-pousse*. The next thing I know is that I was on fire. Bystanders rushed to rescue me, wrapping a large piece of cloth around me to extinguish the flames. The other monk and the *cyclo-pousse* driver vanished in the crowd."

The patient drifted off but a detective who had listened in on the interview completed his story: "It's obvious that the other monk was no monk at all but a Viet Cong trying to stage a fake suicide for the media. The object was to convince world opinion that the Buddhist protest movement had by no means subsided, and that the government was as unpopular as ever. The trouble is that they got the wrong guy and misjudged the bystanders' willingness to thwart their intention by rescuing this poor fellow."

I filed this dramatic story immediately after bidding farewell to Mai, but it was never published. The foreign editors in Hamburg, though generally supporting the U.S. presence in Vietnam, simply did not understand the significance of my tale of false monks with white scalps and of a real monk who was burned against his will. During a home leave, I asked them why they had spiked this piece. They explained that they couldn't find anything about these incidents in the *New York Times* and *Washington Post/Los Angeles Times* news services. Only years later did they realize that the mainstream media in the United States followed an agenda incompatible with their own visions. By naïvely trusting the powerful American press more than their correspondent, they unwittingly abetted the incomprehensible urge of certain U.S. journalists to undermine their own country's position and that of its South Vietnamese allies.

A week later the Prime Minister's office called me: Nguyen Cao Ky was scheduled to fly to Huế the next morning for a meeting with local civilian and military leaders. Would I like to come along for the ride? I immediately agreed. Huế, this beautiful but very xenophobic old capital, had been the hub of the Buddhist opposition against the Ky government and the stronghold of his rival Lt. Gen. Nguyen Chanh Thi and the rebellious monk, Thich Tri Quang. Traveling to Huế in the company of reporters meant that Ky was trying to demonstrate who was now fully in control: himself.

We flew fixed-wing to Phú Bài airport and then transferred to helicopters for the ten-mile hop into the city. To my amazement, the valiant Eberhard Budelwitz was with us, the star of the media Theatre of the Absurd. He swayed merrily in his seatbelts as the army choppers swooped demonstratively over the old imperial capital on the River of Perfumes. On the ground, I took leave from Ky's party for a brief visit with Prof. Horst-Günter Krainick and his wife Elisabetha. Over lunch, Krainick proudly showed me his most treasured possession on the walls of his dining room: a collection of delicate behind-the-glass paintings. He said, "I do hope they are safe here but I fear that Huế is no longer the safe place it used to be." This was the last time I saw the Krainicks. Two years later they would be murdered and I would witness the wanton destruction of his paintings.

I returned to Ky and his entourage in time for their return to their helicopters. As we approached the landing pads, the prime minister grabbed me by the arm and pointed to a lump lying still under his chopper's skids: "What on earth is this? I can't believe it: it's your compatriot Budelwitz!" He had obviously fallen out of the helicopter, which fortunately landed not right on top of him, breaking his bones, but safely framing his vodka-soaked body with its skids, thus providing him with a shady spot where to sleep off his hangover!

Laughing, Nguyen Cao Ky pulled Budelwitz from under the chopper and, with the help of an aide, lifted him onto the aircraft and strapped him in. I enjoyed this incident hugely. After watching the violence at the Vien Hoa Dao and visiting the burned monk in hospital, this was such a wonderfully human scene. Budelwitz had once again excelled in the Theatre of the Absurd.

Matters turned worse for me in the following weeks. Suddenly I fell very ill. I could not hold down any food, could not go anywhere, meet anybody, concentrate on writing, and I experienced abdominal pain, which, as I was told later, must have reached levels comparable to the pains experienced at childbirth or third-degree burns. I lost so much weight that I had to hold my trousers together with a rope. When my illness reached its peak one night I must have screamed so loudly that I woke neighbors and staff in the *Continental Palace*, but there was nothing they could do except feed me green tea because of a curfew that made it impossible for a doctor to visit me in my hotel room.

At six in the morning, my pain had subsided a little. I staggered to my old *Citroën* and told Đức and his street urchins to find a different accommodation.

"You look terrible, Đức," said Đức addressing me by the nickname he had given me which, recall, means German as well as "virtuous."

"I think I am dying," I answered.

"Where do you think you are going, Đức?"

"To the U.S. Naval Hospital in Cholon," I said.

"You are in no condition to drive by yourself. I come with you."

I drove slowly to the American medical compound in Saigon's Chinatown, doubling over in agony at every intersection, with Đức stroking my right arm. I only vaguely recollect what happened next. Obviously I must have stopped at the gate to the hospital to let Đức out because he lacked an ID necessary to enter a military facility. Later I was told that I had abandoned the *Citroën* with the engine still running and the door on the driver's side open. I never saw it again. Worse still, I never saw my friend Đức again. When I returned to the *Continental Palace* months later, he and most of his wards had left Tu Do Street.

In the emergency room, I staggered along a long line of GIs queuing up for a VD check. I remember hearing the gruff voice of a chief petty officer inspecting the men's privates, saying "Ya got it, ya pig, ya got it, ya pig," meaning that they had caught gonorrhea. As I approached him, bent over, he growled, "And you, Sir, have amoebic dysentery, first door to your right, Sir," before resuming his routine: "Ya got it, ya pig, ya got it, ya pig!"

I entered the room he had sent me to, presumably a doctor's office, and passed out. Three days later, I woke and thought I was dead and had gone to heaven. The pain had gone and so had the heat and the humidity. I heard baroque music and saw an angelic creature above me; she was all dressed in white but had lovely black hair. As I came to, I realized that I was alive and in a hospital bed, and that not an angel but a lovely, dark-haired nurse of the U.S. Navy with a rank of a lieutenant commander was looking down on me.

I always thought white naval uniforms on women most alluring, and so I made a feeble attempt at chivalry. But she yanked the sheet off my body and said, "Sir, you are in no condition to flirt. Look at yourself; you look as if you are straight out of Auschwitz." I stared at the sorry skeleton pretending to be my body and asked her to cover me up again quickly.

"You are lucky you are alive," she told me. "You weighed 118 lbs when you came here and were totally dehydrated by your amoebic dysentery. You will stay here for a couple of more days until you are stabilized for travel. We have already contacted your employers. They'll get you home to Germany as soon as you can fly. They have bought three seats on an Air France flight to Paris so that you can stretch out all the way. You will be treated at the Tropical Institute in Hamburg. It was a pleasure dealing with the *Axel Springer* people. What fabulously efficient and decent employers they must be!"

Three days later I was driven to Tan Son Nhut Airport. My luggage was already there. Somebody—I still don't know who—had packed all my belongings at the *Continental Palace*. As the nurse had said, there were three seats reserved for me in the economy section of the Air France Boeing 707. I slept most of the way to Paris-Orly, where I was taken to a connecting flight to Hamburg.

My editor-in-chief, Julius Hollos, the one who made me cancel my wedding four years earlier, picked me up at the airport with a grief-stricken face. He informed me that on the orders of our publisher, *Axel Springer*, I would not be staying at the *Bernhard Noocht Institute for Tropical Medicine* but only be treated there. Springer had a suite reserved for me at the luxurious *Reichshof Hotel*, where I would be much more comfortable than in a hospital to which a company car would take me every morning.

When we arrived at the *Reichshof,* my wife, Gillian, was there, as were my mother and her new husband, all flown into town at Springer's expense. After my three-week treatment, I was granted three weeks extra vacation time in Austria, paid for by Axel Springer who also invited me to tour Scotland with Gillian in his chauffeur-driven Rolls Royce on our next trip to Europe.

Why I left this decent boss two years later to join *Stern* magazine, whose founder and editor had none of Springer's human qualities, I am unable to explain today; sometimes I suspect that the Saigon amoebae had not only attacked my digestive system, but also temporarily afflicted my brain.

Reflection Six

Willfully vanquished

The war we cannot win, should not wish to win, are not winning. The assumed enemy does not exist.

> Prof. John Kenneth Galbraith,
> Chairman of Americans for Democratic Action,
> in *How to Get Out of Vietnam*
> (New York: Signet Books, 1967)

It is unconscionable that extremist groups circulate letters which accuse me of horrific things, saying that I am a traitor. These lies have circulated for almost 40 years, continually reopening the wound of the Vietnam War.

> Jane Fonda,
> commenting in *The Huffington Post* on the reaction in
> America to the 1972 photograph of her sitting on a North
> Vietnamese missile launcher aimed at U.S. soldiers

[I]t is increasingly clear... that the only rational way out... will be to negotiate, not as victors, but as honorable people who lived up to their pledge to defend democracy and did the best they could.

> Walter Cronkite,
> CBS News, 27 February 1968

I have lost Cronkite, I have lost Middle America.

President Lyndon B. Johnson,
to his aides after hearing Cronkite's remark

Rarely has contemporary crisis-journalism turned out, in retrospect, to have veered so widely from reality. Essentially, the dominant themes of the words and film from Vietnam… added up to a portrait of defeat for the allies. Historians, on the contrary, have concluded that the Têt Offensive resulted in a severe military-political setback for Hanoi in the South.

Peter Braestrup,
in *Big Story*
(New York: Westview Press, 1977); p. 508

The enemy… does not possess… the psychological and political means to fight a long, drawn-out war.

Vo Nguyen Giap,
in a speech before the political commissars
of the 316th North Vietnamese Division,
as quoted by Bernard Fall

He who does not win in a people's war or in a guerilla struggle, loses. He who does not lose, wins.

Mao Zedong,
as quoted by Sir Robert Thompson

Chapter Eleven

Varied forms of R & R

Two months after my Near Death Experience in the U.S. Naval Hospital in Cholon I was back on the beat in Vietnam. My medical treatment in Hamburg had been a success, and three weeks in Austria with its moderate climate and wonderful music, food and wine provided the perfect kind of rest and recuperation, or R & R, to use military jargon. I felt well. My weight had returned to 140 lbs, the normal level at that point in my life; I fancied that I would now be ready for the angelic black-haired nurse in the uniform of an American lieutenant commander who so heartlessly rejected my advances by pointing out the lamentable state of my amoeba-infested body earlier in the summer. Of course I never saw her again.

"You look like a man ready for war," observed Lt. Col. Tzschaschel with a bemused smile as he drove me in his black Mercedes from Tan Son Nhut Airport to the *Continental Palace*.

"It seems so," I replied. "What's the news here?"

"The good news is that Ky is pulling off national elections for a constituent assembly amazingly well, despite violent Viet Cong attempts to hinder voters from going to the polls."

"And the bad news?" I asked.

"The antiwar movement in the United States and Western Europe is gathering momentum so quickly that I doubt free elections in South Vietnam will have any impact on public opinion in the West. It's crazy, isn't it?"

"Why crazy?"

"Because Americans are so much under bad media influence that they refuse to recognize what a heroic feat it is to organize a poll in the middle of this country's fight for survival. Just think: even in Britain, the world's oldest democracy, national elections were suspended for the duration of World War II, and yet the British didn't even have enemy forces on their island."

"Interesting point," I said, "It's strange that the American media never mention England in this context."

"Remember what my friend in the ballroom told you before they carried you out of here as a near-corpse?" Tzschaschel went on. "These people only write for each other."

"You are right up to a point, a lot of them do just write for each other," I said, "But this doesn't apply to the whole American press corps here. Many of their correspondents are very fair and conscientious journalists."

"True, but these are not the ones with the greatest influence on public opinion in the United States," Tzschaschel persisted.

"Alas!"

Less than one month later the elections were over. The Saigon government celebrated, justifiably, a voter turnout of 80 percent, an admirable display of democratic will in the face of dire threats to life and property. In the week before the polling, 680 incidents of terrorism were recorded throughout South Vietnam, proving that the Communists tried to prevent the people from legitimizing the Saigon government in a democratic manner.

Some incidents were bloodless: the Viet Cong set up roadblocks in order to confiscate the identity cards of passengers traveling on long-distance buses and "Lams," the three-wheeler collective taxis. This way, the Communists tried to make it impossible for voters to present themselves at polling stations; amazingly, the otherwise inefficient civil service managed to issue substitute IDs.

Other acts of terror were as odious as the slaughter of a village chief and his family whose mutilated bodies I had seen in the Central Highlands one year earlier. Campaign workers and candidates were massacred at such a rate that the government offered them weapons to protect themselves. And yet they continued to campaign intrepidly, with volunteers distributing leaflets showing not names but photographs and pictograms identifying the candidates and their party affiliations for the benefit of illiterates. In fairness to the western media, many of their correspondents did mention this evidence of courage. And when, eleven months later, 83 percent of the eligible voters braved more Communist threats by going to the polls, even the liberal *New York Times* noted in a news report the glaring contrast with the meager 62 percent voter turnout in the U.S. presidential elections of 1964. But this was a straight news story; most of the influential media stars, notably those opining on U.S. television, sniffily ignored this phenomenon.

Soon after the elections, I resumed my routine of traveling to the strategically vital Central Highlands for which I had almost developed an obsession. On the U.S. Air Force C-130 from Saigon to Plei Ku I was wedged between two privates, a Vietnamese by the name of Hương and an American who introduced himself as Mike.

Hương was a slight young man with a wrenchingly sad face. On his lap he carried a birdcage housing a canary to which he whispered sobs. Vietnamese soldiers carrying birdcages to forward positions were a familiar and touching sight often mocked by GIs unaware that the birds might be the only possession in the lives of their comrades-in-arms. As it turned out, this was so in Hương's case. Trying to compete acoustically with the racket of the badly soundproofed plane's four turboprop engines, Hương told me his story in a mixture of broken French, English and Vietnamese. He was on his way back to his unit from a special furlough he had been granted to bury his mother and sister, both killed by the Viet Cong because of their volunteer work during the election campaign.

"VC kill *cat hong*," he said with a gesture suggesting that the two women had their throats slit.

"Everybody dead in my family," he continued, "My father, he killed in combat last year. He *dai uy* (captain). My brother die last month. He *thieu uy* (second lieutenant). VC burn down my hou[se]. I alone now, no family, no hou[se], just him," he added pointing at the bird in the cage. "He all I own."

"How did he survive?" I asked.

"Neighbor enter burning hou[se] after VC go and save him—for me."

"What a sad story!" said Mike, sitting on my right merrily swaying with the jerks of the military transport plane; he was visibly hung over. Mike must have been about Hương's age, 20 or so, and like Hương was a conscript returning to his unit from a furlough—but not from a burial.

"Had a week's R & R in Bangkok. Blew $900," he bragged.

"Nine hundred dollars!" said Hương, "That's more than I make in one year!"

"What did you do with all this money?" I asked Mike.

"Drink and screw my brains out. Three, four different women every day," he blurted out.

Hương gave him a poignant look.

"Was that good?" I asked.

Mike went quiet: "No, not really. I just took revenge on Amanda."

"Amanda?"

"My girlfriend in Madison, Wisconsin. She broke up with me calling me a baby killer. I went nuts when I received her letter containing a picture of herself with her new boyfriend, some hippie."

This was my first introduction to a phenomenon Dr. Emanuel Tanay, a Detroit psychiatrist, termed the Dear John Syndrome: an avalanche of usually spiteful farewell letters from American women to their boyfriends or husbands serving at the front. There had been "Dear John Letters" in every war of the 20th century, but according to Tanay, never nearly as many as in the Vietnam era, a fact he attributed to the lack of popular support for America's military involvement in Indochina.

The most mysterious feature of "Dear Johns" was their shocking cruelty. "The letters are bitter," Tanay told the

Associated Press, "[they were] obviously written for the purpose of hurting or creating injury to the other person... The girls are usually in their early 20s. They haven't been married long enough to have acquired such hatred. But it's there. Some send photographs of themselves with other men in compromising positions. Some send tape recordings of exchanges with another man."

I tried to put myself into this young soldier's situation. I imagined him returning to base from a combat mission in the jungle, collecting his mail and sifting through letters and parcels. He singles out the envelope bearing his sweetheart's handwriting and places it on the pillow of his bunk. He showers, shaves, puts on fresh fatigues, stretches out on his bed and opens the letter. First the nauseating photograph falls out; then he reads the brutal news that Amanda has left him for this peacenik in the picture.

"The effect of such things on men who receive them is destructive," said Tanay. "They feel helpless to cope with it because they are so far away." Tanay added that he became interested in this phenomenon during a visit to Vietnam where he testified at a court martial of a marine who, after receiving a Dear John letter, had grabbed his M-16, run off base and blasted indiscriminately at Vietnamese civilians, killing four men.

Hương reached across me to pat Mike's left hand: "So sorry 'bout that, Mike," he said, "So very, very sorry."

Mike nodded at him gratefully as he continued his narrative:

"That's not all. You see, before I opened Amanda's letter, something bad had happened to me during a lull in combat. We opened our C rations. I went straight for the can of fruit salad, like we always do. It felt funny—light, empty. When I opened it, there was no fruit salad in it but a note saying, 'You live like a dog—you die like a dog!' I went ape-shit. So did my buddies. The company commander pulled my squad out of combat and ordered us back to base, and then I read Amanda's letter... and shiiiit! That's why the battalion sent me on R & R."

"So sorry 'bout that, Mike," Hương repeated, "So very, very sorry." Then we landed in Plei Ku, where I watched the two sad soldiers walk off the airfield with Mike's hefty left arm wrapped around Hương's shoulder, and Hương holding his birdcage with both hands.

The image of these two soldiers consoling each other in their sorrow has stayed with me for over four decades as one of my strongest visual memories of the Vietnam War, for in human terms it was a healthy scene: these young men from two different cultures recognized each other as fellow sufferers in a struggle against a common enemy whose evil deeds Hương had just described vividly in one short sentence.

This scene did not reflect the general relationship between American and Vietnamese soldiers, though, nor did it mirror the rapport between the GIs and the Vietnamese population. According to a study by U.S. historian Guenter Lewy, many soldiers had developed "strong feelings of animosity" towards their host country's population in the second year of the deployment of American forces in Vietnam.

"A survey of marines in Quang Ngai province in 1966 revealed that 40 percent disliked the Vietnamese and these attitudes were especially pronounced among small-unit leaders. Less than one in five of the NCOs had a positive attitude toward the ARVN (South Vietnamese army) or PF (Popular Forces)," wrote Lewy in his book, *America in Vietnam* (New York: 1978), a work *The Economist* lauded as, "Splendid... in many ways the best history of the war yet to appear."

"This dislike was often racism," Lewy went on, "It also resulted from the fact that the soldiers... felt engulfed in a sea of enmity, a situation where no Vietnamese could be fully trusted." He then described the situation American warriors found themselves in: "They suffered the deadly trepidations of enemy activities—ambushes, snipers, mines and booby traps. Buddies were killed, yet no enemy was in sight on whom one could revenge those losses. Seeming civilians were actually combatants;

women or children tossed grenades or planted traps. Gradually the entire Vietnamese population became an object of fear and hatred."

I once witnessed the capture of benign-looking peasant women as they prepared punji sticks from bamboo spikes, hardening them over a fire and rubbing them with human feces. Batteries of these traps were to be planted in grass and undergrowth at such an angle that they would penetrate a GI's canvas boots causing an instant infection, which would require his immediate evacuation and usually result in the loss of his foot.

Lewy cited a Marine lieutenant telling an American doctor, "You walk through the bush for three days and nights without sleep. You watch your men, your buddies; your goddamn kids get booby-trapped. Blown apart. Get thrown six feet in the air by a trap laid by an old lady and come down with no legs." The lieutenant ended his outburst by saying that eventually one had to conclude that the only thing to do was to "kill them all."

"Callousness toward the Vietnamese was also caused by the writings and pronouncements of many American journalists and politicians who, while seeking to end American involvement, for years exaggerated the faults of the South Vietnamese government and gradually created an image of people not worth defending, if not altogether worthless," continued Lewy, a refugee from Nazi Germany. "For all these reasons, some Americans came to regard the South Vietnamese as somewhat less than human, though acceptance of the 'mere-gook' rule has probably been exaggerated. For each misdeed and instance of mistrust and hostility, unbiased observers in Vietnam could see examples of friendship and generosity. Individual American soldiers, and sometimes entire units, adopted orphans and other children and engaged in various programs known as 'civic action.'"

This is also what I observed in my years in Vietnam: I repeatedly saw GIs suffering horrible wounds in their attempts to protect civilians from harm. In one case, I was there when a Viet Cong tossed a live hand grenade into a platoon of marines

147

surrounded by scores of women and children. The platoon leader, a second lieutenant, threw himself on the grenade so that his body would absorb the detonation, which would otherwise have killed and maimed the Vietnamese bystanders. He died instantly, his body torn to shreds by shrapnel, but nobody else was hurt. Several of the women cried and hugged the shocked "leathernecks" in gratitude for the self-sacrifice of their commanding officer.

Ignorance was yet another reason why many U.S. soldiers denigrated the Vietnamese as "gooks," "dinks," "slopes" and "slants." These men had never seen, heard of or read about the bravery of ARVN units, a valor that persisted until the fall of Saigon in 1975 when the South Vietnamese fought on doggedly knowing that everything was lost. This ignorance must in part be attributed to the pervasive parochialism of the American media that, if anything, is even more pronounced today than it was four decades ago. Once U.S. ground forces had landed in Vietnam, very few American correspondents bothered to spend much time with ARVN companies or platoons or, for that matter, the large Thai contingent or even the remarkable two divisions and one brigade from South Korea. Much like America's German, French, Australian, Dutch, Danish or Norwegian allies in Afghanistan at the time of this writing, they were, by and large, arrogantly ignored on television and by most newspapers in the United States.

In the case of the South Koreans this was all the more baffling as they were probably the most effective fighting force in the entire war. They were so ferocious that Communist commanders ordered their troops to retreat rather than fight these fearsome fellow Asians should they come across them in the battlefield. The first time I visited the headquarters of the Korean 9th infantry division, named "White Horse," in Ninh Hoa, I was assigned a batman who slept at the foot of my bed on the division's immaculately kept and litter-free base. The next morning at five, he shook me awake to go outside and watch an astonishing spectacle: everybody, from the commanding general down to the lowly private, practiced Taekwon-Do, a Korean version of karate that involved bisecting a brick with their bare hands, a skill they adopted with abandon in the battlefield.

I accompanied a White Horse platoon on a patrol. Before we moved out, a briefer told me that I could expect an excursion as peaceful as a walk in the park. "Where we are deployed, the Communists have moved out," he told me with a guttural laugh. Yet evidently one Viet Cong fighter had not got the message. As we were crossing a clearing, there was sniper fire from a tree line.

Furiously, the platoon leader ordered his forty men to drop to the ground. He stripped to his briefs and, moving like a cat towards its prey, rushed to the tree where he had spotted the sharpshooter. Holding his dagger between his teeth, he clawed up the tree. Next, the offender's severed head came down, followed by his torso.

"Very, very good," whispered his platoon sergeant full of admiration. "Our lieutenant decapitated a VC with a Taekwon-Do chop. Our lieutenant is a champion."

"But is it possible to sever skin this way?" I asked.

"No, we use a dagger or our teeth for that. Maybe the lieutenant used his dagger this time."

The platoon leader returned, sticking his knife into the ground several times to clean the blood off the blade. Slipping back into his fatigues, he said matter-of-factly:

"No more VC in my sector."

With that we resumed our patrol.

"These are scary people," my interpreter Lanh told me after my return to Saigon, "But the local Vietnamese like these tough Koreans because they keep them safe and relieve them of the nightly dread of visits by Viet Cong terrorists. They also make themselves useful in everyday country life. Many Korean soldiers are rice farmers. At harvest time they help the villagers with their work, bringing along simple pedal-propelled thrashing machines that are nonetheless ten times more productive than our traditional flailing methods but require no big investment and no fuel. This is a very smart policy, don't you think?"

In purely human terms the saddest aspect of the GIs' personal relationship with the people of their host country was perhaps that it was usually limited to two unpopular categories of people: the Communists, who were trying to maim or kill them, and the ladies of the night whose affections were not free of charge. Tragically, the soldiers and the bar girls and prostitutes had more in common than just their carnal encounters, for both were shunned by significant elements of their respective societies. The young Americans roaming Saigon's red light district when off duty might not have realized this at the time they sought solace from their fears and deprivations in the company of bargirls and prostitutes. But they would soon discover the disdain in which they were held back home when they heard the mindless slogan "make love not war." I felt nauseous when I discovered, during stints in the United States in 1967, that the glib cliché mouthed by the smart set of New York, "Vietnam veterans, my least favorite minority," had become the mantra of wannabe progressives on the cocktail party circuit.

The Vietnamese women were, of course, being made aware of their outcast status every time they crossed the street when they were spat on by pedicab drivers who normally inhabited the bottom rung of their country's class system. I spent much time in the countless bars where these two groups mated, not because I enjoyed squalor but because it was there that a personal calamity unfolded in which mostly very decent young Americans and equally decent Vietnamese were united. To write about this was, of course, an important part of my assignment.

For many soldiers, often small-town boys in their late teens or early twenties, these women were their first erotic contacts, and all too often their last. Nearly all the girls were war widows without pensions or vocational skills. Most had several children to raise and mothers and grandmothers to look after, women who themselves might have been war widows but had lost the bloom that might have attracted foreign consorts.

I confess that I had a soft spot for these simple and warm-hearted peasant girls from the Mekong Delta greeting me, as they would any American: "Hey you! Long time no see! You numbah one! You buy me Saigon tea," meaning, "Hello, I haven't seen you for a long time. You are the greatest! Please buy me a brownish looking liquid posing as a shot of whisky that will cost you anywhere between two and ten dollars." Their "*Mamasans*," or Madams, paid them a percentage of the price for the "Saigon Tea" but not of the real drinks they had to encourage their customers to consume, and the *Mamasans* took a cut of the price the women negotiated with their Johns for sex.

Saigon's authorities estimated that at least 30,000 of these women were practicing their trade in the capital in 1967, and that there were at least 100,000 in the entire country. Journalists who befriended them found them to be rich sources of information and an especially reliable barometer of the public mood in South Vietnam. When thousands of them began rounding out their figures to suit GI tastes, we reporters knew that they no longer believed in America's stamina to bring the war to a victorious conclusion, and that they had to find a foreign husband to get them away from their homeland before the Communists took over. Hence they were prepared to do almost anything to catch their man.

The avalanche of body modifications started when the news broke that the exquisite wife of a Vietnamese leader had flown to Japan to have her eyes rounded and her breasts enlarged. I won't mention her name because she is still alive, but when I first saw her after her return from Tokyo, I wanted to shout at her, "Whatever made you do this? You were the perfect beauty, and now you look like a fake Modigliani figure with a Rubens chest superimposed!"

It didn't take many months for local quacks to transform brigade-size numbers of young women. With other correspondents I polled the *Mamasans* of scores of brothels and bars. They estimated that between 5,000 and 10,000 of their girls had undergone such operations. The results were frightening: on Saigon's sidewalks where only recently the abundant flow of delicate and gracile females clad in *Áo dàis* delighted our eyes, monstrously deformed creatures with grotesquely large chests and rears hobbled down the street in ill-fitting miniskirts. Often the operations were so inexpertly done that one or both breasts suddenly sagged several inches and buttocks dropped into the hollows of women's knees.

Once I sat in a Saigon bar next to a sweet girl with hopelessly misshapen features by the name of Ngoc. She kept staring at herself in the large mirror behind a battery of liquor bottles and fumbled constantly with her unusually big nose.

"Does your nose itch?" I asked her. "This could mean that you'll be rich soon, according to a German superstition."

"No, no," she answered with a giggle, "It's just that I had a bigger nose bone fitted, but it never stays in place. So I have to put it straight all the time."

"Why did you do that, Ngoc?"

"Because I had a small, flat nose, like many Vietnamese girls. This is why GIs always called me little monkey. That hurt me very much."

"But small noses can be pretty. Why do you care?"

"I must marry and go to America. When the VC come and catch me, they will kill me and hurt my children."

One afternoon as I left one of these grubby, smoke-filled places we reporters used to call "long-time-no-see bars," my friend Philippe Franchini, the *Continental's* owner and general manager, spotted me and shook his head.

"Why do you frequent these disgusting joints?" he asked.

"Not for any salacious reason, trust me!" I replied. "These places are a font of information for reporters."

"Then let me show you an even better font of information that is less revolting. Let's meet in an hour in front of the hotel."

We did. He drove me up Hai Ba Trung Street, which is named after a pair of sisters revered in Vietnam, much as Jeanne d'Arc is venerated in France, for they led, in the year 40 A.D., an army of 80,000 men that liberated their country from the Chinese invaders. We traveled for a while on this major thoroughfare that parallels Tu Do Street until we reached the old French cemetery in front of which Philippe parked his car. We crossed the street, entered a discreet but seemingly well-appointed townhouse and were met at the door by an elegantly dressed middle-aged woman.

"*Không mỹ!*" she said angrily: no American!

"*Mais non, mais non! C'est un ami allemand. Il parle français,*" explained Philippe: No, no! This is a German friend. He speaks French.

"*Entrez donc,*" she answered with an apologetic smile: Come in, then.

She took us to the *bel étage* on the first floor (second floor in American counting) and guided us into a pleasingly appointed salon vaguely resembling the fine but slightly decadent Paris salons of the 19th century described by Charles Baudelaire. It was filled with prominent and well-dressed gentlemen, many of whom I had vainly asked for interviews in the past: there were two or three senior civilian officials, a couple of generals and politicians, some drinking champagne, others tea.

"What is he doing here?" one general asked Philippe in Vietnamese.

"Don't worry, Uwe is a friend of mine. You can trust him," Philippe Franchini assured him.

"Philippe is right, General," I said. "In responsible journalism we have our rules of engagement, just as you military men have your rules of engagement. I would be a fool if I broke your trust. You can speak to me freely, and I won't quote you by name, or not at all, if that's what you wish. I'll give you my word of honor."

"I must get back to the *Continental*," said Philippe, leaving me in the company of the other guests who gradually relaxed, and of the Madam who whispered into my ear: "Monsieur, I know exactly your taste. Wait here for about one hour and enjoy your conversation with the other gentlemen. Would you like some champagne?"

"Yes, please, I will have a bottle, and let's have glasses for everyone."

A *"boyesse,"* or maidservant, brought the bottle in a cooler and glasses, and Madam disappeared. One hour later she was back in the company of a breathtakingly beautiful woman dressed in an expensive *Áo dài*.

"Pour vous," she said.

"I'll take her out to dinner," I answered bidding farewell to my new VIP friends, some of whom I would develop close professional contacts with that served me well when covering ARVN combat operations in subsequent years.

Madam took me discreetly aside and asked for a substantial honorarium, about $180, which I paid in cash. She had a servant call a taxi, and we drove to the *Royal*, my favorite place in town, where old Jean Ottavi let off a gentle cat-whistle: *"Quelle beauté, cher ami, quelle beauté!"*—What a beauty, my dear friend, what a beauty!

She was an exceptionally witty conversationalist talking in flawless French about European history, music, the visual arts, current affairs, travel and religion. Why, I wondered, would this well-bred and educated woman work for an escort service, even for one as posh as Madam's? She seemed to read my mind. By the time we reached Ottavi's celebrated soufflé course, she told me that she had gambled away her husband's monthly salary playing dominos.

"It's an Asian disease, Monsieur," she explained, "that's why I have to do this."

"Are many of Madam's ladies in the same position?"

"I suppose so."

The next day, over lunch, I told Lt. Col. Tzschaschel how I had spent the previous evening.

"What a damned shame!" he exclaimed.

"Why shame?"

"I mean: what a shame I am being transferred! Now it's too late for you to introduce me to this precious place."

I didn't see Tzschaschel again for 15 years. When we met next, he was a general heading the analysis and evaluation branch of the BND, West Germany's equivalent of the CIA.

Chapter Twelve

Tây Đức vs. Đông Đức

In the Hàn River Harbor of Da Nang a pristine white vessel marked by large red crosses on both sides was moored during much of the Vietnam War. It stood out like a sleek icon of altruism against the all-pervasive grey of all the military craft nearby. Named *Helgoland*, it used to ferry sightseers to German seaside resorts, and, after her six-year stint in Indochina, the *Helgoland* became an Ecuadorian cruise liner stationed in the Galapagos Islands. But from 1966 until 1972, she served as a floating hospital, operated by the West German Red Cross and financed by the West German taxpayer.

Measuring 330 feet in length and 46 feet in width, the *Helgoland* was better equipped and manned than many Western clinics. She was the most modern hospital in Vietnam at the time. There were three state-of-the-art operating theaters, 180 beds, 8 doctors, a nursing staff of 22, plus 8 medical and laboratory assistants, and 34 seamen, cooks, and other personnel. From 1966 until 1972, almost 200,000 sick or maimed Vietnamese civilians were cared for on board this ship and its dockside outpatient clinic. These were islands of relative safety surrounded by a world of terror, bombs, rockets, napalm, and artillery fire. Some patients came from areas controlled by the Saigon government, others from villages that were in the hands of the Viet Cong, at least at night; no questions about their political loyalties were ever asked.

I enjoyed visiting the *Helgoland* for several reasons. After weeks of covering combat operations and feeding on C-rations, it was always good to have a wholesome German dinner and to trade yarns with the ship's nurses, doctors and crewmen over a beer from home. The *Helgoland* also served as a relatively reliable barometer predicting horrors that might take place on land: if she left port unannounced before nightfall, I knew that the captain was taking her to the safety of international waters, because American and South Vietnamese intelligence officers had warned him of an expected Viet Cong attack on Da Nang.

Most importantly, a sojourn on the *Helgoland* produced moving tales about the people this war was supposed to be all about: the South Vietnamese. There was, for example, the story of the first napalm victim a nurse I shall call Isabel had ever seen. He was a nine-year old boy by the name of Le Xien. "When he was carried on board, his arms and legs were burned black and still smoking."

"How did this happen?" I asked Isabel.

"He said he was playing soccer with other children. Suddenly planes appeared in the sky and bombs fell. He remembered being knocked to the ground and feeling absolutely nothing. Villagers took him to a nearby American base and from there he was flown to us by helicopter. During the flight the pain set in."

"Did this make you feel angry about the Americans?" I asked her.

"No, it just made me feel more perplexed about the nature of this war. You see, this happened right next to the American base where both of Le Xien's parents worked, the father as a garbage man and the mother as a cleaning woman."

"Did they visit him on the *Helgoland*?" I wanted to know.

"No, and this was the next tragedy in Le Xien's life: no sooner was he in our ward than he received the news that his parents had both been killed," said Isabel.

"How?"

"We never found out."

Chances were that the family lived in a government-controlled village the Viet Cong visited at night, and this cleaning woman, this garbage man might have lost their lives because they had worked for "the enemy." We shall never know.

Next, Isabel had an equally perplexing encounter while sunning herself on My Khe Beach—Da Nang's most beautiful—in her off duty hours.

"A young GI approached me and asked courteously, 'May I sit with you for a little while?'"

"By all means," Isabel answered, "But why are you so drunk?"

"I drank so much because I wanted to forget that I killed three children yesterday," said the GI.

He continued, "I am a helicopter door gunner. We flew over a Viet Cong-infested area. Below us I spotted a group of people dressed in black pajamas. When they saw us they tried to run away in three different directions. So I opened fire and got three of them. For a brief moment I felt like a hero."

"And then?" Isabel pressed him.

"Then we swooped further down and I saw three dead children on the ground, killed by my bullets."

The GI shook inconsolably.

"Please forgive me, Fräulein, for crying like this in the presence of a lady, but I am only 18. At home I am not even allowed to vote or drink a beer. And now I have the deaths of three children on my conscience. I don't know how I will ever be able to live with myself."

During another visit on the *Helgoland*, I spent the evening in the company of a woman with that glorious blend of qualities only the nursing profession seems to produce in such intensity: feistiness, compassion, down-to-earth practicality, humor and *joie de vivre*. She was a sturdy drinking pal who kept her beer perfectly cool by storing it in the ship's morgue—in short, she was a mensch of the kind some of us reporters feel most akin to.

She described vividly her fondness for a 49-year old epileptic rice farmer who had literally lost his whole face in an explosion of unknown origin. "You must meet him," she said, "He spent many months with us, but now he is in a hospice just outside the city. We love him and miss him a lot. I'll take you to him tomorrow on my day off. Now let's have another beer."

And so we did.

The next morning, I rode on the back of her small motorbike clinging to her waist as she weaved wildly through the chaotic traffic in downtown Da Nang. We ended up in the suburbs at a simple but immaculately kept nursing home run by Vietnamese Catholic nuns.

We found him in the garden on a swing bench being pushed to and fro by neighborhood children. There was nothing left of the front of his head: he had no eyes, no brows, no cheekbones, no nose, no lips, and no chin.

When he heard the nurse's voice, he cried and grabbed her hands. It was uncanny to watch a man without eyes weep, but weep he did when he told me, "These German nurses are so loyal! They are my only visitors, my only friends."

"What about your family?" I asked him.

"They are dead," he replied.

"And your neighbors?"

"They don't come," said the featureless man, shaking with sobs, "In this country maybe people don't want to see a man who has lost his face."

At lunchtime one day, a group of nurses relaxed on the *Helgoland*'s deck observing with amusement a seemingly drowsy South Vietnamese military policeman on a bridge nearby. He was slouched over the railing looking aimlessly—or so it appeared—at the muddy water below. What the Germans could not see at first was the object of his attention: a tiny piece of straw moving purposefully in an upright position toward the hospital ship.

Abruptly, the MP aimed his M-16 rifle at this barely discernible target and fired off a volley of rounds. The water turned red and a wounded Viet Cong frogman drifted to the surface. This guerilla had used the straw to breathe through while swimming long distance toward his target for a terror attack. He had a limpet mine strapped to his body. When I interviewed a military spokesman about this incident, he said, "We are not quite sure what this frogman's target was; he was contradicting himself during interrogations. One moment he said he had orders to blow up the bridge, but then he claimed that the mine was really intended to blow the *Helgoland* out of the water." If this was true, the lives of some 250 Vietnamese and European civilians had been at risk.

The limpet mine was also a present from Germany—though not from Tây Đức (West Germany) but from Đông Đức (East Germany).

This fascinating detail underscored the geostrategic dimension of this war: yes, it was a Mao-style People's War, but it was also the hot theater of the global Cold War between East and West, and this very much included the conflict between the two German states.

One of the most lethal gifts from the East German government to its Vietnamese comrades was a fiendish landmine known around the world as PPM-2. I saw its devastating impact many times when driving on National Route 19 between Plei Ku in the Central Highlands and Qui Nhon by the South China Sea: bits of human bodies were strewn all over the road and had been propelled into bushes and trees—heads, legs, arms or perhaps just hands, feet, fingers or toes intermingled with remnants of shattered vehicles.

These scattered fragments of women and children made up the bulk of the fatalities on Route 19 every day. Traveling between their villages and market towns in flimsy three-wheeler Lambretta buses, these civilians were far more vulnerable to anti-personnel mines than soldiers riding in tanks, armored personnel carriers, or on trucks and jeeps that had their floorboards covered by sandbags to absorb explosions.

American officers showed me unexploded mines that their men had dug up on Route 19. They were black and had a plastic exterior and a plastic pressure plate, plus a piezoelectric fuse triggering a blast of 110 grams of TNT. The East Germans planted thousands of these devices in the 875-mile "death strip" along its western border, not to keep out foreign invaders, but to prevent its own people from fleeing to the free part of their own country.

The difference between the ways the two Germanys were involved in Vietnam was glaring. According to the Woodrow Wilson International Center in Washington, East Germany supplied North Vietnam, and by extension the Viet Cong, with $200 million worth of military materiel ranging from automatic weapons, mines, grenades, ammunition, trucks, engines, and anti-aircraft batteries. East Germany also trained officers and supplied musical instruments for military bands. In addition to these, East Germany's feared intelligence service, known as Stasi, trained and equipped its North Vietnamese equivalent.

Militarily, North Vietnam was East Germany's most important client state outside Europe. This close relationship continued almost until the regime of the so-called German Democratic Republic (GDR) collapsed as a result of the peaceful revolution against its totalitarian rule in 1989, and its territory became part of the free Federal Republic of Germany the following year. Before that happened, though, the GDR'S People's Army continued training officers from Communist-ruled Vietnam, and completely equipped its new officers' academy in Saigon, now called Ho Chi Minh City.

By contrast, West Germany ranked second only to the United States in humanitarian and economic aid to South Vietnam, but this was the only form of assistance Bonn provided. West Germans advised South Vietnam on how to fight juvenile delinquency, helped restructure its trade unions and trained their leaders, and donated large amounts of rice when the Mekong Delta, once the "Rice Bowl of Asia," was no longer able to feed the nation as a consequence of the war. West Germans also built state-of-the-art slaughterhouses to provide South Vietnam with safely butchered meat.

But the most important aid West Germany gave was medical. There was the *Helgoland*. There was the medical school in Huế. There was also a hospital in Da Nang run by the relief services of the German branch of the Knights of Malta, a lay order of Catholic nobility, with outposts in An Hoa and Hoi An.

All Germans working in these centers were volunteers, chiefly young Christians, whose exemplary comportment and dedication won them the affection of the thousands of Vietnamese civilians they served. But this did not spare several of them from being captured, shot, or subjected to months-long death marches along the Ho Chi Minh Trail from South to North Vietnam, from being starved and denied medical care, and from being held under inhuman conditions in Communist prisons in a glaring violation of the Geneva Conventions on warfare.

It was not "by mistake" that they were being deprived of their liberty, mistreated and killed, for their captors knew very well that they were not combatants. The three German faculty members of the Medical School of Huế had to dig their own graves before being shot in the back of their heads six weeks after their arrest during the North Vietnamese occupation in 1968, and despite international pleas with Hanoi to spare their lives.

Monika Schwinn, a young pediatric nurse of the Knights of Malta relief service, related in the weekly magazine *Der Spiegel* a telling statement by one of her captors: "We are holding you not because you are Monika Schwinn. We are holding you as citizen of a country that is in cahoots with the enemy." Monika Schwinn spent nearly four years in seven Communist prison camps, including, as the only woman, the infamous "Hanoi Hilton," where she heard the screams of American pilots during torture sessions and where she met John McCain, the future senator and Presidential candidate. She told *Der Spiegel* how she managed to survive her ordeal: by her faith in God, by her knowledge that she was innocent of any crimes because she had come to help the Vietnamese people, not to hurt them, and by reminding herself of her own defiant motto: *"An mir beißt ihr euch die Zähne aus"* — you will break your teeth on me!

Why did the Vietnamese Communists murder German doctors, nurses, and the diplomat Hasso Rüdt von Collenberg, a brave young nobleman whom they captured while he was trying to evacuate German citizens from their Saigon residences during urban warfare in the aftermath of the Têt Offensive? Why did they summarily execute him, according to eyewitnesses, even though his white *Volkswagen* bore diplomatic license plates and he showed them his diplomatic passport, which should have guaranteed his immunity?

There can only be one explanation: from the mid-1960s, East German propagandists spread the lie almost every day that West Germany was militarily involved in Vietnam, and the North Vietnamese and Viet Cong media repeated this falsehood with equal regularity. At first they claimed that German soldiers were fighting in South Vietnam disguised as Americans. Later they asserted that entire units of the German *Bundeswehr* (Federal Defense Force) were participating in combat operations.

It is true that young Germans were sent to fight in Vietnam—but not by the West German government. They came, rather, as American or Australian conscripts. I once ran into three German-speaking soldiers in three different uniforms in a Saigon bar: American, Australian and New Zealand. All three had emigrated from Germany, as had hundreds of thousands of young Europeans in the 1960s and 1970s. The U.S. and Australia drafted young immigrants into their armed forces and deployed many of them to Vietnam. New Zealand did not have national service but enlisted new citizens as volunteers.

I even ran into a young bomber pilot from Heidelberg by the name of Helmut Bubbel. He was a Marine Corps captain flying an A-6 Intruder on missions over North Vietnam from the aircraft carrier Coral Sea. He told me that after a number of sorties he had developed a personal relationship with a North Vietnamese anti-aircraft gunner whom he recognized by the signature rhythm in the way he fired his cannon.

"Firing a flak can be like singing," Bubbel explained to me during a visit on the Coral Sea. "Two people might sing from an identical score but interpret it differently. It's the same with gunners. They shoot to different meters."

"So what happened to him?" I asked Bubbel, who had migrated to California with his father in 1953.

"The last time we 'met,' I was dive-bombing his gun emplacement," said Bubbel. "This became clearly a duel between us. I knew that we had recognized each other. He fired at me relentlessly with his familiar meter. I thought, 'One of us will have to bite the dust today.' I could see his fire bursts and literally look into the barrel of his flak. I couldn't have been more than 80 meters away from him when I released a bomb and went on a steep climb. Once I had reached a safe distance I looked back and could see that I had made a perfect hit. It was quiet down there."

"What did you do then?" I asked.

"I went back and flew a lap of honor over his smoking gun emplacement saying, 'Respect, you brave little man! What a shame that a soldier of your valor has had to die!'"

"This reminds me of World War I tales about famous flying aces such as the 'Red Baron' Manfred von Richthofen."

"It was like that, in a way. At least I know that I admired this guy, and I suppose he admired me."

Unlike most German immigrants in the enlisted ranks, Helmut Bubbel was already a United States citizen; he could not have become a commissioned officer otherwise. But he did still own a German passport and showed it to me. I remember urging him:

"Don't carry this on you when you take off on a bombing raid. If you're shot down the Communists will present it as evidence that West Germany is a party to this war. This would give them an excuse to kill more West German civilians in South Vietnam. Too many have already been murdered."

"You are right. I must not do this," he promised.

In truth there were never more than three men in West German military uniforms in South Vietnam: soldiers working at the embassy. One was the defense attaché who sometimes had an assistant attaché with the rank of a major. A sergeant major did their office work.

During her imprisonment in North Vietnam, Monika Schwinn met two diplomats from the East German embassy in Hanoi. The encounter with the representatives of the country that spread lethal lies about an alleged West German combat role in Vietnam was an eerie experience. After all, these lies had most probably contributed to her ordeal—hers as well as the plight of fellow German inmate Bernhard Diehl and the death of three other Knights of Malta aides who succumbed to illness and malnutrition on their way up the Ho Chi Minh Trail.

She found these "diplomats" distasteful. "Their behavior and their manner of speech were so primitive that I was ashamed that these men were Germans," she wrote in *Der Spiegel*. She made the point that they voiced no compassion for her lot and offered no help. "Actually, they came to interrogate me." They wanted to know whether her father, who died in combat in World War II, had been a member of the Nazi Party, and what military rank he had held. They urged her to end her series of hunger strikes against the conditions of her imprisonment and told her to show some understanding for the behavior of the North Vietnamese, adding, "After all, German members of the French Foreign Legion have killed innocent people here." He neglected to mention that 1,400 German deserters of the Foreign Legion fought on the side of the Communist Viet Minh, and that Ho Chi Minh had adopted two of these: Walter Ullrich, who became a Viet Minh lieutenant by the name of Ho Chi Long, and Georg Wächter alias Ho Chi Tho.

When Monika Schwinn responded that the torments of her long march had reduced her capacity for understanding, one of the East German diplomats screamed at her, "Well, for God's sake, they couldn't have picked you up [from the Viet Cong] in a streetcar!" As for her three colleagues who died, he shrugged, saying, "Unpleasant things do happen in a war."

The most tragic victims of this lethal Cold War game of Germans against Germans acted out in Southeast Asia were of course South Vietnamese civilians who were deprived of doctors and nurses to heal their wounds and give love to orphaned children. Soon after the Viet Cong had kidnapped the medical personnel of the Knights of Malta clinic in An Hoa, they tried to overrun a nearby combat base of the 5th U.S. Marines. I arrived in An Hoa while the battle was still raging.

"You are a German journalist?" asked the regimental G-2 (intelligence officer). "Then you must go over to the German clinic just two kilometers down the road; your people are in real trouble there. Actually, there is only one doctor left."

He assigned me a jeep and a driver who took me to a ruin that, until the previous night, had been a neat little medical center. Outside, a long line of Vietnamese civilians waited for admission, some with limbs missing, some with grievous head injuries, some with their dead children in their arms, all casualties of the Communist attack.

Inside a young German doctor was working frantically to save lives. On a makeshift operating table I saw an unconscious woman with her bowels spilling out of a huge wound on her left side.

"Are you a doctor?" he asked.

"No, a journalist."

"Never mind, I need help now. There's nobody left here to give me a hand. The VC kidnapped them all. Go wash your hands over there, put on some surgical gloves and make yourself useful."

In order to put the woman's organs back in their place, he had to cut her belly open. Then he needed an extra pair of hands to first push her innards back into the open wound on her left side. That was my job!

As we were busy with this patient, a team of Marine medical officers entered the room. They had just finished tending to their wounded and were now ready to help their exhausted German colleague.

A quarter-century later, I attended the morning conference of a high-brow Berlin daily newspaper where I worked as an editorial consultant. My job was to help its editors and publishers modernize this fuddy-duddy publication in the hope that it would become the leading broadsheet of the capital of reunified Germany.

That morning the discussion turned to topics for feature stories from the former East Germany.

"Here is an idea," I said, "How about producing an in-depth report on the East German manufacturers of PPM-2 mines, the remnants of whose victims I saw all over Route 19 in Vietnam? How about searching East German archives for material about the propaganda mill that accused West Germany of complicity in the Vietnam War, probably resulting in the death of our doctors and nurses in Vietnam?"

Oh, did I step into a hornet's nest by suggesting this! I might as well have spoken well of Hitler. This was not supposed to be a left-wing paper, but several of its smug younger editors became so irate that I wondered if Communist East Germany had really disappeared. So much had the ideology of the 1968 student movement that glorified Ho Chi Minh taken root among that generation of German university graduates that any suggestion of inhuman behavior on the Communist side was considered a heresy.

It didn't surprise me that the older editors, who should have known better, found it imprudent to come to my support. Lutheran theologian Dietrich Bonhoeffer once bemoaned the "dearth of civil courage" in his country when the Nazis were in power. At that editorial conference in the early 1990s I felt that this deficiency was definitely lingering on in certain places. This was one of my most disagreeable experiences with German colleagues in my entire journalistic career.

That evening, I entered my apartment with an ashen face. My wife told me that she had never seen me like that before. Being British, she knew a remedy: a stiff whisky, and another one, and then a third.

Gloriously inebriated, I spurted out something I had never thought I was capable of saying: "Could it be, Gillian, that the wrong people were reunified the right way?"

"Sleep it off, darling," she said, "You'll feel better in the morning."

And so I did. "Of course, I don't really believe that we Germans didn't deserve to be reunified peacefully," I said, "But since yesterday's editorial conference, I know what can make people feel that way."

Perry Kretz

Capt. Helmut Bubbel (left) preparing for a sortie.

Perry Kretz

Mission accomplished: Capt. Bubbel (right)
returning to aircraft carrier USS Coral Sea.

Chapter Thirteen

Prelude to Têt

*T*ết *1968 will be uneventful,* my Saigon sources assured me when I contacted them during my Christmas break at my new home in Hong Kong. They said that both sides would call a seven-day ceasefire from January 27 until February 3, enabling the Vietnamese to celebrate the dawn of the Year of the Monkey. Good! This allowed me to take a brief leave of absence from Vietnam and turn my attention to another part of my territory. I was after all my employers' "Far Eastern correspondent," which meant that in theory I was to cover most of Asia, though the constant changes of events in Vietnam obliged me to neglect even its next-door neighbors. Now I had an opportunity to even out this deficit.

I went to Laos.

I was looking forward to this trip, which I hoped to be an excursion into a less intense theater, not that the "Land of a Million Elephants" didn't have its own nasty war to keep an eye on. But Laos was a mellow, pleasant, though slightly goofy place filled with placid citizens who were less highly-strung, but to my mind also less intriguing, than the Vietnamese. They had a benign king by the name of Sri Savang Vatthana who had learned every Marcel Proust novel by heart, or so I was told; a few years later the Communists interred this gentle monarch, his wife, his son, the crown prince, and his brothers in the hellish "Reeducation Camp Number One," where he is thought to have died one year later.

Laos was also richly endowed with adolescent Buddhist monks who were definitely no radicals. After sundown they slunk about the grounds of their pagodas, smoking cigarettes and pinching the bottoms of Western female visitors tenderly, which, I believe, enticed many women to stroll around these holy grounds in the cool of the evening!

I once asked the abbot of a large pagoda in Vientiane why he and most of his colleagues at the helm of Laotian monasteries were imported clerics from Thailand. "Well, young man," he answered, "Laos does not seem to produce serious Buddhist scholars."

Getting to Laos was half the fun. Not having to fly to Vientiane spared me the irritation of wartime airports, which always made arrivals at Tan Son Nhut in Saigon an ordeal. Instead, I took the leisurely sleeper train from Bangkok to Nong Khai in northeastern Thailand. In those days there was no bridge connecting Nong Khai with Vientiane, the administrative capital of Laos on the other side of the Mekong, and so I was treated to a marvelously hilarious border crossing.

After my arrival at Nong Khai station early in the morning, I chartered two pedicabs, one for myself and another one for my luggage. We glided past mendicant monks in saffron-colored cowls on our way to a structure resembling the airline terminal of a Western city. It featured porters, immigrations and customs booths staffed with officious and crisply uniformed public servants, plus ticket counters fit for handling Boeing 707 passengers. I purchased an airline-style ticket, checked in my suitcases, and proceeded to the waiting area.

Eventually, my ferry's departure was announced. I went to the gate and what did I see outside? Rickety, shaky, slippery steps leading down a muddy embankment to an "international ferry" for which the Thais and Laotians had built architecturally pretentious terminals on the Mekong's southern and northern shores. The boat looked as if it had been designed by the British cartoonist William Heath Robinson and was propelled by the diesel engine of a retired pre-World War II London bus. It was an alarmingly leaky vessel but Eban, my Ivy-League traveling companion, assured me that the 15-minute trip across the river was too short for this boat to sink.

"I know, I know, Eban," I said, "I have been on this floating coffin before, and I can swim. Still, I wouldn't like to be bitten by a poisonous water snake."

"Or eaten by Penis Head Fish roaming these muddy waters," he continued my sentence. Both of us laughed moronically; we had drunk too much during the previous night.

I met Eban in the train's dining car, which offered Thai whisky, appropriately called *Mekong,* for only three dollars per 70-centiliter bottle. Eban had been an agricultural advisor to Laotian farmers before being promoted to a senior USAID position based in the Philippines. Now he was embarking on an inspection of his former place of work.

"When I was stationed in Laos, my job was to teach farmers in one particular area how to produce two rice harvests every year," he told me with a wry smile. "This has turned out to be a frustrating but funny business."

"Why frustrating?" I asked.

"Well, when I returned to the same area last year, I found the farmers frolicking or snoozing under shady trees, while their fields lay fallow."

"It seems your agricultural wisdom did not impress them," I taunted him.

"I must have made an impression on them, though," Eban replied. "I shook the village chief awake and asked: 'Did I not teach you last year how to produce two harvests?' The chief smiled and answered, 'O yes, you did, and we are very grateful. We had two harvests last year. So now we don't need a harvest this year.' With that he dozed off again."

Eban and I parted ways in Vientiane. As a high-powered civil servant he checked into the antiseptic western-style Lan Xang Hotel on the banks of the Mekong, where American officials and media pundits liked to stay because it offered air conditioning, an international cuisine, and a swimming pool.

I, on the other hand, preferred the spooky ambiance of the *Hôtel Constellation* on dusty downtown *Rue Samsenthai*, which featured in John Le Carré's spy thriller *The Honourable Schoolboy*. There was no air conditioning in my $25-room, just a ceiling fan and a mosquito net above my bed, a cold-water shower, a bidet, a toilet, and a window overlooking not the Mekong, but a duck pond. The *Constellation* resembled the simple French country inns, most of which have since sadly fallen victim to modernity. The *Constellation's* cuisine matched its setting: sturdy French fare accompanied by chilled *Beaujolais* wine in pop-top cans, but always served at the innkeeper's insistence with an immaculate white napkin slung over the waiter's right wrist.

"Welcome back! Your favorite dish is on the menu today," said Maurice Cavaliere, the *Constellation's* proprietor as the taxi dropped me off at lunchtime, "*Pigeon rôti aux Petits Pois!* I found very good pigeons in the market this morning, fresh and succulent!"

Chain-smoking Maurice was one of my favorite characters in all of Indochina. Born in Kunming, the son of a French botanist and a Chinese noblewoman and a graduate of the prestigious *École Supérieure de Commerce"* in Paris, he was more than just a great hotelier: he was also a reliable source of information, and for good reason. The *Constellation* was the watering hole of a most eclectic crowd of people. There were spies from all over the world, including a luscious Chinese woman in her early forties whom regulars at Maurice's bar knew to be in the employ of Mao Zedong's régime at the height of the Great Proletarian Cultural Revolution; her French colleagues told me that it was her job to seduce American spooks and flyboys and spy on them in compromising situations right there, at the *Constellation*, perhaps in the room next to mine.

There were German veterans of the French Foreign Legion on obscure missions. There were smugglers and cops and many pilots on perilous assignments. Of the 24-odd airlines operating out of Laos, only one, *Royal Air Lao*, was a legitimate carrier. Another, *Air America*, was owned and operated by the CIA and flew the most daredevil missions, including bombing raids on the

Ho Chi Minh Trail. I once foolishly had an *Air America* helicopter drop me under heavy fire into a mountaintop base of a Laotian tribe allied with the United States. Amazingly, the chopper returned the next morning, still under heavy enemy fire, to get me safely back to Vientiane. These were the bravest men I ever met—and I met them all at Maurice's bar.

There were 20-odd other "charter" airlines shuttling between the Golden Triangle in the Thai-Laotian-Burmese tri-border area and Vientiane, Saigon and destinations beyond. At one point I covered the strange encounter between one of these planes and the *Royal Air Force* over an outer island of Hong Kong. The RAF forced the alien intruders to land in what was then a British Crown Colony. The plane was registered in Laos; on board the British airmen found huge amounts of gold destined to be dropped over a rendezvous point off Hong Kong and picked up by a junk; gold smuggling was big business in Laos then, and its operators and pilots got drunk telling great stories at the bar of Maurice Cavalière's *Hôtel Constellation.*

Maurice brought me a *Pastis,* a refreshing anise-flavored liqueur that turns milky with the addition of water and is the perfect aperitif for the tropics.

"It gives me pleasure to have you stay with us again. But why *are* you here. Shouldn't you be in Saigon?" he asked.

"Occasionally I do have to produce copy from other parts of my territory, Maurice, and this seems as good a time as any," I said. "The Americans told me they didn't expect any trouble during the truce that will begin tomorrow."

"Well, I don't know. Do you trust their information? Do they still know what they are talking about? We get different intelligence here, and it is quite troubling," said Maurice. "But check with Mee. She really has her ears to the ground. I've taken the liberty to tell her that you were coming. She'll have dinner with you here tonight. Is that alright with you?"

"Very much so, thanks!!

"Pigeon for two then," Maurice said with a chuckle and turned to the other guests at his bar.

So I was going to see Mee again, and that was good news. Mee was not her real name. I just chose it from a list of Akha tribal names as a *nom de guerre* for this strange and fierce beauty I had met a couple of years earlier.

The bizarre beginning of our friendship merits a lengthy flashback to a late Thursday afternoon in the monsoon season and the wild days that followed. I sat in the *Constellation's* lounge putting my notes in order. To keep the rain out, Maurice had shut the French windows on the Rue Samsenthai side of his hotel. Suddenly, crash, bang, wallop, a strange object broke through the door violently, shattering its glass and wooden frame. It turned out to be a leather-clad creature resembling a curvaceous *boudin noir* (blood sausage) in the saddle of a Harley Davidson.

She stopped at the bar. She yelled, "*Maurice, mon Pastis s'il te plaît!*" Utterly unperturbed, with his *Gitane* cigarette dangling from his lower lip, Maurice handed her the potent aperitif. As she drank I noticed a strange tattoo on the top of her left hand. Then she went into reverse gear, a unique feature of Harley Davidson motorbikes, backed her machine away from the bar, glass crunching under her tires, and roared off into the tropical downpour.

"Maurice, *what* on earth was that?" I asked.

"That was Mee," he replied with a shrug, "She comes every Thursday evening for her *Pastis* when she is in town. I forgot it is Thursday."

"And?"

"And what?"

"What about your shattered French windows?" I wanted to know.

"Oh that! She'll send over a couple of people to clean up the mess and repair the damage first thing in the morning. I'll just lower my metal shutters now and call it a day. There won't be any more guests on a rainy night like this. Let's have dinner in the back room."

"Who is Mee?" I asked Maurice while we were eating.

"An amazing woman; very, very rich and still only in her mid-thirties. She is a retired freelance opium courier! Until last year she owned a large truck and regularly drove it *by herself* loaded with opium from the Golden Triangle (a poppy-growing region in the Thai-Laotian-Burmese tri-border area) across Laos and the Ho Chi Minh Trail into South Vietnam."

"Was she never stopped?" I inquired.

"I am sure she was, but she had her way to pacify nosey officials. She invited them to the top of her cargo and persuaded them that what they smelled was not opium," said Maurice with a deadpan face.

"But opium reeks, how could they miss it?"

"*Cher ami*, she *is* a very beautiful woman, haven't you noticed?"

"I have, Maurice, and I'll be at your bar next Thursday."

"I'll leave my new door open, rain or shine."

"One more thing, Maurice," I went on. "What is that weird tattoo on her left hand all about?"

"Ah, that's an Akha tribal mark. She belongs to the ferocious Akha, a mountain people living in the Golden Triangle, though her mother is a Meo, also called Hmong. Most Akha are illiterate, so is Mee."

"But, Maurice, I just heard her speak French to you!"

"Yes, she speaks French, plus a dozen other languages, even German. She likes Germans, having been in the arms of a Foreign Legionnaire or two in her day. But she can't read or write any language; that's not part of the Akha upbringing. Yet she is very intelligent. As you might have noticed, she is also rather tall for a mountain tribeswoman."

"Like Charlemagne! He was multilingual, illiterate, willful, bright, and very tall," I interjected.

Maurice burst out laughing: *"Félicitations* (congratulations)! Charlemagne! You just coined the perfect nickname for that imperious lady!" He popped open another can of *Beaujolais*. The Sino-French hotelier in Laos and his German guest ended the day lifting their glasses to honor a 9th-century emperor.

The following Thursday the door was open. I was at the bar at cocktail time. She rode in on her Harley, stopped next to me, engine running and placed her order: *"Maurice, mon Pastis, s'il te plaît!"* Then she noticed me and asked:

"Qui êtes vous?" — Who are you?

"Un journaliste allemand." A German journalist.

"Warum sitzen Sie dann hier herum statt sich auf dem Lande umzusehen, wo viel passiert?" she told me off in German: Why are you hanging around here instead of looking around the countryside where so much is happening?

"To meet you, Mee. I watched you crash through the French windows last week."

"Ah yes," she replied. "That was quite wild, wasn't it? Be ready tomorrow morning at seven. I'll pick you up for a ride."

With that, Mee went into reverse and left the bar.

Punctual like a Prussian, she arrived at the *Constellation* at seven o'clock sharp and beckoned me to sit behind her. As we roared off in a northeasterly direction, I clung to her leathery waist, indulging in the scent of her black ponytail flapping against my face. She had obviously washed her thick mane that morning with a very expensive French shampoo.

What happened during this wild two-day outing is a different story for a different day, except to say that we visited areas in Eastern Laos controlled by three competing armies: the royalists, the neutralists, and the Communist Pathet Lao. All three welcomed Mee, whom they obviously knew well, and tolerated me because she introduced me not as a journalist but as her lover from Europe, which, in truth, I was not and would never become. But this turned out to be a useful white lie. At the Pathet Lao post we were warned to go no further lest we risk falling into North

Vietnamese hands. "The North Vietnamese are not very nice people," the Pathet Lao officer told Mee, ogling at her leather-covered curves lustfully.

"It's getting dark, Mee," I said as we drove back.

"You are right. It's too dangerous to return to Vientiane tonight," she replied.

"So where are we going to sleep?"

"On the porch of that house on stilts over there."

"Do you know the owners?" I asked.

"No. We just go there and unroll our sleeping mats. That's what these porches are there for. Hospitality to strangers is a Laotian tradition."

So we stopped at the farmhouse. Mee asked me to help her carry her duffle bag, two sleeping mats, light blankets and mosquito nets. An old lady came out of the house and brought us two bowls of chicken and rice with a pot of tea, which we used to clean our teeth after the meal.

Mee had brought along two pop-top cans of *Beaujolais* to accompany dinner. Before she shed her leather gear to crawl under her blanket, she dug into her duffle bag again and produced two Colt 0.45-inch pistols, handing me one of the guns. "It is always good to have one of these by your bedside, just in case we get surprise visitors tonight," she said and throwing me a kiss, she fell asleep.

We arrived at her walled-in compound in the center of Vientiane at mid-day. In the courtyard I made out an E-Type Jaguar and a brand-new black Mercedes 280. Mee directed me to a luxurious bathroom to take a shower; a servant brought me a fresh shirt and fresh underwear.

When I came out she had changed into a plain shirt and jeans. "Please stay for lunch," she said guiding me to a large but sparsely furnished dining room, the most memorable feature of which was its floor covered with blackish tiles. During the beautifully prepared French meal served by a uniformed butler, she asked me point-blank:

179

"What do you think an Akha-Meo-German baby would look like?"

"Probably very pretty," I replied.

"We could have one. I am only 35. I would love to have children. Would you like to marry me?"

"But, Mee, I *am* happily married, and I love my wife."

"That can be taken care of with one or two of those," she said coolly, pointing at the tiles on the floor.

"What, slay her with a tile?"

"No, no, no! Buy her out! These tiles are pure gold. I used to be in the gold trade, you know. These are my savings," she said making circular motions with her arms to indicate that all her floors were covered with this precious metal.

Well, in Asia it is bad form to say "no" outright and it might have been a dangerous thing to do, given Mee's fierce nature. So I answered evasively: "I must discuss this with Gillian first."

"You do that, *lieber Freund* (dear friend)," she responded with a smile. "My driver will take you back to the *Constellation* now."

When I told Gillian about this episode, she said, hopefully in jest: "You should have accepted: imagine, two bricks of gold! We could have divorced and remained lovers."

As it turned out, Gillian and I stayed married, and I gained a fascinating friend in Laos. We saw each other every time I visited Vientiane, but the question of siring an Akha-Meo-German amalgam never came up again. I thought about this spectacular episode in my life with a grateful smile as I dressed for my pigeon dinner with Mee on that Saturday, the 27th of January 1968, the day the Têt ceasefire in Saigon commenced. In retrospect, it became the day when my career as a journalist was saved.

Mee arrived at the *Constellation* in her Jaguar E-Type, looking magnificent in her white dress with blue polka dots, which she had just brought back from a "business trip" to Bangkok, as she told me while having her *Pastis*.

"I didn't expect you here this time of the year," she said, "You are a reporter. Shouldn't you be in Saigon for Têt?"

I told her what my American sources had said. She sighed, "It is frightening to see how confused the Americans have become. This is scary for those of us not wanting to live under Communism. My sources predict that something horrific is going to happen in Vietnam over Têt. But I have an idea: check with the French in Paksong. Go tomorrow. I'll announce you to their commanding officer."

Paksong was the coffee capital of Laos at the Bolaven Plateau in the Laotian Panhandle. Because of its refreshing climate the French Military Advisory Mission to the Royal Lao Army had established a comfortable rest and recuperation camp there for its officers. As I was to discover, it was also an important French listening post given its proximity to the Ho Chi Minh Trail, the westernmost branches of which were only 40 miles away from the French R & R center.

After dinner Mee called Paksong and told me, "The major is expecting you tomorrow for lunch. I'll drive you to the airport first thing in the morning. You'll fly to Pakse, rent a car at the airport, and drive 50 kilometers east. It's an easy trip."

In the morning at Vientiane airport, she gave me a warm hug and said, "I really do believe you should be in Saigon now. Call me from Paksong as soon as you know more."

I can't remember the French major's name. He briefed me well about the Ho Chi Minh Trail, and then assigned me a room above the Center's entrance. I woke in the middle of the night hearing Vietnamese voices below my window. One was a woman's voice belonging to the Center's Vietnamese housekeeper. The other voice was male, grating, and thoroughly unpleasant.

I heard him say repeatedly, "*Mỹ*," meaning American. She replied, "*Báo Chí Đức*," meaning German journalist. The two squabbled agitatedly for a while, clearly about me, and I fell asleep again.

The next morning at breakfast, the major told me: "We had a visitor last night."

"I know, I heard him. He sounded like a North Vietnamese talking to your housekeeper about me," I said.

"Indeed, about you and some other things I can't talk to you about. You are of course welcome to stay here as long as you wish, but if I were a journalist I would hurry back to Saigon. That's where the big story is going to be."

By that time I had been around French military and intelligence types long enough to heed the major's advice without any further argument. These people were better informed about the former French Indochina than anybody else.

I called Mee to tell her I was returning to Vientiane that evening. "Do you know anyone at the South Vietnamese embassy?"

"All of them. What do you need?"

"I must renew my visa and I fear that the embassy will be closed tomorrow in anticipation of Têt," I said.

"You are right. They will be closed, but that's not a problem a $100 donation in an envelope with New Years' greetings couldn't solve. I'll fix this for you. All you have to contribute is a crisp $100 note."

She picked me up at Vientiane Airport, drove me to the *Constellation* and sent her chauffeur to the South Vietnamese vice consul's home the next morning to take him to his office, where Mee and I were already waiting in her E-Type with my passport and the envelope including my $100 note.

The vice consul gave me my visa. I wished him *"hạnh phúc têt,"* meaning, happy New Year.

"Let's hurry," said Mee, "Your *Royal Air Lao* plane to Bangkok leaves in a little over an hour. You are booked on the last *Air Vietnam* flight from Bangkok to Saigon tonight. Here's your ticket."

At the airport I reimbursed her for the fare and embraced her.

"Maybe I shouldn't have done this. You are flying into hell. I don't want you to get killed," she told me in an uncharacteristic emotional outburst.

I gave her a kiss and boarded my plane. In Bangkok I ran into my teammate Friedhelm Kemna, who worked exclusively for *Die Welt* but not for the other *Axel Springer* papers, although we filled in for each other when one of us was "on the road."

"What are you doing here? You are supposed to be in Laos," he said.

"The French and my Lao friends told me that something big was going to happen in Vietnam. And you? Weren't you supposed to hold the fort in Hong Kong?"

Kemna, a bachelor in his forties who had served as a young German cavalry lieutenant in World War II, gave me a sheepish look and said, "Sometimes my desire for European women gets the better of me. Pan American has beautiful German stewardesses and they always stay in the *Siam Intercontinental*. So I had a little outing to Bangkok."

"And were you also warned of a big crisis in Saigon?"

"Yes, at the German embassy," he said. "That's why I am also booked on the last plane to Tan Son Nhut today."

When we arrived, hundreds of thousands of Vietnamese were in the streets. We were later told that nearly half a million had come out to enjoy the first evening without a curfew. Firecrackers detonated all around us as a taxi took us to the *Continental Palace*.

I was too exhausted to go out to dinner. With the noise of firecrackers in my ears, I fell asleep. When I awoke a few hours later in the middle of the night, it became clear that my American sources had been woefully wrong prognosticators and Maurice, Mee and the French major in Paksong dead right: Nothing was uneventful about Têt 1968 in South Vietnam and, thanks to Maurice, Mee and the major, I did not commit the massive blunder of missing the Têt Offensive that started while I was in bed that night—in Saigon.

While the war peaked in Vietnam, the King's Palace in Luang Prabang, the royal capital of neighboring Laos, still seemed like a pocket of peace.

Chapter Fourteen

Têt 1968: Saigon

I woke shortly after three in the morning, growling at the Têt revelers: "Isn't it time for you to go home?" But when I went over to the window and looked down at Lam Son Square I was amazed: there wasn't a human soul where, a few hours earlier, tens of thousands had welcomed the Year of the Monkey. Even the *White Mice*, Saigon's policemen, were gone; only rats scurried about. I realized that what I was hearing was not the sound of firecrackers but the rat-tat-tat of automatic rifle fire—and not somewhere out there across the Saigon River, but right in town within walking distance from my hotel.

I put on a pair of jeans and a dark-colored polo shirt, and took my steel helmet and flak jacket from my aluminum trunk the hotel staff had brought to my room from the *Continental's* basement. As I came downstairs, the lobby was filling up with people who would not normally have been there so early: receptionists, telephone operators, room boys, kitchen staff, waiters, and American contractors with their paid companions.

"Ne sortez pas! VC! Couvre feu!" the night watchman, a wizened French-speaking Indian from Madras, urged me: don't go out! Viet Cong! There's a curfew on.

"The curfew does not apply to me because I am an accredited correspondent," I said, "I must go outside to see what's going on."

He unlocked the door and I quickly turned right and then right again. I walked up Tu Do Street in a northwesterly direction following the increasingly angry sound of a nearby firefight. Commonsense made me stay close to walls. The streetlights were turned off. At first I felt chillingly alone until a gut feeling told me that somebody might be watching me. I ducked, walking warily in measured steps lest hasty movements drew unwelcome attention. Fearing that my white face might betray me in this terrifying darkness, I turned it away from the street and faced toward the facades of the buildings on Tu Do, and edged sideways like a crab.

At the first intersection, I quickly glanced over to the opposite side on my left. There was the *Café La Pagode*, where *Mamasan*, Đức's boss, normally squatted next to her pile of newspapers. Where was Đức now, I wondered? Was he alive? Was he an ARVN soldier—or a Viet Cong? The last time I saw him was eighteen months before when he accompanied me to the Naval hospital in Cholon.

Something made me glance up at the floors above *La Pagode*. Did I see shadowy figures scampering on the roof, or was this just my imagination? If so, were these Viet Cong snipers? This question continued to trouble me as I scuttled block by block toward *Notre Dame* Cathedral, turning around and scanning roofs and sidewalks quickly at brief intervals.

Had Viet Cong fighters been there they might either not have seen me or just not opened fire on a solitary figure so as not to make their presence known prematurely. I wasn't taking chances. I turned sharp right, still hugging walls. At the next intersection, I ran across the street as fast as I could and turned left. Then I was on Hai Ba Trung. Still ducking and hugging buildings, I approached a scene of battle. I wasn't alone anymore. Others moved in my direction, all staying on the sidewalks close to the houses. I made out the familiar voices of colleagues and the whispers of strangers in French or English spoken with a British accent.

Arriving on Thong Nhut Boulevard, I felt, as so often in Saigon, as if someone had dropped me on a stage of the Theatre of the Absurd during a particularly demented scene. To my right, soldiers of the Royal Gurkha Rifles had taken up position in full battle mode behind the gates of the British Embassy, the protection of which was their responsibility. Across the avenue I witnessed a bizarre spectacle: a helicopter trying repeatedly to land on the roof of the six-story U.S. embassy; again and again automatic weapons fire from within the compound fought it off.

Viet Cong sappers had blown a hole into the wall surrounding this four-acre terrain. They held the chancery grounds until eighteen of them were killed and one captured in a battle lasting hours, taking the lives of three American marines and two military policemen, all outgunned by the Communists. A chopper swooped down, dropping three cases of M-16 ammunition in an effort to resupply American security people as they were shooting it out with the Viet Cong. Then it transpired that not a single M-16 existed in the chancery for which these munitions were intended.

I scanned the spectators lining the sidewalk on my side of Thong Nhut Boulevard, and my cartoonist's mind kicked in, just as it had done in my high school days, always at the most inappropriate moment. Then I had developed a passion for drawing caricatures of my mathematics teacher—during tests, which I inevitably failed. This time, my passion for comics found an entirely different target: in my head I sketched the hilarious contrast between neatly placed civilian feet and the military chaos across the road.

Next to me I spotted a pair of feet in woolly socks and leather sandals, and I thought, "This can only be a German!" With the sound of the firefight across the street in my ears, my eyes scanned the stranger from his flip-flops on up. I pinched myself. "Am I having a bizarre dream?" I wondered. What I saw was German uniform trousers, topped by a German officer's jacket with a badge identifying the wearer as a helicopter pilot. His epaulettes were garnished by one silver pip framed by two silver oak leaves. A peaked officer's cap completed the picture: in the midst of combat in central Saigon I stood next to a German major in sandals. As it turned out, he was the assistant West German defense attaché.

"Neue Kleiderordnung, Herr Major?" I asked him: new dress code, major?

"Wie meinen Sie das?" he shot back: what do you mean?

I pointed to his feet and said: *"Uniform, Wollsocken, Sandalen."* Uniform, socks and sandals!

"Gucken Sie sich gefälligst Ihre eigenen Füße an," he retorted: Look at your own feet.

I did, and saw a sorry sight: below my helmet, flak jacket and jeans, I saw a pair of feet covered in coagulated blood and stuck in blue shower sandals made of rubber. I hadn't even noticed that I was injured, probably by flying glass.

"Nur Tarnung, Herr Major," I replied: just camouflage! We both laughed.

Our mirth drew the attention of other bystanders who joined in, unaware that the topic of our jollity was footwear. They laughed because they assumed that we, too, were reacting to the tragic absurdity of what we were witnessing on the other side of the street.

"I thought you were in Laos," said a British journalist, "What brought you here?"

I told him that I had followed the advice of Maurice, Mee, and the French major in Paksong to return to Saigon for Têt.

"They were right," commented the Englishman shaking his head. "It's unfathomable. An innkeeper, a retired opium courier, and a French officer in Laos knew what was coming. The South Vietnamese military knew it too. Gen. Cao Van Vien, the ARVN chief of staff, knew. Three days ago, he ordered the corps commanders to place their troops on alert. But American military spokesmen in Saigon seemed to be blissfully ignorant about the Viet Cong intentions."

"You are right about Gen. Cao," said the German major, "He gave this order after the ARVN had captured, in Qui Nhon, eleven Viet Cong officers carrying audiotapes containing a pre-recorded address to be broadcast to the people of the 'liberated' cities of Saigon, Da Nang and Huê, presumably today."

"Two days ago, I was at a pre-Têt poolside party with 200 MACV intelligence specialists," the English reporter continued, using the acronym for U.S. Military Assistance Command

Vietnam. "Nobody there seemed to have a clue that the Communist offensive was imminent."

It was by now daybreak. Bit by bit we learned astonishing details of what had transpired on that battle torn piece of real estate. There was a particularly dramatic scene at a villa housing George Jacobson, a special adviser to Ambassador Ellsworth Bunker. Aware that a Communist fighter had entered this house, Jacobson rushed to his bedroom window, shouting at a GI below, "Throw me a gun."

Thus armed, Jacobson confronted the Viet Cong soldier pointing the gun at him. A life-and-death scuffle between the two men ensued. Eventually Jacobson managed to shoot the stranger. An American reporter came by to tell us that Gen. William Westmoreland, the commander of U.S. forces in South Vietnam, was about to show up at the embassy, however, I couldn't wait because I had to file my story. As I returned to the *Continental Palace,* I saw sporadic house-to-house fighting in the side streets, which were covered with bodies. I ran for my life. Sharpshooters popped up suddenly at one spot, fired a few rounds, then disappeared just as quickly only to surface again at a different place, thus creating an illusion of omnipresence and unpredictability. In my own story, written on January 31, 1968, I read, "The shootings took place only meters from my hotel."

The *Continental's* elegant lobby looked like a refugee camp. Droves of foreign residents of the Saigon districts stricken by the Viet Cong offensive were seeking shelter. Some called loudly for food because there was nothing to eat in the capital where all bakeries, shops, and restaurants were closed, but Monsieur Loi, the *Continental's* general manager, announced that the hotel had barely enough supplies to feed its registered guests.

In the midst of this pandemonium, young Baron Hasso Rüdt von Collenberg stood out as a model of composure. This pale and boyish-looking first secretary at the German embassy was an incredibly brave man. Journalists loved him for his dry sense of humor and analytical mind. By the time we ran into each other in the lobby of the *Continental Palace* he had been up most of the night driving around in his white *Volkswagen* in order to bring German citizens to safety.

He had arranged temporary lodgings for Arno Knöchel, his Vietnamese wife and their ten children. Knöchel, a former staff corporal in the Foreign Legion, was the factotum of the West German embassy. He was squatting in its courtyard, which was a woefully unsafe place, given the embassy's location at the edge of Cholon, Saigon's embattled Chinatown. It had taken von Collenberg three trips, ducking sniper fire, to ferry the 12 Knöchels to the city center.

"The Viet Cong have kidnapped our doctors in Huế and also Prof. Otto Söllner, a conductor heading the National Conservatory there," said von Collenberg as he made his way out the *Continental's* teeming lobby, "We don't know anymore than this. Will you be going there?"

"As soon as I can catch a military flight to Da Nang, maybe tomorrow," I answered, "From there I'll hitch a ride on a military convoy to Huế."

"Good luck! I hear that Huế is completely in the hands of the Viet Cong," von Collenberg told me.

"I will try to attach myself to an American or South Vietnamese unit fighting its way back into the city."

"Be careful—and keep me informed," he pleaded.

"I'll do my best. I know they are friends of yours," I promised.

"Yes, I stayed with them so often when visiting Huế. They are such cultured and decent people. They gave up so much in Germany to help the Vietnamese. Actually, they were supposed to go home but extended their tour of duty over here. They told me they had fallen in love with Vietnam and its people and didn't want to desert them. And now we don't know where they are or whether they are still alive."

"I'll contact you as soon as I can when I'm in Huế, this is a promise. Where will I find you?"

"At the embassy, even at night for the duration of this crisis. I have put up a camp bed in my office."

I went up to my room, showered and bandaged my wounded feet before writing my story. Just then, my teammate Friedhelm "Freddy" Kemna came in from the press center with a comprehensive account of the situation in the whole country: Some 80,000 Viet Cong and North Vietnamese troops had attacked 100 towns and cities in South Vietnam. President Nguyen van Thieu had declared martial law.

Freddy spread out a map of Saigon on my bed, encircled the worst trouble spots with a blue marker and said: "There's heavy fighting at the race track and at Tan Son Nhut; but I think the airport has by now been cleared. The VC attacked the ARVN and Navy headquarters near Tan Son Nhut, and the Presidential Palace but never managed to penetrate the perimeter. The good news is that the South Vietnamese mounted an effective defense and fought extremely well. The national radio station is still in Viet Cong hands, but the South Vietnamese cleverly cut the lines to the transmitters, so the VC can't use the station for propaganda purposes. The Fifth Arrondissement—Cholon—is the worst battleground. It's a mess..."

"Oh, my God!" I said.

"Why?"

"The Fifth Arrondissement! That's where Josephine lives!"

"So that fabulous woman is still on your mind, is she?" Freddy asked, "It's almost three years after you had split up. I thought she had married a Chinese grain merchant with a grand villa."

"Yes, she has, but I don't think she'll be at that villa. She is probably with her mother in her little house in the Fifth Arrondissement during Tết, and that has me worried."

"Let's eat something and then start writing," Freddy suggested. "Do you have food in this room?"

"I have brought some tins of German pumpernickel from Hong Kong, and I always keep C-rations. They include canned cheese. Let's have some bread and cheese, then."

We ate. Then I hit the keyboard with Freddy standing on my left side and filling in the details he had learned at the Press Center. Under a joint byline we wrote the Tết cover story with sidebars for *Die Welt,* and then I did additional pieces for my other papers.

Every time I finished two or three typewritten pages, Freddy grabbed the manuscript and rushed across the road to the Press Center where recently two telex lines to Manila had been installed—two for 600 accredited correspondents. There were three pretty and humorous telex operators, all three of them friends of mine because I had brought them bales of silk for new Áo dàis from Hong Kong.

"You have worked wonders with those ladies," said Freddy, beaming, when he came back. "There were two long lines of journalists waiting to file their copy, but these girls sneaked our manuscript right in before anybody else noticed. It's good to have friends in low places."

"Freddy, would you mind staying put, checking with the Press Center and updating our story, please? I must take a look around town."

"How?" Friedhelm Kemna yelled, "You don't have a car anymore. There are no taxis, no pedicabs, nothing!"

"There are ways," I answered. "Let me talk to the concierge. He is also a friend of mine."

I am embarrassed to say that I have forgotten the concierge's name if I ever knew it; like so many of his kind in well-run hotels, he was a gentleman of extraordinary character.

"Can you please find wheels for me?" I asked him.

"No and yes," he replied with a smile.

"What do you mean?"

"I say no because there are no civilian cars on the road today. But I say yes because you may use my Honda."

"But, I have never ridden a motorcycle before!"

"You can ride a bicycle, can't you? I'll teach you how to accelerate and brake. That's all you need to know."

He went to the courtyard, rolled out his Honda, started the engine, showed me how to shift gears and then watched as I drove off jerking forward like a grasshopper when releasing the clutch. The concierge never asked me for a rental fee or even a deposit for lending me his prize vehicle. Months later, I asked him, "Were you not worried that I might not return your Honda in one piece to you?"

"I figured that I had a fifty-fifty chance," he answered, "But you needed transportation there and then, and I wasn't sure I'd ever need a motorcycle again, given what had happened at Têt. So I felt it was the right thing to do to lend you mine."

It is remarkable how differently eyewitnesses remember world events, or rather, which aspects on these events remain foremost on their minds. I for one was deeply moved by the acts of basic humanity, generosity and bravery I witnessed on that first day of Têt 1968. Hasso Rüdt von Collenberg and the concierge provided two outstanding examples, but there were others. Today I am certain that I owe my life to the courage of ordinary Vietnamese who took great risks to protect me.

I knew the route to Josephine's house well, but this time it became a wild zigzag course around Viet Cong bodies and pockets of house-to-house combat. As I rode slowly through one eerily quiet street, staying close to the walls, an elderly man jumped at me from a doorway, knocked me off the Honda and held me down to the ground ordering me gently but firmly, "*Ne bougez pas!*"—don't move!

He crawled over to the motorcycle the wheels of which were still spinning in the air. He turned off its engine, came back and whispered, "VC," pointing to the windows of buildings further down the block. Then he pulled me inside his house, leaving the Honda where it was. Twenty minutes later he went outside again, came back and said, "VC gone. You can go now. But do use different street. This one is very dangerous."

Amazingly, the Honda was barely scratched. As I zigzagged on, I was warned three more times, twice by Vietnamese women and once even by children shouting, "VC, VC," in clear defiance of the Viet Cong's stated purpose of the Têt Offensive, which was to trigger a popular uprising against the Americans and their "Saigon puppets," as the Communists phrased it. From what I experienced, the offensive had the opposite effect. As the world learned later, nobody in all of South Vietnam followed the Communists' orders.

Josephine was standing at the gate of her mother's little house with a baby in her arms and her two sons from a previous marriage clinging to her pajama pants.

"I knew you were coming," she said.

"How?"

"I just knew. I can't explain."

"Are you alright?"

"Yes, now I am fine. We saw the Viet Cong outside our door. That was scary, but they didn't come in. Thank God the telephone is working. My husband called first thing this morning. He'll be here soon to take us to safety."

"Will he take you abroad, Josephine?"

"Yes, I think so, probably to Singapore. My husband is Chinese and is well connected in Singapore."

She turned briefly to the house, handed the children to her mother, and came back to say goodbye.

"*Comme la mer, comme le ciel*," she said softly, just as she had three years earlier while we were swimming off the *Baie des Cocotiers* in Cap St. Jacques: she loved me like the sea, like the sky. Then she went inside.

I never saw Josephine again.

Zigzagging back to the *Continental Palace*, I stopped by the Press Center to have my name placed on the manifest of a U.S. Air Force flight to Da Nang the following morning, if possible.

"How will I get to Tan Son Nhut?" I asked the desk sergeant.

"We'll pick you up at your hotel tomorrow at 0300 hours—tomorrow or the following day, whenever we have space available. We'll call you," he said.

In my room at the *Continental Palace* I bashed out another brief feature story before going out to dinner with Freddy. We wandered through deserted streets to the *Royal* and were not surprised to find it open; nothing could prevent old Ottavi from putting a meal on the table.

"All I can offer you is fresh artichokes from Dalat, some stale bread and my *Soufflé au Grand Marnier,*" he said.

"Fresh artichokes from Dalat! Where did you get artichokes from?" Freddy asked, "Dalat is in Viet Cong hands, isn't it?"

Ottavi smiled mysteriously and said, "Well, we have our ways."

Artichokes were my favorite vegetable in my Vietnam days, so much so that my English friends called me "Artichoke Charlie of Hamburg." Devouring six artichokes each, Freddy and I agreed that he would hold the fort in Saigon while I would travel "up-country" to Da Nang and Huê. Later we would reverse our roles to allow him to go to the Mekong Delta.

As it happened, I had to wait for a couple of days before I commenced what turned out to be the most traumatic journey of my professional life.

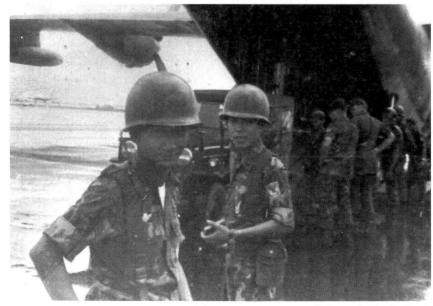

South Vietnamese Airborne soldiers on their way from
Saigon to Huế. They were instrumental in defeating the
Communists in the Tết Offensive.

Chapter Fifteen

Têt 1968: Inferno in Huế

Da Nang was a miserable place in early February 1968. It was cold and drizzly. I might as well have flown to a Northern European destination. The streets were deserted, except for military traffic. I had hoped to spend the night on the *Helgoland* in Da Nang in order to find out how the ship had fared during the Têt Offensive, and to eat some hearty German food, for I was starved. Since leaving Vientiane I had not had a square meal. But the *Helgoland* wasn't there. Wisely, the captain had taken her to the safety of international waters.

So I went to the MACV press compound, which lacked charm, but had a passable restaurant and a very good bar. I had a dry martini, ate a steak, drank a bottle of wine, took a hot shower, and felt ready for an adventure that afforded me none of these luxuries for a while. It was still dark when I joined a convoy of American Marines early in the morning. I wore two sets of jungle fatigues on top of each other, to which I would add a third before long, and I was grateful for the extra warmth my flak jacket gave me.

Several journalists from the press compound dared the perilous journey by road to the vicinity of the Communist-occupied imperial city. This was our best chance to get there quickly. The cloud ceiling was so low and the security situation around Phú Bài airport so unstable that we might have had to wait days for a seat on a military flight.

Before we were allowed to board a truck, we were each handed an M-16. "We know that this is against the rules," a sergeant major explained. He was alluding to the Geneva Convention that stipulated that war correspondents be unarmed. "But," he added, "We will be traveling through very dangerous terrain and could be ambushed. In that case you will have to defend yourselves. Here's your choice: carry a gun or stay behind."

We made it to Phú Bài south of Huế without incident, except for one scene that tickled my sense of irony. Next to me, on the back of the truck, sat a team of *Stern* magazine reporters: a photographer and a writer. The photographer was Hilmar Pabel, one of the most celebrated practitioners of his craft in German journalism, and a wonderfully seasoned old trooper. The picture of me on the cover of this book is his handiwork. Hilmar took it during a lull in the fighting in the old city of Huế.

His colleague, though, was another matter. He was a young Austrian writer steeped in the pestilential hard-left stereotypical thinking that poisoned Western Europe's intellectual life in those days and would culminate in the calamitous May 1968 student uprising in Paris, which in turn infected the entire continent and much of the rest of the western world.

His name was Peter Neuhauser. Aside from his Marxist ideology, he was actually a likable, burly fellow, not unlike the leathernecks with whom we traveled. That's why they loved him, being oblivious of his pro-Communist views. "You look like one of us. All you need is a haircut," they said. So when we arrived at the staging area of the Fifth Marines behind Phú Bài Airport, they yanked Peter into a tent, gave him a crew cut, shoved an M-16 in his hands and shouted with glee: "Behold our new gunnery sergeant!" From that moment on they called him "Gunny," and Peter, of all people, pro-Viet Cong Peter, seemed to enjoy his new status hugely, which showed in the photographs Hilmar Pabel took of him. This didn't help his career. The pictures of Neuhauser in a martial pose, along with more pertinent images of Pabel's films, ended up at *Stern* magazine's Hamburg head office a few days later, causing outrage among his peers who failed to see the humor in this. He was never sent on a foreign assignment again.

The next morning, as Peter and I accompanied a battalion of Marines battling its way inch by inch into Huế, he seemed to experience an epiphany of sorts, albeit a brief one. On the road into Vietnam's former imperial capital we saw scores of dead civilians, individuals and groups, women, old men and children, all elegantly dressed for the New Year. From the position of the bodies we could see that many women had been trying to shield the children with their own bodies against the killers.

"Your Communist buddies did this, Peter!" I told him cruelly.

He went white. "Surely not," he replied, "These people were killed by American airplanes."

"No, Peter, this is not what casualties of air raids look like," I retorted, "Look at these head wounds, look at these body injuries. Look at how some of these women had held up their hands protectively. They were shot at close range. Believe me, I have seen this before: This is the handiwork of killer squads. What we have here is evidence of a war crime. These people were liquidated for whatever crazy reason Communists might have to liquidate women, children and old men."

Peter Neuhauser fell silent but I knew I hadn't convinced him; he admitted as much when we next met months later in Hamburg. Neuhauser died a few years later of natural causes, still an unreconstructed leftist. Decades on, I feel occasional pangs of sorrow that even the sight of scores of murdered innocents on the road to Huế had not brought this otherwise pleasant young man to his senses. My days in his company taught me one of the most frightening lessons of this whole Têt episode: nothing, not even the most irrefutable evidence, can trump an ideologue's fixed ideas.

Phú Bài and Huế are only ten miles apart, but it took us almost a day to reach the MACV compound near the southeastern shore of the misnamed River of Perfumes. Sporadic fighting without air support, due to bad flying conditions and the need to clear the road of bodies, slowed us down. The compound was located in the new European section of the city, an area of broad boulevards with comfortable French villas, a charming *Cercle Sportif,* or sporting club, and a *Cité Universitaire,* with apartment buildings for faculty members built in the egregiously ugly 1950s-style of the low-cost housing projects littering the northern outskirts of Paris.

By the time we arrived, the Americans and South Vietnamese had brought this side of town under their control to some extent, at least during the day, while the Old Town with its imperial enclosure, or Purple City, which was patterned after the Forbidden City in Beijing, was still firmly in Communist hands.

The MACV compound consisted of a former hotel with a dining area on the ground floor, officers' billets on the upper two floors, and an annex with 20 suites. Next to the annex were the so-called hootches: open-bay structures for the enlisted men. The place was teeming with an eclectic assortment of people: military men, journalists, intelligence operatives, aid workers, Vietnamese employees of the Americans and civil servants plus their dependents who had found refuge here from the fighting and from Communist death squads that were still roaming the city looking for supposed counter-revolutionaries to be killed on sight.

"Sorry, guys, all bunks are taken, all blankets too. You gotta make ya'selves comfortable on this here concrete floor," said the quartermaster sergeant welcoming us to what used to be the dining area. "There are C-rations over there in the corner and lots of paper body bags to keep ya guys warm. Take as many as you want. It's gonna be cold tonight."

The compound was closed by nightfall. Nobody could come in, nobody could go out. We heard ferocious battles raging north of the river, but also occasional firefights just outside the compound's perimeter. I squeezed myself into a narrow space between Vietnamese families, spread out three body bags on the ground in lieu of a mattress, covered myself with three more body bags that were intended to transport fallen soldiers and bore markings showing where the head and the feet were to be placed. I used my knapsack as a pillow. My neighbors spoke French. In whispers they told me how on the day before Têt, Communist death squads had gone from door to door with lists containing the names of people to be tried before so-called people's tribunals and then summarily killed.

"Do you think the German professors were on those lists?" I asked the man on my right.

"They definitely were, just like the French priests and other foreigners who were also led away," he replied.

In the middle of the night, bursts of automatic arms fire in our immediate neighborhood woke us: rat-tat-tat, rat-tat-tat, rat-tat-tat, rat-tat-tat, rat-tat-tat.

"Executions," said the Vietnamese man on my right. "AK-47 Kalashnikov."

"How do you know?" I asked.

"This has become a familiar noise by now. What you heard was no firefight. These were five volleys from one automatic gun—very purposeful."

"How close was this?" I asked.

"No more than 100 meters away."

Forty years later, I befriended in southern California Di Tonthat, a member of Vietnam's extended imperial family. We discussed the events of Têt 1968 in Huế and discovered that his father, two uncles, and two cousins could have been the victims of this execution. Di's father, Nguyen Tonthat, had been the mayor of Dalat and later worked as a civil servant at the social security administration in Saigon, the offices with which I was familiar; they were next door to the *Café La Pagode* on Tu Do Street.

In January 1968, Nguyen Tonthat had flown to Huế to spend Têt with his brothers and nephews in their villa. Di and I studied a street map of Huế. "This is where the house was," he said, pointing to a spot not even 100 yards from the dining area of the MACV compound. "We only recovered the body of one of my uncles. We couldn't even bury my father."

Whether I was really an aural witness of their execution or of another murder I shall never know, but that moment stuck in my memory, primarily because it was followed by yet another of my many surreal experiences in Vietnam: something big, warm and quacking crept under my three body bags. It turned out to be a white goose with a yellow beak and grayish-black feathers on its wings. I have always loved geese, especially when roasted and served with red cabbage at Christmas. But I have never had a goose cuddle up to me before, and this one was seriously disturbed. Along with scores of Vietnamese refugees, this frightened bird had fled into the American compound at the beginning of the Têt Offensive and been waddling about the grounds ever since, sometimes inspecting the sleeping quarters. The GIs had named him Garfield. Being a watchful goose, Garfield took up an observation post every night, always at the same place and always looking out toward the street. But when he heard the bursts of gunfire right next door he took fright and sought cover next to me. I shooed him out of our bedroom back to his observation post.

At dawn, we journalists were allowed to leave the compound on condition that we carried an M-16 for our own protection. Peter Neuhauser, Hilmar Pabel and I each accepted one but, at my suggestion, deposited these guns disobediently with the sentry. We were on our way to the kidnapped German doctors' apartments. "Imagine if we run into a Viet Cong patrol carrying arms," I argued, "We'd be dead. Unarmed, we might at least claim the status of noncombatants, though I am not hopeful that this would mean anything to them."

Shivering in the cold drizzle, we walked west on Le Loi. This once elegant boulevard seemed deserted and looked in sorry shape. Its villas were pockmarked, its trees felled or mortally wounded. As we approached the *Cercle Sportif*, where I'd sometimes had dinner with the German professors, and where Elisabetha Krainick used to swim every day, I was vaguely hoping that a faithful servant might be there to make us coffee, but of course this was a foolish thought; there was nobody about—nobody except U.S. Marines racing past us in jeeps and armored vehicles. For a moment the cloud cover lifted, and we glanced across the River of Perfumes. We could see the Viet Cong flag—red and blue with a yellow five-pointed star in the center—flying over the citadel, and we could hear the sounds of furious combat.

The apartment building where the Krainicks lived overlooked the Phú Cam Canal, as did a U.S. tank parked on the estate's northern flank. Vroom! It fired off a round across the canal. Vroom! The whole building shook as we walked up to the Krainicks' place on the fourth floor. It had been taken over by an entire platoon of leathernecks and looked in a horrible mess. Clothing, books, scientific papers and private documents were strewn everywhere. To my horror, Peter Neuhauser pilfered through them and slipped some of the Krainicks' family photographs into his pocket.

"Have you no shame?" I asked him.

"That's what you have to do if you work for an illustrated magazine," he replied coolly and left.

The platoon leader was a stocky 23-year old second lieutenant from New Mexico. I knew at first sight that he was a fool, and he spoke like one. He pranced around in a white T-shirt, wearing neither a flak jacket nor a helmet. Vroom! The tank fired off another round.

"What is the tank shooting at?" I asked him.

The lieutenant took me to an open glass door leading to the balcony and pointed at an elaborate French-style villa on the other side of the canal:

"VC snipers," he said. "They are shooting at us."

"And you are standing there in a white T-shirt, presenting these guys with a perfect target?"

"Sir, I am a marine, we are trained to fight and die."

"Doesn't it cost the American taxpayer $500,000 to train a professional officer?" I challenged him. "Even if you don't have any fear for your own life, do you really think you should put such a big investment at risk gratuitously? Should you chance leaving your men leaderless?" He stared at me uncomprehending.

As I walked out through the front door and headed down the stairs, I heard a scream the like of which I had never heard before. It didn't sound human. I turned around. The lieutenant came staggering towards me holding the left side of his chest from which blood spewed. He stumbled, fell, rolled down the stairs and was dead. The snipers had got him.

I walked over to the university hospital where Professor Horst-Günter Krainick, Dr. Raimund Discher, and Dr. Alois Alteköster had worked. It was 75 percent destroyed by the fighting. Seeing my fatigues, most of the Vietnamese civilians avoided my eyes. They were too scared to be seen fraternizing with an "American," even though a badge on my helmet identified me as a West German journalist: West German, like the doctors who had founded the medical school. They obviously feared that the Communists might return and take revenge on people who had been seen "collaborating" with the enemy — people like me.

An older gentleman quietly pulled me to the side to tell me frightening stories of kangaroo trials by so-called people's tribunals. They were set up by the North Vietnamese. The accused were Huế residents belonging to the old aristocracy, the bourgeoisie, and the South Vietnamese civil service, as well as foreigners, active Roman Catholics, and priests; in short, anybody suspected of being unfavorably disposed to the revolution.

"They weren't arrested at random, Monsieur," he stressed, "Their names were on lists the Communist cadre carried with them. At the tribunals they were not given a chance to defend themselves. They were convicted, taken off and shot."

"How many?"

"Who can tell? Hundreds? Thousands?"

To this day no precise figure of victims is available. The estimates range from 2,500 to 6,000.

"The worst part of this offensive came when the fighting reached the psychiatric ward," continued the old man who never gave me his name or position, but he sounded like a French-educated academic. "The patients went wild, running amuck, attacking each other in their confusion. You can't imagine what it was like. Many died because they were incapable of escaping the crossfire. It was like a scene out of the Inferno in Dante's Divine Comedy."

"And where were you at that time?"

"Hiding among the patients, Monsieur, pretending to be one of them, which I wasn't, but it saved my life."

He advised me to walk over to the university's main auditorium, which was crammed with hundreds of homeless people, all still festively clad, all in various stages of bewilderment with blank expressions on their faces; many were injured, with very few nurses or doctors, if any, available to treat them. They had no running water, no electricity, and no sanitation facilities.

"Take a look at the *Lycée Quoc Hoc*, too," the old man had suggested, and this was sound advice. This beautiful high school on the southern bank of the River of Perfumes was one of the most splendid national institutions. Founded by Ngo Dinh Kha, the father of the South Vietnamese President Ngo Dinh Diem, in 1896 as an elite national academy, it was meant to give imperial princes and the sons of mandarins a blend of French and Far Eastern education. The alumni rolls read like a Who's Who in Vietnamese Politics, North or South. Ngo Dinh Diem attended it, as did Ho Chi Minh, née Nguyen Sinh Cung, as well as Gen. Vo Nguyen Giap and the North Vietnamese Prime Minister Phạm Văn Đồng, son of the highest-ranking mandarin. When I arrived at its campus, it looked like yet another refugee camp. Somebody told me that some 8,000 people had sought shelter on the school's luscious grounds, many shivering in the cold and waiting for food and water, although I was in no position to verify that number. It was huge.

On my way back to the MACV compound I spotted a telling graffito on the wall of a large villa. It read, *"cat dau mỹ,"* meaning: decapitate the Americans. As I looked more closely I noticed that the word, *mỹ* (American) had only recently replaced the term, *pháp* (French). I am jumping ahead of myself now, but this piece of information fits here: On my next visit to Huế a few weeks later, I happened across the same graffito again, and now it had been changed to *"cat dau cong,"* which translates into: cut the Communists' head off! This told me that the revulsion over the behavior of fellow Vietnamese had trumped any dislike of foreigners the burghers of Huế might have previously held, a xenophobia so strong that until Têt 1968 the Americans had kept an extremely low profile in this city. The 25-day battle of Huế, the shooting, clubbing to death and burying alive of thousands of its residents, and rendering 116,000 of a population of 140,000 homeless, had resulted in the Communists' most significant failure: if ever they had possessed the hearts and minds of anybody in Huế, they had lost them now.

I walked quickly back to the MACV compound to telephone my story to my teammate Friedhelm "Freddy" Kemna in Saigon, and to give Baron von Collenberg at the embassy an update about the German doctors. There was only one telephone line out, with a long queue of reporters waiting to put a call through. My turn came after two hours. Then I had to work my way through a succession of military exchanges in the hope that all were staffed by intelligent operators, which they weren't.

At the top of my voice, I shouted into the field telephone: "Huế, please give me Phú Bài! — Phú Bài, give me Da Nang! — Da Nang, give me Nha Trang! — Nha Trang, give me Qui Nhon! — Qui Nhon, give me Tan Son Nhut! — Tan Son Nhut, give me Tiger (the Saigon military exchange)! — Tiger, give me the PTT! — PTT, *donnez moi l'hôtel Continental, s'il vous plait."*

After two failed attempts, I finally got through to my hotel, praying that my nemesis, an opium-saturated Indian from Madras, wasn't on telephone duty that evening. But he was!

"Ici Monsieur Siemon-Netto, donnez moi Monsieur Kemna, s'il vous plaît," I said: Siemon-Netto here, please give me Mr. Kemna.

"Monsieur Siemon-Netto n'est pas ici," the opium head answered: he isn't here.

He hung up!

Thank God, the kindly American colleague behind me in the queue also lived in the *Continental Palace* and had a copytaker waiting for him there. He dictated his story and then asked his counterpart to keep the line open and fetch Freddy, whose room was on the same floor. So, in the end, I did manage to give my story to Freddy and asked him to pass on my message to Baron von Collenberg.

Then I needed a drink. Thank God, I had a hip flask of whisky in my knapsack. After the grisly experiences of that day, a few gulps from the flask plus some slices of pumpernickel were perfect bliss. Then I had to wait for the American military to move.

The Old City of Huế and its citadel were still in the hands of some 10,000 North Vietnamese soldiers. We were told that the 1st ARVN division, while fighting well, had a hard time trying to move in from the northwest in an effort to retake the citadel, and expected elements of the 1st U.S. Marine Division to attack from the southeast. When that happened, I intended to attach myself to one of its platoons.

What happened next was so traumatic that I am left with only fragmentary recollections of the day I joined a Marine platoon as it set out to cross the River of Perfumes at three in the morning. I remember that this unit was unusually large, numbering 53 men. I also remember that its leaders were of a vastly higher caliber than those in charge of the platoon I had met in the Krainicks' apartment. Sadly, I saw most of them get wounded or killed before the day was out.

I remember us running into house-to-house combat almost from the moment we hit the river's northern shore. The North Vietnamese seemed extremely well entrenched, firing at us out of every window. I found my story about this battle in the Amsterdam newspaper, *De Telegraaf*, which was a client of the Springer Foreign News Service. It focused on my most harrowing experience of that day, but one about which I now only have a hazy memory. I was running alongside a black lance corporal. We got pinned down by sniper fire from an upper-floor window and threw ourselves to the ground, with the lance corporal "spraying" the window with volleys from his M-16, to keep the sharpshooter at bay. But then the marine's gun jammed, as these weapons all too often did in Vietnam. The sniper resumed shooting at us immediately, whereupon the black man lobbed a hand grenade into the window. At once the firing stopped and the lance corporal gave off a whoop.

Next, a woman came out of the door showing the American lance corporal the blood-soaked corpse of a child. He went berserk. "Oh, my God, oh, my God, what have I done? I have killed a little baby! Please help me, God! Oh my God, oh my God!!!" he screamed whirling around like a dervish, while North Vietnamese snipers continued firing at us from the other windows. The platoon sergeant had to subdue his comrade with force and then lead him away from this scene of combat.

It was three in the afternoon when I first found time to look at my watch during a lull in the battle. I turned around: where were all the men I had been with twelve hours earlier? I counted ten, maybe 15. The others had either died or been wounded; another platoon replaced us. It was time for me to get out. I made my way back to the River of Perfumes. Amazingly, the Communists had left the main bridge standing. I walked across it and found myself at a helicopter landing zone (LZ) covered with severely wounded men, hundreds of them, many groaning in agony.

"Major," I asked the officer in charge of the LZ, "What's happening here? Why aren't these casualties being flown out?"

He pointed at the sky: "Bad flying conditions!"

"But, Major, I have seen worse. The ceiling is high enough," I protested.

"Yes, but you see, we Marines haven't got enough helicopters."

"What about the Army? I have been told that ten miles from here at Phú Bài two Army helicopter battalions are on standby."

"Sir, we are Marines, we wouldn't call upon the Army!"

I remember thinking to myself: a maple leaf on the lapel of a major's uniform is clearly not a certificate of a high IQ. It was time to get out of there. The Theatre of the Absurd showed signs of madness here. I had seen the best and the worst of mankind in these few days: heart-rending self-sacrifice and bravery contrasting with the unimaginable cruelty of the Communists and the meat-headed mindlessness of a couple of certifiable halfwits in uniforms.

I remember tears welling up in my eyes thinking of all the dead Vietnamese I had seen in Huế, mostly women and children, and of the maimed young Americans on those stretchers. I had seen them fight so bravely, despite the growing anti-war sentiment in their homeland. I had witnessed the self-sacrifice of so many trying to protect the lives of Vietnamese civilians. And here hundreds of these warriors lay moaning in agony, with nobody giving them the comforting news that they had just vanquished the enemy.

More than half the 80,000 Communist soldiers who participated in the Tết Offensive were killed; the Viet Cong infrastructure was smashed. This was a big military victory. It was a hard-won victory for the Allies, but a victory it was. All things being equal, this should have been *the* Allied triumph bringing this war to a successful end. We combat correspondents could testify to this, irrespective of the pacifist and defeatist spin opinion makers, ideologues and self-styled progressives in the United States and Europe put on this pivotal event. But as I looked at these wounded warriors I feared deep in my heart that, in the end, their own compatriots might betray them because, as North Vietnamese defense minister Vo Nguyen Giap had prophesied, democracies are psychologically not equipped to fight a protracted war to a victorious conclusion.

The German national Sunday newspaper, *Bild am Sonntag*, titled my story from Huế, *"Ich habe genug vom Tod,"*—I have had enough of all that dying. I was anxious to get out of Huế. One look at this LZ told me that I had no hope of getting a ride on a helicopter anytime soon, but I did notice a Vietnamese Navy Landing Craft Utility (LCU) nearby. I rushed over to the vessel, and found its skipper, a Vietnamese naval lieutenant with the leathery complexion of a Comanche chief.

"We are about to sail," he said, "Welcome to progress: This is the first time since the beginning of the Tết Offensive that an LCU navigates this river. Expect trouble!" We headed east and immediately met small arms fire from the northern shore, a barrage of bullets ricocheting off the ship's hull. But the vessel continued its journey toward the Tam Giang Lagoon, though I didn't stay on board long. The shooting subsided as the LCU gathered distance from Huế. I fell asleep. In the middle of the night, the lieutenant shook me and said, "You'd better get off here." He had stopped at the landing site of a small MACV base on the southern bank of the river.

I don't remember how I made it from there back to Da Nang, probably by helicopter. All I know is that I arrived at the press compound a total mess. I hadn't shaved for eight days. My hands were filthy, my fingers brown from cigarette smoke, and I stank of death and dirt. I can't even recall if I was hungry or not; my digestive system had completely shut down since leaving this press center more than a week earlier.

I borrowed underwear and a fresh set of fatigues from an American officer and asked one of the compound's cleaning women to wash my own clothes as quickly as possible. As I showered, dark-grey water came pouring down from my hair and my body. Getting rid of my stubble was the highlight of the day. I went to the bar, had two stiff, dry martinis but couldn't eat anything. So I stretched out on my bed and slept for four hours, then wrote my story and phoned it to Freddy in Saigon.

Toward the end of the day, I went over to the *Helgoland*, which thankfully had returned. The bridge announced that the ship was leaving the pier and asked all visitors to leave. "Stay with us," the nurses and doctors pleaded with me, "You look dreadful. Have a good meal, have some good drinks, leave the warzone for a night and relax." The ship's horn tooted. I couldn't move, even if I had wanted to. My German friends gave me a very good time in international waters.

These joyful moments didn't last long. In the morning I returned to the press center. My clothes were back, and I was lucky to catch a helicopter ride back to Huê. In the MACV compound I ran into Peter Braestrup, the Saigon bureau chief of *The Washington Post.*

"They have found a mass grave," he said, "We are going there now, why don't you come with us?" A military truck took us and other correspondents to a site at the southwestern outskirts of Huê that had recently been wrested from Communist control. There were hundreds of women, men and children in that grave, some evidently burned, some clubbed to death, others buried alive, according to a South Vietnamese officer.

"How do we know they were buried alive?" I asked him.

"We found this site when we noticed women's freshly manicured fingernails sticking out of the ground," he answered, "These women had been trying to claw their way out of their grave."

Peter Braestrup thrust his left elbow in my side and pointed to an American television team—a reporter, a cameraman and a soundman—standing aloofly at the gravesite, doing nothing.

"Why don't you film this?" Peter asked them.

"We are not here to film anti-Communist propaganda," answered the cameraman.

"This is madness, Peter," I said, "I have had enough of this for a while."

"I don't blame you. We are losing this war after the military had won it. It's all in the head."

This was my lucky Huê day. I found a ride to the airport. There was an *Air Vietnam* DC-6 about to take off for Saigon, and it had a seat for me. Freddy Kemna was anxiously waiting for me at the *Continental Palace.* He had been a good sport as a placeholder and copytaker, but now he wanted to go to the field himself, meaning the Mekong Delta, with another German correspondent. "I prefer the Delta this time of the year. It's warmer," he joked.

It was a Thursday, and I longed for nothing more than Donald Wise's *Stammtisch*, the regulars' table for European correspondents at *Aterbéa's*, where no one was allowed to speak about the war, about Vietnam, about American politics or anything remotely connected with this whole enterprise.

After the meal, Donald said, "Now that this is over and we can speak about the war again, let me make a suggestion: how about you and I sharing a taxi to take us to the assorted battle fronts right here in Saigon every morning? It's very expensive because the taxi owner risks having his car blown up. I think it's worth it. The Americans don't pay much attention to these small combats because they are mainly Vietnamese operations. But this is nonetheless important."

So we found a chauffeur with military experience and an air-conditioned Buick. He came by the *Continental Palace* every morning to take us from one urban battle to the next. One morning we found ourselves in a pitched skirmish at the southeastern outskirts of Saigon where South Vietnamese forces controlled one side of a road and the Viet Cong or North Vietnamese the other. There was a burning house to our left. We heard a woman scream, "There's a little girl in that house! Help!"

We were lying on the ground. Donald rose to his full height of six foot two. He adjusted his helmet and then, with an umbrella dangling from his right arm, walked in measured steps right along the embattled road toward the burning house. Both sides stopped firing. Donald went into the house and came out with the little girl in his arms, his umbrella still dangling. He took her to an ambulance on the ARVN side, handed the child to the driver and said, "Take her to the hospital, my man—take her now!"

Then he threw himself on the ground again and the firing resumed.

We returned to the center of town, had lunch at the *Royal* and drove to southwestern Saigon where, according to our driver, a fierce house-to-house battle was raging between the Viet Cong and South Vietnamese rangers. As we drew closer, we saw the rangers in chaos because they had lost all their officers and senior NCOs. In the midst of this chaos, upright and unperturbed, with his head hanging sideways, walked our colleague Hans von Stockhausen, a German television correspondent.

The tilt of his head dated back to World War II when von Stockhausen was a young major in the cauldron of Stalingrad where he'd had half his skull shot off; he was the last casualty to be flown out of Stalingrad in a *Luftwaffe* plane before it fell to the Red Army. Military surgeons replaced the shattered skull bone with a silver plate, which weighed his head heavily to one side. This didn't stop this good-humored scion of an ancient military family from covering every war he could find as a reporter. Donald Wise nicknamed him thus "The Galloping Major."

"Ah, Herr Vise," the major shouted, "Zere is no system here, zere is no system here. You vere a field-grade officer, I vas a field-grade officer. Now let's together bring some system into this mess."

And so Donald Wise, the former British lieutenant colonel, and Hans von Stockhausen, the former German major, quietly taught the surviving young sergeants and corporals of a South Vietnamese Ranger company how to organize their defenses in house-to-house combat, and before long the battle was over.

Years later, Donald Wise kept reminding me, "I fell in love with the Galloping Major. What a character! I can't wait to discuss 'ze system' with him again."

We drove back to the *Continental Palace*. After a few days, I took the *Air Vietnam* Caravelle jet home to Hong Kong. Gillian awaited me at Kai Tak Airport. She looked very fetching in her miniskirt showing off her magnificent suntanned tennis player's legs and flashing me the sweetest smile. She had brought *Schnudel* on a leash, a native of the New Territories, half chow and half poodle, white and fluffy with a blue tongue. I loved this young dog and his wicked habit of welcoming our female guests—but only the pretty ones—with a nip in the rear.

"Let's celebrate your return with an early dinner at the *Peninsula*," Gillian suggested as we got into our red *Volkswagen*, "I know you are looking forward to a steak tartar and a bottle of Australian red." Gillian's most wonderful feature is her bubbly personality. She regaled me with hilarious anecdotes from the British Crown Colony's social scene; I don't think I had ever enjoyed an evening more than that first one with her after weeks of trauma.

But when we arrived at our apartment on Victoria Peak later in the evening, she abruptly turned serious. Looking me straight in the eyes, she asked, "What is it with you, darling? You seem so distant. You haven't even embraced me or given me a real kiss. Is everything alright?"

I can't recall now whether I told her the truth right there and then or a few days later, but eventually I gave her the honest answer: "I haven't embraced you as I should have, nor have I given you a proper kiss because I did not want to defile you. Ever since Huế at Têt I've felt desperately dirty." I was haunted by a sense of dereliction I had never experienced before. For weeks I had the irrepressible urge to take a hot shower and scrub myself several times a day. Now, almost half a century later, I am noticing occasional recurrences of this urge. I attribute these flashbacks to the incontrovertible fact that I am growing old.

Photographer Perry Kretz (left), General Ngo Quang Truong, commander of I. Corps, and the author, during battle for Huế, 1972.

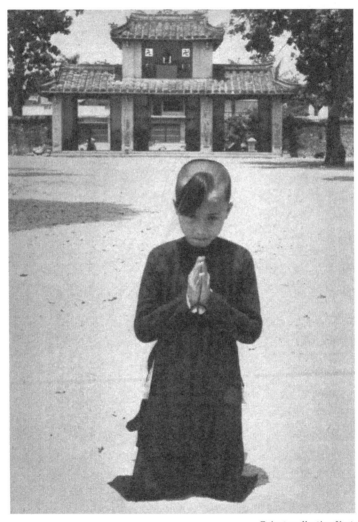

Symbol of Buddhist piety in ancient Huế:
A kneeling novice outside the Tu Dam Temple.

Chapter Sixteen

A long farewell to the absurd

It dawned on me in the weeks following Tết 1968 that the Theatre of the Absurd had ceased to be a laughing matter, even for observers with a sardonic sense of humor. Of course Eberhard Budelwitz, my infallible absurdity barometer, had grasped this much earlier. In his last bizarre commentary before being recalled to Germany for detoxification and subsequent assignment to another Asian capital he articulated this realization non-verbally this time as he had in the past; he did not ask nutty questions at the *Five O'Clock Follies*, for instance questions about submarines for Buddhist monks as a possible defense against leathernecks urinating outside the monks' pagoda. No, he made his point in a desperate act of inebriated lunacy.

This happened in the *Continental Palace* while the *Time-Life* bureau gave a roaring farewell party for correspondent James Wilde, a red-faced and short-tempered Irish-American who had entered the hall of fame of aphorisms about the Vietnam War with a blood-curdling remark: "The stench of death massaged my skin; it took years to wash away."

Jim was being transferred to Canada, and we were teasing him with questions about his new assignment. "How are you going to keep your blood pressure up on those dry Sundays in Ottawa?" someone asked him. Then, out of the blue, he was gone. After a few more drinks we began to worry about him and organized a search party, which logically began with Jim's room. His door was ajar. Peering inside, we saw a combat zone. His closet was open and his clothes were strewn all over the place. One of the large French windows had been yanked out of its frame and smashed on the floor. There were bloody footmarks throughout, leading right up to the window.

James Wilde was in his bed, shaking, with his sheet pulled over his head.

"Go away, go away!" he cried.

"Jim, it's us, your friends! What happened?" we said.

"Oh it's you? Thank God!" he said, "I just went to my bathroom to relieve myself, then stretched out on my bed for a little rest, and fell asleep. The door opened and in came this naked Kraut scaring the s..t out of me…"

"What naked Kraut, Jim?" I asked, "I am right here, and I am dressed."

"No, you idiot, not you! I am talking about that other Kraut who always asks boozy questions about submarines for Buddhist monks and things at the *Follies*. Anyway, he went straight for my closet, took out all my clothes, put on a jacket, went to the window, ripped it out, smashed it on the ground, trampled dementedly on the broken glass, and then jumped head first out of the window. It was frightening, guys, really frightening!"

"Where is he now?" asked William Tuohy of the *Los Angeles Times*.

"I don't know, probably dead on the sidewalk. I heard a thump."

We looked out of the window and down on a generous canopy providing additional shade for the patrons of the *Continental's* terrace below. On this canopy lay our colleague Eberhard Budelwitz, fast asleep, dressed only in Jim Wilde's jacket. His hands and feet were covered with blood, but otherwise he was intact. We hauled him inside, put some of Jim's underwear on Budelwitz, and then carried him to his own room, without waking him up. This was the last time I saw Budelwitz. I continue holding him in high esteem for his incisive though seemingly bizarre questions, and particularly for this last performance in Saigon, which in the final analysis did not strike us as bizarre after all. His urge to throw himself out of the window as an exclamation mark behind his reporting career in Vietnam resonated well with some of his peers.

Not that any of us really had suicide on our minds; I certainly didn't, and I don't believe Budelwitz did either. Even in his inebriated state, he possessed sufficient wisdom to realize that a hop out of a window and onto a canopy wouldn't be lethal. But in his whacky way he made a powerful point: What we had just experienced at Têt was the Theatre of the Absurd taken to its most ludicrous level. This incident convinced me that the Latin axiom, *in vino veritas* (in wine is truth), also applied to Screwdriver cocktails, at least in Budelwitz' case.

Six weeks at home in Hong Kong after my Têt ordeal did little to satisfy my longing for a return to sanity. Two parallel political developments made some Hong Kong-based correspondents wonder about who was really unhinged: was it us, or was it the world we were supposed to cover? Next door, in Communist China, the *Great Proletarian Cultural Revolution* was reaching its peak. We received reports of the Pearl River being clogged with the corpses of Communist cadres clubbed to death by young *Revolutionary Guards*. Some were sighted in Hong Kong waters, with their arms tied with wire behind their backs but carrying Mao Zedong's *Little Red Book* in their pockets.

Still, from a geopolitical perspective, the news about the Soviet-Chinese split and Beijing's refusal to have Soviet arms supplies to North Vietnam transported by rail across Chinese territory was even more dramatic. This should have been received as good news in the United States but it was barely noted in the American media. An even more sensational piece of information followed.

Gillian and I attended a small dinner party at the home of the station chief of a Western European intelligence service. The guest of honor was an American naval captain who mastered six Chinese dialects and held a Ph.D. in Sinology. We knew that he was the U.S. military intelligence officer in charge of analyzing provincial broadcasts and internal communications in the People's Republic. His place of work, the massive American eavesdropping station, was only a few minutes' walk away from my apartment.

"Tell me, gentlemen," he suddenly asked the two journalists present, "Do you also find it sometimes as difficult as I to get the attention of your top editors when you have some hot news?"

"Do I ever!" I replied.

"I don't," said my American colleague, "But why are you asking?"

"Well, you see, hardly anything I send back to Washington reaches the President in any consequential form, regardless of how important my news might be."

"For example?" I asked.

"For example, I had told my superiors of mounting evidence that an armed conflict was likely between the Chinese and the Russians. Some guy at the Pentagon watered it down before it reached the chief of military intelligence. He watered it further down before Defense Secretary McNamara got it. McNamara again watered it down before sending it on to the White House."

"So what did Lyndon Johnson get to read?" asked my American colleague.

"A meaningless one-liner saying that according to Hong Kong Station, the Russians and Chinese aren't getting on—or something banal like that."

"Why are you telling us this?" I wanted to know.

"Because I believe that the President of the United States should be prepared for military clashes between these two Communist world powers. He will if he reads that story in the press. Go and write about it, but please do so on background: not for attribution."

That night we filed our pieces, and the following morning the world, including presumably LBJ, knew how serious the Sino-Soviet conflict really was. This dangerous situation took a while to reach its climax, but one year after our dinner conversation, Chinese and Russian forces did clash at the Ussuri River.

Driving home from the spooks' party, I regaled Gillian with the tale of Eberhard Budelwitz's auto-defenestration as the ultimate performance of the Theatre of the Absurd. She laughed.

220

"I get your point," she said, "What we have just heard was yet another act of the Theatre of the Absurd."

"Yes, top-level Theatre of the Absurd."

"Frightening," she said, "It's enough to want to throw oneself out of the window."

"Only figuratively speaking, please!"

Then, on February 27, 1968, big news broke: CBS Evening News anchorman Walter Cronkite, home from a flying visit to Vietnam after the Têt Offensive, pronounced sonorously before an audience of some 20 million viewers the Vietnam War unwinnable. This flew in the face of everything many combat correspondents, including Peter Braestrup and I, had lived through at Têt. We knew then what historians are saying now: the Americans, South Vietnamese, and their allies had defeated the Communists militarily.

But Walter Cronkite's opinion trumped reality, turning a military victory into a political defeat.

"I have lost Cronkite, I have lost Middle America," said Lyndon B. Johnson, and announced one month later a partial halt of bombing over North Vietnam along with his decision not to seek re-election. With that the Theatre of the Absurd crested.

It so happened that on the day Johnson made this announcement, on March 31, 1968, Gillian and I traveled together to Saigon. It was her first time in Vietnam. Most war correspondents kept their families in Hong Kong, Singapore or Bangkok, not only for their safety but also for a sound professional reason: a combat reporter must be able to join a battle on an *ad hoc* basis without first having to discuss this at great length the night before with his wife at the dinner table.

Gillian was never overly convinced of this argument and became even less so after landing in Saigon. On our *Cathay Pacific* flight I had warned her how unpleasant the South Vietnamese immigrations officer could be. But when she showed her British passport, the man's face lighted up.

"*Ah, Madame Siemon-Netto, soyez la bienvenue à notre pays!*" he said, "*Je connais votre époux, bien sûr, mais il m'est une honneur de vous rencontrer.*"—Welcome to our country. Of course I know your spouse but now it's an honor to meet you.

"What a charming chap," said Gillian, giving me a strange look.

"I have flown in here umpteen times, and he never bothered to even say hello to me," I growled. "But wait till you get to the customs guy. He'll give us a hard time."

Well, he didn't give us a hard time; instead he greeted Gillian just as warmly as the immigration officer. He did not even look at our luggage but simply waved us on. Gillian gave me an even funnier look.

"Normally these guys inspect every one of my knickers," I mumbled. "But wait until we have to fight for wheels to get us to the *Continental Palace.* Taxis are no longer allowed to drive up to the terminal."

Just then a young man, who probably was an Air Force lieutenant moonlighting as a chauffeur, offered to drive us to our hotel in his air-conditioned *Buick.* At this point Gillian stared at me with an expression of deep distrust.

Monsieur Loi, the *Continental's* general manager, welcomed us with a huge smile and guided us personally to Suite 214 where 25 red roses awaited Gillian, compliments of the house. These beautiful flowers intensified her suspicion!

"Why have you kept me away from this charming place for so long?" she demanded to know.

That evening at the *Royal,* Monsieur Ottavi rolled out the red carpet: artichokes, onion soup, *foie-gras,* and *canard à l'orange,* accompanied by a bottle of *Château Cheval-Blanc,* the finest red wine from Saint Émilion. Ottavi's famous *soufflé au Grand-Marnier* followed, together with a bottle of *Dom Pérignon* champagne. Where had he hidden these treasures in all the years past?

On our way back to the *Continental Palace,* Gillian stated tersely, "So is this where you are taking your mistresses!"

"Look, darling, whatever you might think, there is something important you must hear," I said when we reached our room, pointing to the large French windows, the panes of which I had carefully Scotch-taped during one of my previous stays as a protection against flying glass in case of a Viet Cong rocket attack.

"When you hear a thud tonight," I went on, "you must immediately come with me to the bathroom and stay there until the attack is over. The bathroom is the safest place in this suite because it has no windows and will therefore offer the best protection against flying glass."

Not dignifying me with an answer, Gillian curled up in my bed, which, as I had explained to her, had probably once been Graham Greene's.

Two hours later, the Viet Cong lobbed a barrage of rockets from handmade bamboo launchers across the Saigon River into the city, killing hundreds of people, including 19 women and children who had sought shelter in a Catholic church. We spent most of the rest of the night sitting in the bathroom. For Gillian, this was lesson 101 about the Vietnam War: for all its charms, Saigon was indeed a dangerous place.

More importantly, this was an unmistakable message from the Communists to the rest of the world, especially to deluded utopians fantasizing that peace was nigh after the American bombing halt and Johnson's announcement on that very day that he would not seek re-election. One did not have to be member of *Mensa International* to grasp the significance of this attack: with the help of Walter Cronkite and likeminded communicators, a military victory had been turned into a political defeat for the United States and South Vietnam. A staggering number of Communist soldiers had fallen during the Têt Offensive, but the Viet Cong made—from their perspective—the best possible use of the irrational reaction in the United States to this appalling bloodbath, a reaction confirming Vo Nguyen Giap's conviction that democracies were not psychologically equipped to fight a protracted war. In the arrogant, defiant and callous manner of totalitarians, the Communists retook the initiative by murdering and terrorizing more civilians.

This time our stay in Saigon was brief because we had been given visas to visit Cambodia, a rare occurrence. Prince Norodom Sihanouk, the Cambodian chief of government, seldom allowed Western journalists into his realm, the easternmost part of which the Viet Cong used as a staging and supply area for their war against South Vietnam. Before we boarded our plane to Phnom Penh, though, I paid Wilhelm Kopf, the West German ambassador in Saigon, a courtesy visit.

Unexpectedly, Hasso Rüdt von Collenberg entered, apologizing for interrupting our conversation. The young baron's face looked even paler than usual. He whispered something sounding like code. Kopf's chin sagged to his chest. Following intuition, I ventured a guess:

"They have found the bodies of the German doctors in Huế haven't they?" I said.

Hasso von Collenberg stared at me distraught and answered, "Yes, but it's not official yet. We must first inform Bonn."

"I understand. Tell me off the record then: what happened?"

"They found the bodies of Professor and Mrs. Krainick, of Dr. Discher and Dr. Alteköster in a mass grave about 20 miles west of Huế. They were blindfolded and had their arms bound with wire behind their backs. They were made to kneel before being shot through the back of their heads, and then dumped into the ditch."

As the ambassador and I were listening to him, we could not know that this description would soon apply to von Collenberg's own fate a few weeks later when the Viet Cong murdered him not far from the embassy in a side street of Cholon, Saigon's Chinatown.

The young diplomat told us that the Rector of Huế University had identified the bodies of his German colleagues, and that their condition allowed one significant preliminary conclusion: they must have been alive at least six weeks after their abduction. Given Hanoi's efficient command structure, the execution of these four West Germans could therefore not have been a "mistake" committed in the heat of battle; they weren't "collateral" damage of an act of war. Despite pleas from around the world, Hanoi did not act to save these innocent lives, although it had plenty of time to do so. Thus we must assume that the executions of these, and thousands of other guiltless people, had been intentional and accordingly were classed as war crimes either ordered by a government or committed with the regime's connivance.

One year later, at the Paris peace conference, which ultimately led to America's withdrawal from Vietnam, I ran into a reporter of *Giai Phong*, the Viet Cong news agency. He told me that he had covered the Tết Offensive in Huế. Comparing notes, we found that at one point we were less than 100 yards apart. I wanted to ask him: "Why did your people massacre thousands of women and children? Why did they murder my West German friends whose only 'crime' was to heal Vietnamese, regardless of their political loyalty?" Alas, I didn't. It seemed useless to ask him these questions; he was not alone. There were always "minders" within earshot, and at any rate, the Viet Cong had already given Western journalists at Communist receptions in posh Paris salons their ridiculous version of what had transpired in Huế. They said this was the work of the CIA.

To this day, I am unsure about the origin of this preposterous fib. Was it the brainchild of some boneheaded party apparatchik in Hanoi? Or was it the invention of yet another West German physician, the frenzied psychiatrist Erich Wulff who had played an unsavory role during his tenure in Huế? In 1963 he had agitated against the government of President Ngo Dinh Diem and the United States, and passed medicines and surgical instruments secretly to the Viet Cong. Later, after being made to leave the country, he testified before Bertrand Russell's *International Vietnam War Crimes Tribunal*. When I met him in Huế in 1965, he accused his neighbor Horst-Günter Krainick of nurturing a racist bias against the Vietnamese people and vented his outrage against Krainick's wife for swimming in the *Cercle Sportif* every day and socializing with Americans. Neither I nor any other acquaintance of the Krainicks' had ever detected anything other than a great love for the people they had come to help.

In 1968, Wulff wrote, under the pseudonym Georg W. Alsheimer, a revolting polemic titled, *Vietnamesische Wanderjahre*, or Years of Travel in Vietnam (Frankfurt: Suhrkamp, 1968). In this book he claimed that a top CIA official by the name of Bob Kelly had told him about a CIA terror program called *Black Tactics*. According to Wulff, this program consisted of young men dressed up as Viet Cong killing old men, women and children, to stir up hatred against the Communists.

The North Vietnamese and Viet Cong explanation of the Huế massacre corresponded to Wulff's version. In fairness to most Western correspondents, they found this tale unconvincing. In the meantime, Erich Wulff offered yet another harebrained story at leftist gatherings in West Germany: he ventured to suggest that Dr. Discher, Dr. Alteköster and the Krainicks might have been killed by their own students as an act of revenge for bad grades or, alternatively, by jealous Vietnamese colleagues.

Again, I am jumping ahead of my narrative. At this point in my tale I was still in the ambassador's office in Saigon. The expression of sorrow in Hasso von Collenberg's face was indescribable. I remember thinking: "What a noble mind! What a decent and brave man! Since the beginning of the Têt Offensive he had driven about Saigon day and night making sure that German citizens were safe. He never went home, but slept on a cot in his office. He had prayed that the Communists would spare his friends in Huế, which was all he could do, and now they were dead. Our government should be so proud of him!" If it was, it didn't show it. All that is left of his memory are his photograph and two paragraphs of text in a 2011 German Foreign Office brochure titled, *Zum Gedenken* (In Memoriam). The West German foreign minister at that time was Willy Brandt, a social democrat who had given *détente*, or the thaw in the relations with the Soviet bloc, the highest priority in his policy. One can only surmise that he thought it might be helpful to this objective to fuzz over the murder of one of his envoys.

With dark premonitions, Gillian and I boarded our plane to Phnom Penh, embarking on a journey back in time, or so it seemed. Cambodia's capital was then still the way Saigon had been in balmier days: very French but also very exotic, quirky, glamorous and peaceful. Lissome, bikini-clad wives and daughters of French military and civilian advisers lined the swimming pool of the hotel *Le Royal*, but in reality they were just decorative trimmings. In truth only one person mattered in all of Cambodia: Prince Sihanouk, who was once its king and would become king again. But at the time of our visit he contented himself with playing a host of different roles: he was the chief of government, chief producer and star of countless films, chief radio and television commentator, chief choreographer of the Royal Ballet, editor-in-chief of a high-brow magazine, chief saxophonist and composer-in-chief writing orchestral pieces resembling Charlie Chaplin's romantic tunes. He was also the obedient husband of the magnificent Princess Monique, a stern disciplinarian. She was the daughter of an Italian bricklayer and a wily Vietnamese woman. When Monique was 15 she caught Sihanouk's eye at a beauty contest. So her mother slipped her through a back door into the royal palace. Monique never slipped out again. Sihanouk, then king, fell in love with her and married her almost instantly. They remained together until his death at the age of 89 in 2012.

Sihanouk's form of neutralism was amusing. Boulevards named after Mao Zedong, John F. Kennedy and Charles de Gaulle crisscrossed Phnom Penh. It was fun watching Sihanouk handle diplomats from both sides of the East-West divide with equal irreverence. At the opening of a new hotel in Sihanoukville he hopped into a swimming pool, the water of which was brown and seemed dirty because the staff had forgotten to replace it with fresh water. "Excellence!" he yelled at the Chinese ambassador standing aloofly at the rim of the pool, "If your Chairman Mao can swim in the cold Yangtze, you can surely join me in a balmy dip." Immediately, the ambassador shed his Mao jacket and jumped, while Sihanouk, laughing, focused on the Soviet ambassador, saying in his high-pitched voice, "And you, Sir, should tell your government to tear down the Berlin Wall!" Not until two decades later, an American president, Ronald Reagan, said the same words to Soviet leader Mikhail Gorbachev.

With my colleague Ronald Ross of the *Minneapolis Tribune* and his wife Marilyn, Gillian and I hired a chauffeur-driven *Peugeot* station wagon to take us to the temples of Angkor. Throughout this journey through an enchanting and unthreatening countryside we wondered how much longer Cambodia would be spared the grim fate of neighboring Vietnam. Sihanouk had dark forebodings. He had warned us: "The *Khmers Rouges* want to kill all my little Buddhas," meaning his people. The *Khmers Rouges* numbered only about 300 men then. Their leader was a former schoolteacher named Saloth Sar, alias Pol Pot, who, during his student years in Paris, had been part of Jean Paul Sartre's entourage. Seven years after our visit to Cambodia, Pol Pot joined the ranks of 20th century's worst genocidal fiends, alongside Hitler, Stalin and Mao Zedong by killing one third of his fellow countrymen—almost two million people.

After our return to Phnom Penh, Sihanouk invited a group of visiting foreign correspondents on an excursion to the Parrot's Beak area by the South Vietnamese border. The stated objective of this trip was to show us evidence of armed incursions by ARVN and U.S. forces into neutral Cambodia's territory, but he also had an ulterior motive. The Parrot's Beak was known to be a North Vietnamese and Viet Cong base and rest area, and also constituted the terminus point of the Ho Chi Minh Trail. Driving east, some of us found evidence of a violation of Cambodia's neutrality by Hanoi more compelling: On car ferries crossing estuaries of the Mekong River our *Peugeot* was wedged in between *Land Rovers* filled with military types whose signature footwear gave them away as Vietnamese Communists. They wore sandals made from worn rubber tires: Ho Chi Minh Sandals they were called.

We knew then that happy Cambodia was merely a paradise on parole. We enjoyed its humor, beauty, sensuality, good food and its idiosyncratic ruler whom cliché-mongers in the Anglo-Saxon media loved to label mercurial. Nobody enjoyed all this more than a cheerful young freelance journalist named Sean Flynn. He was Errol Flynn's son. Two years later, he became one of the first Westerners for whom paradise in parole turned into hell. The *Khmers Rouges* captured him, held and probably tortured him for about twelve months, and then killed him.

Following our trip to the Parrot's Beak, Gillian and I returned to the *Royal*, where a telegram was awaiting us: Egon Vacek, the foreign editor of *Stern* magazine, invited us to join him at the *Siam Intercontinental* in Bangkok, and there I made the biggest blunder of my career. Vacek offered me a very generous salary and the glamorous position of *Stern*'s North American correspondent based in New York and Washington. I accepted, which meant leaving the *Axel Springer* Corporation after my contract expired in the fall of the following year.

Today I realize that this was my own ludicrous act in the Theatre of the Absurd. Springer had been a wonderful employer, and the company tried to persuade me to stay. Herbert Kremp, the erudite editor-in-chief of *Die Welt*, Springer's flagship newspaper, offered me even the prestigious post of Tokyo correspondent, which would have allowed me to return to Indochina frequently. I dared not accept this challenging assignment without a thorough knowledge of Japanese.

Stern seemed attractive at the time because, as a magazine, it offered me a better opportunity than daily newspapers to write big and colorful feature stories. I also liked Egon Vacek, my future boss, a seasoned former foreign correspondent and a political moderate at a time when *Stern* drifted further and further to the left. When he died of cancer a few years later, I was left without allies within the increasingly leftwing power structure of the biggest weekly magazine in Western Europe. No more need be said here about this mistake, which resulted in the most unpleasant episode of my professional life.

But my love affair with Vietnam did not end there and then. As I was fulfilling the last year of my *Springer* contract, my sense of dark presentiment intensified. When I returned to Saigon from my trip to Cambodia and Thailand, my friend Lanh, the German-speaking ex-trombonist of the French Foreign Legion, came to see me at the *Continental Palace*.

"I am learning Russian now," Lanh announced.

"Why not Chinese?" I asked him.

"Because the Russians will be here before long, not the Chinese. You'll see! A Russian will inhabit your suite, or perhaps an East German!"

"God forbid!"

"Yes," said Lanh, "God forbid!"

Seven years on, after the Communist victory, Russians and other East Europeans would indeed be billeted in the *Continental Palace*, but by that time Lanh had fled to Paris.

One emblematic scene of my last elegiac months as *Springer's* Vietnam correspondent remains deeply ingrained in my mind: I traveled with Vice President Nguyen Cao Ky on an *Air France* Boeing 707 from Paris to Saigon. Ky had led the South Vietnamese delegation at the Paris peace talks where his wife, Tuyet Mai, charmed everybody with her beauty and the elegance of her borrowed mink. But on the journey back, all this glamour seemed to have faded. I sensed that Ky had lost his normal exuberance. We talked for many hours about many things, but most of what he said sounded like vain attempts to reassure himself; he knew that the Americans were determined to leave Vietnam. The only real questions to be resolved at the peace talks were: how and when?

As we spoke, he kept looking at the door to the cockpit.

"Why are you staring at the cockpit all the time?" I asked him.

"Because all I am really longing for is being a pilot again," he answered softly, and I detected a trace of despair in his voice. "Go chat with Tuyet Mai a little," he said abruptly, turned on his side and closed his eyes. As it transpired, he would never become a pilot again. The lowly job of a liquor store manager in Huntington Beach, California, was all fate held in store for him.

This snapshot of our *Air France* flight to Saigon told me more about the real story behind the Paris peace talks than anything I had heard in several weeks of covering them. It seemed symbolic for the fate of all of South Vietnam.

I took up my new position as *Stern's* North American correspondent, on September 1, 1969. The very next day Ho Chi Minh died. His obituary was my first *Stern* article, and writing it directed my mind straight back to the horrors of Huế because I had to describe the significance of the *Lycée Quoc Hoc* he had attended as a young boy. This revived my memory of the thousands of starving and freezing people I had encountered on the grounds of that school, all driven from their homes by Ho's Tết Offensive. In the obituary, I also made a point of describing Ho as "the man from the land of the wooden spoon" because he hailed from the Central Vietnamese province of Nghe Anh, the people of which were so poor and stingy that, when they traveled, they carried with them wooden spoons, which they would dip into the complimentary *nuoc mam,* or rancid fish sauce, to add protein to the only dish they could afford to order in restaurants: a bowl of rice.

My long farewell to Vietnam continued throughout my three and a half North American years with *Stern.* Even if I had wanted to, it was impossible to take a leave of absence from Vietnam. Not a day went by when it didn't dominate the news. There were the interminable peace marches, there was the killing of four demonstrators at Kent State University in Ohio, and there was the murder trial of Lt. William Calley, which I covered in Fort Benning, Georgia. As a platoon leader, Calley had played a pivotal role in the massacre by American soldiers of between 347 and 504 civilians in the South Vietnamese village of My Lai. Attending Calley's court-martial, I couldn't help recalling the refusal of an American television cameraman to film a mass grave in Huế, saying, "I am not here to spread anti-Communist propaganda."

Of course I was gratified when Calley received a life sentence and was outraged that he was the only U.S. officer tried for this war crime. I was beside myself when President Richard M. Nixon ordered his release. But the fact that his crime overshadowed the genocidal behavior of the Communists in the public mind troubled me because the difference between these two events had been lost in the hysterical rhetoric that has become the most unbearable feature of a media-driven culture: Calley's crime violated stated U.S. government policy and internationally accepted standards of warfare. The North Vietnamese and Viet Cong atrocities, on the other hand, were committed as an integral part of a government policy that included a military strategy based on terror. To my mind it constituted massive malpractice by the media that they have not made this crucial point unmistakably clear to the general public.

In the spring of 1972 I returned to Vietnam for the last time. More than anything I wanted to see Huế again, the city where seven years earlier I had spent an enchanting night on a sampan listening to the songs of a beautiful girl with long black hair. I remembered her hauntingly sensuous voice and the exotic tunes of the trapeze-shaped Đàn Đáy, the three-stringed instrument she strummed as we floated down the River of Perfumes. In an almost perverse way, I pined for this martyred city I had left in an armored landing craft after spending frightening hours in house-to-house combat during the Têt Offensive. I kept recalling the three sets of fatigues I wore, one on top of the other, all reeking of dirt and death. I also felt a morbid and yet melancholy urge to retrace my stops along Le Loi Boulevard, and take one last look at the ugly *Cité Universitaire*, where the murdered German doctors had lived.

This time I traveled in the company of *Stern* photographer Perry Kretz, a tough German-American who was wholly bilingual in a unique way: he spoke a New York-accented English and *Kölsch*, the hilarious dialect of Köln (Cologne). It was very good to have him as a companion because he had seen battle many times before, starting in the Korean War where he had served in combat as a soldier in the U.S. Army. Perry could be relied upon not to panic.

We knew that a tough assignment lay ahead of us. The Communists had just launched their Easter Offensive, their largest campaign so far. Its aim was not so much to conquer territory, as to gain bargaining chips for the Paris peace talks. An enormous invasion force poured into South Vietnam from Cambodia, Laos, and especially, in a most brazen manner, across the so-called Demilitarized Zone separating the North and the South; part of this force was, as I found out later, 25,000 elite soldiers just back from training in the Soviet Union and other Warsaw Pact countries, including East Germany.

The North Vietnamese had already taken Quang Tri, where in 1965 during my memorable visit with the International Control Commission, I had been the interpreter for a Polish major when he needed treatment for a head wound from a volleyball accident. But the Communist advance toward Huế was stopped, not by the Americans, who by that time had withdrawn all but 69,000 men from Vietnam, but by the best of ARVN: the Airborne, the Vietnamese Marines, the First Division and the Rangers, all superbly led and defying the fabrication spread by some U.S. reporters that ARVN could not fight.

In truth, they proved more disciplined and professional than their northern adversaries. "The North Vietnamese brought 100 Soviet-built tanks across the DMZ but then didn't know how to handle them," an American advisor told us on the flight from Saigon to Huế, "They had to abandon scores of these tanks. Drive up National Route 1, and you'll find part of the road lined with abandoned Soviet armor."

233

Perry and I engaged a driver with the looks and demeanor of an archetypal upper class Huế intellectual. He was a reserved and earnest young man, near-sighted with thick eyeglasses and a fine command of French. His name was Hien. He owned a jeep in good condition and equipped with sandbags as a protection against shrapnel in case we hit a landmine.

First we drove up to the Citadel, which I had not been able to visit at Tết 1968 because it was under Communist control. However, at this time we found battle-weary South Vietnamese soldiers resting in hammocks strung between cannons dating back to the early 19th century. These guns were symbols of hope and pride for them, especially at a time when their elite units—and not the Americans, who were about to depart—had stemmed a new massive invasion by Communist forces. The cannons reminded them that their country had been divided before for 200 years. It was a South Vietnamese prince, Nguyen Anh, who ended this division by defeating the northern Tay Son Dynasty in 1801/1802 with the help of 300 French mercenaries.

Nguyen Anh then proclaimed himself emperor, assuming the title, Gia Long. He seized bronze pieces of armory from the beaten Tay Son forces and ordered them melted down and recast as nine big guns, naming five of them after the five elements metal, wood, water, fire and earth, and the other four after the four seasons spring, summer, autumn and winter. They had never fired a shot in anger but were only used for ceremonial purposes.

"This historical detail is very much on our mind," said Brigadier-General Bui The Lân, the commander of the South Vietnamese Marines who had established his headquarters in the Citadel. I had known Gen. Lân for years. In the eyes of many U.S. officers, foreign military attachés and reporters in Saigon, this wiry Hanoi-born soldier ranked among the toughest and most capable commanders in this conflict.

"If Huế falls, the game is over for us," Lân continued. "This is why our government has deployed our best units north and west of here. If Vietnam is ever reunified, then Huế must become its capital again. The North Vietnamese know it too, which is what their current offensive is all about."

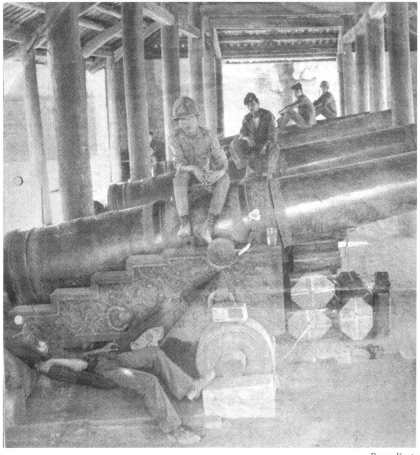

Perry Kretz

ARVN soldiers relaxing on early 19th century
cannons in the Citadel of Huế.

No love for the Viet Cong: Huế teenagers
volunteered to fight the Communists.

Perry Kretz

South Vietnamese soldiers tending to
wounded North Vietnamese POWs.

Perry Kretz, General Bui The Lân (or Laan) of the
Vietnamese Marines, and the author in Huế.

On the following day, a North Vietnamese prisoner of war confirmed this to me.

"What was the object of this operation, according to your officers?" I asked him.

"To take Huế and establish a revolutionary government in the Forbidden City immediately," he replied.

We interviewed him at a forward position some 20 miles north of Huế. He was squatting on the ground, handcuffed and blindfolded while a South Vietnamese captain was fanning the flies from his face, a sergeant slipped a lighted cigarette between his lips, and a corporal gave him water. Perry and I were very moved by these gestures of compassion toward an enemy fighter at a time when the South Vietnamese were fighting for their country's survival.

The soldier was only 17. He hailed from Nam Dinh, a city 50 miles just south of Hanoi. After three months' basic training he was sent with the 66th North Vietnamese regiment to Quang Tri where his first battle turned out to be his last. "Three quarters of the men in my battalion died, and I was wounded in the head," he told me, "then I was captured."

We drove north on National Route 1, which the French called *"La Rue Sans Joie,"* or Street Without Joy, because so many soldiers and civilians had died there during the first Indochina War. We knew that we would not get far because the forward-most North Vietnamese units were reported to be very close. The object of this trip was to put the state of this route in a historical context, comparing it with what I had read in Bernard Fall's books; I also wondered if the buffalo boys I had written about so much previously were still there; as it turned out, they were not, and this was an ominous sign. National Route 1 had become an eerie thoroughfare. Ours was the only vehicle on this road that was the dividing line between North Vietnamese positions to the west, and the South Vietnamese units to the east. Mortar and howitzer rounds were flying overhead in irregular spasms.

Perry sat in the passenger seat next to Hien, and I was in the back, staring with increasing alarm over Hien's shoulder at the speedometer. Its needle rarely passed beyond the 30-kilometer mark. His nose pressed against the inside of his windshield, near-sighted Hien dawdled dangerously along this perilous stretch of road.

"Drive faster, Hien," I begged him, "We are getting sniper fire. Only speed can save us."

"I must check the surface of the road for mines, Monsieur," said Hien, "But my eyes aren't good enough to spot them."

"Then let me drive, my eyes are fine," I said.

"No, Monsieur, I can't do that. This car is only insured in my name," he answered disingenuously and Perry went apoplectic.

"Ya hoid him, ya schmuck, drive faster!" Perry howled in a tone that might have commanded respect in New York, but was definitely not the ideal way to persuade a Hué intellectual.

Hien threw a fit. He slammed on the breaks. The jeep came to a halt at the worst place one wants to be stuck in the middle of a war: at an unprotected spot on an open highway, exposed to all sides, with artillery rounds from both sides whooshing overhead.

Louder and louder Hien and Perry argued in four languages: Hien with a high-pitched voice in a mixture of Vietnamese and French, and Perry shouting partly like a New Yorker, partly like the native of the Rhineland he was. The Theatre of the Absurd reached a level where death had become a distinct probability. I grabbed Hien's car key and said, "I want to survive this and am running for cover. If you calm down before you are dead, join me in the ditch." Then I jumped out of the back of the jeep and ran, ducking, some 500 yards until I found a cavity by the side of the road deep enough to serve as a foxhole.

Hien and Perry continued to argue, but not for long. They joined me in my foxhole until the battle had simmered down. Miraculously, Hien's jeep survived unharmed.

"I'll drive," I said, turning the jeep around. I hit the accelerator and zigzagged back in the direction of Hué, trying to avoid snipers and at the same time weave my way around patches in the surface of the road that seemed to suggest the presence of mines.

As we drew nearer to the city, we came across only one other civilian vehicle. It was a three-wheeler Lambretta bus, or Lam, the driver of which seemed unperturbed by sniper fire and mortar shrapnel. Suddenly he stopped, and so did we, intrigued by the Lam's cargo and passenger. We saw two tiny coffins and a woman with black-lacquered teeth. She threw herself on the coffins and screamed, "O my children, my children, why did you leave me behind?"

"What happened?" I asked the Lam driver. Hien translated.

"They died last night in a North Vietnamese artillery attack that completely destroyed our village over there," answered the driver, pointing at a cluster of ruined huts a few hundred yards south along National Route 1. Eight South Vietnamese soldiers emerged from foxholes near the road and grabbed the two coffins. They buried them at the edge of a field, cautioning the wailing mother not to get too close.

"Mines!" they warned.

From a short distance, the woman threw a fistful of candy into the grave before the soldiers closed it.

We continued our journey. At the outskirts of Huế we came across dozens of armed teenagers squatting on a wall. They looked too young to be soldiers.

"Who are they?" I asked Hien.

"Militia boys," he said. "They have all volunteered to fight the Communists."

"This seems new," I ventured, "especially here in Huế where people tended to stay aloof from the war."

"No more," Hien explained. "We used to hate foreigners, first the French, then the Americans. But after Tết we just hate the Communists—all of us: from schoolboys all the way up to the Dowager Empress."

"What? There is still an empress around?"

"Of course. She is Emperor Bao Dai's mother. Her name is Hoang Thi Cuc," he answered, "We address her as *Đức Từ Cung*, which translates into 'most virtuous kind lady.'"

"*Đức*," I said. "That's my nickname and it also means German. So we have something in common."

For once the earnest Hien permitted himself a smile and a little jest:

"Except that she is a *Đức Sang-Bleu*" — a virtuous blueblood.

"So she has not joined her son in his exile in the South of France?"

"No, she lives right here in a villa off Le Loi Boulevard."

"Do you know her, can you arrange an interview?" I asked.

"Yes, I know her well. But, no, she won't give you an interview. Empresses don't give press interviews, just audiences. I think I can arrange this for you, though."

Two days later, Hien drove us to the empress's residence. The first thing I noticed was a graffito on her garden wall. "*Cat dao*," it said: cut the head off. But the next word, *mỹ*, meaning American, was whitewashed over, clearly a political statement.

A very thin courtier wearing a well-worn tunic instructed us how to behave in the presence of Her Majesty. We were to greet her with our hands folded before our face. We were not to touch her and not to speak first. It was her privilege to open a conversation.

We were led into her living room, and there, in an elaborate arm chair in front of an even more elaborate family altar bearing photographs of her late husband, Emperor Khai Dinh, and her far-away son Bao Dai, sat *Đức Từ Cung*, a tiny 83-year old lady dressed in the gold-colored *Áo dài* reserved only for monarchs. She chain-smoked *Bastos* cigarettes made from strong black tobacco.

Jasmine tea was served in gold-rimmed porcelain cups. *Đức Từ Cung* spoke softly in Vietnamese, with her courtier translating. She made it clear that she saw herself as the placeholder for her son, the rightful ruler of Vietnam. She would never voluntarily leave Huế unless the Communists came for good. But she hadn't left during their three-week reign of terror at Tết 1968.

"One cannot desert one's people," she insisted. "The people of Huế are still monarchists. They come to see me all day long—the rich and the poor, noble and common, high and low. President Thieu and Vice President Ky recently sent their wives to me to pay their respects, and Col. Thon That Khiem, the governor of Thua Thien Province consults me all the time."

Listening to her was a melancholy experience, much like meeting Prince Norodom Sihanouk of Cambodia in 1968. Was this yet another episode of the Theatre of the Absurd? I didn't think so. Compared with what I had lived through in Huế, it struck me as a glimpse of what normal cultured life in this country should have been like, and it saddened me when I heard that, in order to finance the monarchist movement, she sold off porcelain vases from the imperial family's ancestral temples.

There was one more thing to do before leaving Huế for good: As a railroad buff I wanted to pay a final visit to its old train station. Of course, rail travel in Vietnam had long been interrupted, but I was always moved by the way in which the Vietnamese maintained at least the appearance of its continuity, meticulously refreshing timetables and fare schedules.

"Let's be there at eight o'clock in the morning," Hien suggested.

We arrived a little earlier. Walking the platform, we noticed a faded sign informing us that Saigon was 1,041 kilometers away and Hanoi 688 kilometers. A diesel locomotive stood there, engine running. Together with one luggage car it made up the *Trans Indochina Express* that was once legendary.

The stationmaster appeared, unrolled a red flag, waved it, and blew a whistle. The locomotive tooted, and at eight o'clock sharp the train left the station. Five minutes later it was back, having traveled no more than one kilometer, roundtrip. The engineer, a man in his fifties named Duong, turned off the engine. The stationmaster rolled up his red flag, and thus their workday ended. Once again they had proven that the Trans Indochina Express was still around.

Strangely, this scene did not seem absurd to me, but instead virtuous, or *đức* in Vietnamese, for it attested to hope in the face of calamity. As we left the station, 20 *cyclo-pousse* drivers were waiting outside with their pedicabs lined up in perfect order.

"Why are you here?" Perry Kretz asked the lead rickshaw coolie.

"Where else should we be?" he replied.

There and then I understood that there was logic to the Theatre of the Absurd.

Perry Kretz

Receiving an audience: Dowager Empress Đức Từ Cung

At a station without trains in Huế, pedicab
drivers wait for phantom passengers.

Epilogue

The fruit of terror and the virtue of hope

More than forty years have passed by since I paid Vietnam my farewell visit. In 2015, the world will observe the 40th anniversary of the Communist victory, and many will call it "liberation." The Huế railway station, where a locomotive and a baggage car left on a symbolic 500-yard journey every morning at eight, no longer qualifies as Theatre of the Absurd. It has been attractively restored and painted pink. Once again, as in the days of French dominance, it is the most beautiful station in Indochina, and taxi drivers do not have to wait outside in vain. Ten comfortable trains come through every day, five heading north, five going south. Collectively they are unofficially called Reunification Express. Should I not rejoice? Is this not just as in Germany, where the Berlin Wall and the minefields have gone, and now high speed trains zoom back and forth between the formerly Communist East and the democratic West at speeds up to 200 miles an hour?

Obviously I am glad that the war is over and Vietnam is reunified and prosperous, that the trains are running, and most of the minefields cleared. But this is where the analogy with Germany ends. Germany achieved its unity, in part because the Germans in the Communist East toppled their totalitarian government with peaceful protest and resistance, and in part thanks to the wisdom of international leaders such as Presidents Ronald Reagan and George H. W. Bush, Chancellor Helmut Kohl, and Soviet leader Mikhail Gorbachev, and partly because of the predictable economic collapse of the flawed socialist system in the Soviet Bloc. Nobody died in the process, nobody was tortured, nobody ended up in camps, nobody was forced to flee.

There is an incomprehensible tendency, even among respectable pundits in the West, to refer to the Communist takeover of the South as "liberation," thus following, perhaps unwittingly, the contemptible line of Harvard Professor John Kenneth Galbraith who arrogantly wished for South Vietnam to "go back to the nothingness it so richly deserves."

This invites the question: liberation from what and to what? Was South Vietnam "freed" for the imposition of a totalitarian one-party state that ranks among the world's worst offenders against the principles of religious liberty, freedom of expression, freedom of speech, freedom of assembly, and freedom of the press? What kind of "liberation" was this that cost 3.8 million Vietnamese lives between 1955 and 1975 and has forced more than one million Vietnamese to flee their country, not only from the vanquished South, but even from ports in the North, causing between 200,000 and 400,000 of the so-called boat people to drown?

Was it an act of "liberation" to execute 100,000 South Vietnamese soldiers and officials after the fall of Saigon? Was it meant to be a display of generosity by the victors to herd between one million and 2.5 million South Vietnamese to reeducation camps, where an estimated 165,000 perished and thousands more have sustained lasting brain injuries and mental health problems resulting from torture, according to a study by an international team of scholars led by Harvard psychiatrist Richard F. Molina?

And who were the liberators? Does nobody bother to consider the biography, history and words of the man who launched this war of conquest? One of his names his youthful admirers chanted on the campuses of virtually every Western university: Ho-Ho-Ho-Chi-Minh. But that was not his real name. Today we know that it was one of the 170 (!) pseudonyms he had given himself, being a top agent of the Soviet-led *Comintern*, or Communist International, since the 1920s. This was no secret by the time I arrived in Vietnam in 1965. It could be found in the textbooks that lay on most reporters' bedside tables.

Those who wanted to know had no difficulty finding out from reliable and impartial sources what his real goal was. He said so himself: He wished none other than to help bring about the global victory of Marxism-Leninism.

Had independence of Vietnam from France been his primary objective he would not so diligently have betrayed and liquidated all Indochinese freedom fighters not following the Soviet party line, including nationalists, monarchists and Trotskyists.

When I lived in Saigon, it was perfectly known that Ho had been responsible for the murder of at least 200,000 landowners in the Stalinist-style agrarian reform in northern Vietnam between 1953 and 1956. Some sources even claim that 500,000 were killed. Countless others committed suicide to avoid being tortured to death. Following the examples of Stalin and Mao Zedong, Ho's primary reason for these massacres was not so much the redistribution of wealth but the "neutralization" of all potential "class enemies."

As we approach the 40th anniversary of the Fall of Saigon, it is well worth remembering that it was to a political movement with this blood-curdling history that the Congress of the United States delivered South Vietnam when it voted to stop almost all further military aid to this bleeding country, thus accepting the view of Prof. Galbraith and likeminded intellectuals that "the assumed enemy does not exist."

Since the mid-1960s, political and historical mythographers in the West have either naïvely or dishonestly accepted Hanoi's line that this conflict was a "People's War." Well it was, if one accepts Mao Zedong's and Vo Nguyen Giap's interpretation of the term. But the Saxon genitive implies that a "People's War" is supposed to be a war *of* the people. In truth, it wasn't. Some 3.8 million Vietnamese were killed between 1955 and 1975. Approximately 164,000 South Vietnamese civilians were annihilated in a Communist *democide* during that same period, according to political scientist Rudolf Joseph Rummel of the University of Hawaii. The Pentagon estimated that 950,000 North Vietnamese and more than 200,000 South Vietnamese soldiers fell in combat, in addition to 58,000 U.S. troops. This was no war *of* the people; it was a war *against* the people.

In the all too often hypocritical rhetoric about the Vietnam War over the last 40 years, the key question has gone AWOL, to use a military acronym meaning absent without leave, and the question is this: Did the Vietnamese people desire a Communist regime? If so, how was it that nearly one million northerners moved south following the division of their country in 1954, while only about 130,000 Viet Minh sympathizers went in the opposite direction?

Who started this war? Were there any South Vietnamese units operating in North Vietnam? No. Did South Vietnamese guerillas cross the 17th parallel to disembowel and hang pro-Communist village chiefs, their wives and children in the northern countryside? No. Did the South Vietnamese regime massacre an entire class of people by the tens of thousands in its territory after 1954 the way the North Vietnamese had liquidated landowners and other potential opponents of their Soviet-style rule? No. Did the South Vietnamese establish a monolithic one-party system? No.

As a German citizen, I had no dog in this fight, as Americans would say. But to paraphrase the *Journalists' Prayer Book*, if hardened reporters have a heart at all, mine was, and still is, with the wounded and abandoned Vietnamese people. It belongs to these sublime women who can often be so blunt and amusing; it belongs to the cerebral and immensely complicated Vietnamese men trying to dream the perfect dream in a Confucian way; to the childlike soldiers going to battle carrying their only possessions— a canary in a cage; to young war widows who had their bodies grotesquely modified just to catch a GI husband and create a new home for their children and perhaps for themselves, rather than face a Communist tyranny; to those urban and rural urchins minding each other and water buffaloes. What a hardened heart I had, it belonged to those I saw running away from the butchery and the fighting—always in a southerly direction, but never ever north, until at the very end there was no VC-free square inch to escape to. I saw them slaughtered or buried alive in mass graves, and still have the stench of putrefying corpses in my nostrils.

I wasn't there when Saigon fell after entire ARVN units, often so maligned in the U.S. media and now abandoned by their American allies, fought on nobly, knowing that they would neither win nor survive this final battle. I was in Paris, mourning, when all this happened, and I wish I could have paid my respects to five South Vietnamese generals before they committed suicide when the game, that they should have won, was over: Le Van Hung (born 1933), Le Nguyen Vy (born 1933), Nguyen Khoa Nam (born 1927), Tran Van Hai (born 1927) and Pham Van Phu (born 1927).

As I write this epilogue, a fellow journalist and scholar of sorts, a man born in 1975 when Saigon fell, is making a name for himself, pillorying American war crimes in Vietnam. Yes, they deserve to be pilloried. Yes, they were a reality. My Lai was reality; I know: I was at the court martial where Lt. William Calley was found guilty. I know that the body count fetish dreamed up by the warped minds of political and military leaders of the McNamara era in Washington and U.S. headquarters in Saigon cost thousands of innocent civilians their lives.

But no atrocity committed by dysfunctional American or South Vietnamese units ever measured up to the state-ordered carnage inflicted upon the South Vietnamese in the name of Ho Chi Minh. These crimes his successors will not even acknowledge to this very day because nobody has the guts to ask them: why did your people slaughter all these innocents whom you claimed to have fought to liberate? As a German, I take the liberty of adding a footnote here: why did you murder my friend Hasso Rüdt von Collenberg and the German doctors in Huê? Why did you kidnap those young Knights of Malta volunteers, subjecting some to death in the jungle and others to imprisonment in Hanoi? Why does it not even occur to you to search your conscience regarding

251

these actions, the way thoughtful Americans, while correctly laying claim to having been on the right side in World War II, wrestle with the terrible legacy left by the carpet bombing of residential areas in Germany and the nuclear attacks on Hiroshima and Nagasaki?

Reminiscing on her ordeal on the Ho Chi Minh Trail in the news magazine *Der Spiegel*, the West German nurse Monika Schwinn recalled her encounter with North Vietnamese combat units on their way south as one of her most horrifying experiences. She described the intensity of hatred in the facial expressions of these soldiers and wrote that her Viet Cong minders had great difficulty preventing them from killing the Germans on the spot. Nobody is born hating. Hate must be taught. Fostering murder in the hearts of young people involved a teaching discipline at which only the school of totalitarianism excels. In his brilliant biography of SS leader Heinrich Himmler, historian Peter Longerich relates that even this founder of this evil force of black-uniformed thugs did not find it easy to make his men overcome natural inhibitions to execute the holocaust (Longerich, *Heinrich Himmler*. Oxford: 2012). It was the hatred in the eyes of the North Vietnamese killers in Hué that many of the survivors I interviewed considered most haunting. But of course, one did have to spend time with them, suffer with them, gain their confidence and speak with them to discover this central element of a human, political and military catastrophe that is still with us four decades later. Opining about it from the ivory towers of a New York television studio or an Ivy League school does not suffice.

In a stirring book about the French Foreign Legion, Paul Bonnecarrère relates the historic meeting between the legendary Col. Pierre Charton and Gen. Vo Nguyen Giap after France's defeat at Dien Bien Phu (Bonnecarrère. *Par le Sang Versé*. Paris: 1968). Charton was a prisoner of war in the hands of the Communist Viet Minh. Giap came to pay his respects to him but also to gloat. The encounter took place in a classroom in front some 20 students attending a political indoctrination session. The dialogue between the two antagonists went thus:

Giap: "I have defeated you, *mon colonel*!

Charton: "No you haven't, *mon général*. The jungle has defeated us... and the support you have exacted from the civilian population—by means of terror."

Vo Nguyen Giap didn't like this answer, and forbade his students to write it down. But it was the truth, or more precisely: it was half of the truth. The other half was that democracies like the United States seemed indeed politically and psychologically ill equipped to fight a protracted war. This realization, alongside the use of terror tactics, became a pillar of Giap's strategy. He was right and he won. Even more dangerous totalitarians are taking note today.

To this very day I am haunted by the conclusion I was forced to draw from my Vietnam experience: when a self-indulgent throwaway culture grows tired of sacrifice it becomes capable of discarding everything like a half-eaten donut. It is prepared to dump a people whom it set out to protect. It is even willing to trash the lives, the physical and mental health, the dignity, memory and good name of the young men who were sent to war. This happened in the case of the Vietnam veterans. The implications of this deficiency endemic in liberal democracies are terrifying because in the end it will demolish their legitimacy and destroy a free society.

However, I must not end my narrative on this dark note. As an observer of history, I know that history, while closed to the past, is always open to the future. As a Christian I know who is the Lord of history. The Communist victory in Vietnam was based on evil foundations: terror, murder and betrayal. Obviously, I do not advocate a resumption of bloodshed to rectify this outcome, even if this were possible. But as an admirer of the resilient Vietnamese people, I know that they will ultimately find the right peaceful means and the leaders to rid themselves of their despots. It might take generations, but it will happen.

In this sense, I will now join the queue of the pedicab drivers outside the Huế railway station where no passenger arrived back in 1972. Where else would my place be? What else do I possess but hope?

Perry Kretz

ARVN soldiers bury two young boys killed in a Communist artillery attack on their village near Huế. Their distraught mother has to stay behind because the burial ground is mined.

also by Uwe Siemon-Netto

The Acquittal of God: A Theology for Vietnam Veterans

The Fabricated Luther: Refuting Nazi Connections
and Other Modern Myths

29347641R00162

Made in the USA
San Bernardino, CA
20 January 2016